THE CAMBRIDGE REVISION GUIDE

GCE O LEVEL

BIOLOGY

Ian J. Burton

PUBLISHED BY THE PRESS SYNDICATE OF THE UNIVERSITY OF CAMBRIDGE
The Pitt Building, Trumpington Street, Cambridge, United Kingdom

CAMBRIDGE UNIVERSITY PRESS
The Edinburgh Building, Cambridge CB2 2RU, UK   www.cup.cam.ac.uk
40 West 20th Street, New York, NY 10011-4211, USA   www.cup.org
10 Stamford Road, Oakleigh, Melbourne 3166, Australia
Ruiz de Alarcón 13, 28014 Madrid, Spain
33A Tanjong Pagar Road, Singapore 088456

© Cambridge University Press 2000

This book is in copyright. Subject to statutory exception
and to the provisions of relevant collective licensing agreements,
no reproduction of any part may take place without
the written permission of Cambridge University Press.

First published 2000

Printed in Singapore by C. O. S. Printers Pte Ltd

Typeface Times11/13pt.   *System* PageMaker

ISBN 0 521 648467 paperback

AUTHOR'S NOTE

This book was written to help all students taking examinations in Biology at GCE O Level, and School Certificate. It should be of great value also to those taking GCSE examinations involving Biological Sciences. Students should note, however, that syllabuses differ and are constantly under review.

ACKNOWLEDGEMENTS

I am indebted to the following for their invaluable help in the production of this book: The University of Cambridge Local Examinations Syndicate, for its kind permission to reproduce a number of illustrations, and for the use of past papers and diagrams; Professor Helen Nair, The Institute of Biological Sciences, University of Malaya for her painstaking scrutiny of the text and for her helpful advice; Sue Bremner for her help with the artwork, and to Dr. John Gill for his photographs of liver and onion cells.

I am grateful to the following for permission to reproduce photographs:

Figs. 4a and E Biophoto Associates; Figs. 5a and 67b Centre for Cell and Tissue Research, University of York; Figs. 24a and 24b Gene Cox; Fig. 67a Dr. O T Bonnett; Fig. D, the Wellcome Trust Medical Photographic Library; Fig. H, Norvatis Horsham Research Centre.

CONTENTS

Revision Hints for GCE O Level Biology Students   xii

TOPIC 1:   Cell Structure and Organisation   1

TOPIC 2:   Specialised Cells, Tissues and Organs   4

     A – Root hair cell   4
     B – Xylem vessels   5
     C – Red blood cells   6
     D – Muscle cells   7
     How cells combine to improve their efficiency   7

TOPIC 3:   Diffusion and Osmosis   9

     Understanding the processes of diffusion and osmosis   10
     A – The movement of molecules by diffusion   10
     B – The movement of molecules by osmosis   10
     How water is taken up by a plant   12
     The effect of osmosis on plant and animal cells   13
     A – The *intake* of water by osmosis   13
     B – The *loss* of water by osmosis   14
     Active transport   16

TOPIC 4:   Enzymes   17

     How enzymes work – the 'lock and key' hypothesis   18

TOPIC 5:   Nutrition   20

     Chemical structure of nutrients   20
     Carbohydrates   20
     Fats   20
     Proteins   20
     Tests to show the presence of carbohydrates, fats and proteins   21

A – Carbohydrates	21
B – Fats (The ethanol emulsion test)	21
C – Proteins (The biuret test)	22
Sources and functions of nutrients	22
Deficiency diseases	22

TOPIC 6: Plant Nutrition — 25

Photosynthesis	25
The importance of photosynthesis to the living universe	26
What does a plant need to photosynthesise?	26
Things to remember when performing experiments	26
Waste product of photosynthesis	30
The rate of photosynthesis	31
Limiting factors	33
How plants obtain raw materials	33
Leaf structure	34
How a leaf is adapted for photosynthesis	34
How a leaf is involved in the process of photosynthesis	36
Mineral nutrition in a plant	37
The importance of nitrogen-containing ions	37
The importance of magnesium ions	38
The use of nitrogen-containing ions in agriculture	38

TOPIC 7: Animal Nutrition — 39

Problems caused by an unbalanced diet	39
The human alimentary canal	41
The functions of the main regions of the alimentary canal	42
Summary of chemical digestion in the alimentary canal	44
The need for chemical digestion	45
Teeth and the part they play in mechanical digestion	45
The importance of proper tooth care	46
The absorption and assimilation of food	47

	Villi	47
	Assimilation	48
	The role of the liver in glucose and amino acid metabolism	49
	Fat metabolism	49
TOPIC 8:	Transport in Flowering Plants	50
	The path taken by water through a plant	51
	Transpiration	52
	Conditions affecting the rate of transpiration	53
TOPIC 9:	Transport in Human Beings	54
	Dual circulation	54
	The main blood vessels of the body	54
	The heart and how it functions	55
	A comparison of the three types of blood vessel	57
	Differences between arteries, veins and capillaries	57
	Blood: features and functions of the main components	59
	Red blood cells (RBCs)	60
	White blood cells	60
	Platelets	61
	Plasma	62
	How substances in the capillaries reach the cells of the body	62
TOPIC 10:	Respiration	64
	A – Aerobic respiration	64
	B – Anaerobic respiration	64
	Gaseous exchange in man	65
	The differences between inspired and expired air	66
	The structure of the respiratory organs	69
	During inspiration	70
	During expiration	70
	How alveoli are adapted for the process of gaseous exchange	71

	The effect of respiratory diseases on the process of gaseous exchange	71
TOPIC 11:	Support, Movement and Locomotion	73
	How muscles move bones at a joint	74
TOPIC 12:	Excretion	75
	The kidneys	75
	Kidney dialysis	76
TOPIC 13:	Homeostasis	78
	The skin	78
	The part played by the skin in temperature regulation	79
	The concept of control by negative feedback	80
TOPIC 14:	Coordination and Response	81
	A – Nervous coordination in human beings	81
	The eye	81
	How the eye produces a focused image	82
	Accommodation	83
	The 'pupil' (or iris) reflex	83
	The brain and nervous system	84
	The functions of the major parts of the brain	84
	Spinal cord	85
	Nerves	86
	Reflex action	86
	B – Chemical coordination in human beings	88
	Hormones	88
	Diabetes	89
	C – Chemical control of plant growth	89
	Herbicides	89

Tropisms	89
Taxic responses	91

TOPIC 15: The Use and Abuse of Drugs — 92

Drug abuse	92

TOPIC 16: The Diversity of Organisms — 95

Microorganisms (and their importance in biotechnology)	95
Viruses	95
Bacteria	96
Fungi	96
The role of microorganisms in decomposition	97
The roles of bacteria and fungi in food production	97
Industrial biotechnology	98
Antibiotic production	99
Single-cell protein production	99
Insects	99
Activities of insects which affect the ecosystem	100
Plants	101

TOPIC 17: The Relationship between Organisms and the Environment — 102

Energy flow	102
Food chains and food webs	102
Energy loss along a food chain	103
Pyramids of numbers, biomass and energy	104
The carbon cycle	105
The nitrogen cycle	106
The water cycle	107
Parasitism	108
Malaria	108
Control of malaria	109

TOPIC 18:	**The Effects of Human Activity on the Ecosystem**	110
	Deforestation	110
	The dangers of deforestation	110
	Pollution	111
TOPIC 19:	**The Need for Conservation**	113
	The threat of extinction	113
	Maintaining a continuous supply of commodities from trees	113
	Maintaining fish supplies	113
	Conservation of other species	113
	Recycling	114
TOPIC 20:	**Reproduction**	115
	Asexual reproduction	115
	Tissue culture	116
	Sexual reproduction	116
	Sexual reproduction in plants	117
	Pollination	117
	Fertilisation in flowering plants	120
	The development of the fruit	120
	Germination of seeds	122
TOPIC 21:	**Sexual Reproduction in Human Beings**	125
	The male reproductive system	125
	The female reproductive system	126
	A comparison of male and female gametes	127
	The menstrual cycle	128
	Factors affecting the menstrual cycle	129
	Fertile and infertile phases of the menstrual cycle	129
	Human fertilisation	129
	Development of the embryo	130

The nutrition and excretion of the fetus	130
The dietary needs of a pregnant woman	131
The value of breast feeding	131
Birth control	132
Sexually transmitted diseases	133
Syphilis	133
Gonorrhoea	134
AIDS	134

TOPIC 22: Inheritance ... 135

Variation	135
A – Continuous variation	135
B – Discontinuous variation	135
The chemical structure of chromosomes	136
The unit of inheritance	138
Genetic inheritance	138
Variation as a result of mutation	139
Monohybrid inheritance	140
A – With complete dominance	141
B – With codominance	144
The inheritance of sex	146
Selection	147
Evolution	148
Artificial selection	148
Genetic engineering	149
Public concern over genetic engineering	149

REVIEW QUESTIONS ... 150

Multiple Choice	150
Questions from past examination papers	163
Answers	173
Glossary	179

REVISION HINTS FOR GCE O LEVEL BIOLOGY STUDENTS

It is often easier to *understand* Biology at O Level than it is to *remember* the information when you really need to – during examinations, for example. Committing facts to memory can be difficult. Many students think the task is too big, and they hardly know where to begin. Don't be discouraged!

Outlined below is a step-by-step revision method I devised myself when, as a student, I was faced with the same problem. By using revision tools, like the method described, you can make the most of your time and improve your knowledge of the facts.

It cannot be stressed too much that examination results depend on knowledge. About 50% of the marks awarded in the exam are for simple knowledge alone, and interpretation questions rely heavily on a good knowledge of the subject.

The success of this revision method relies on your following the technique carefully. It *does* work, but you must be prepared to spend the necessary time. You may even enjoy the experience!

Revision sheets

You will notice that key words, terms and phrases in this book have been written in SMALL CAPITALS or **bold**. All words in small capitals are listed alphabetically in the Glossary on pp. 179–192. Use the Glossary to check on the meaning of these words or phrases. Bolded words are also important. Make an effort to remember these highlighted words, terms and phrases.

Revision sheets can be constructed in the following way:

1 Take a sheet of paper and draw a vertical line so that three-quarters of the sheet is on the left of the line (see p. xiv). Read a page of the Cambridge Revision Guide, and each time you come to a word or phrase in SMALL CAPITALS or **bold**, write a simple question to which that word or phrase is the answer (see examples on p. xiv).

2 Write these questions on the left-hand side of your sheet of paper, leaving a space between each, and number them. Continue on further sheets of paper if necessary.

3 If there is a diagram in the text, draw a quick sketch of it on the left-hand side of your sheet with numbered lines pointing from important parts of the diagram to the right-hand side of the page (see example on p. xiv).

4 When you have reached the bottom of the page in the Revision Guide, close the book and see how many of the answers you can write down in the right-hand column on your sheet. When you have attempted all answers, check them against the book. You will probably be surprised at how well you do – but remember: *you* wrote the questions *around* the answers!

5 Continue until you have a list of questions and anwers to the entire topic.

6 Take a second sheet of paper and use it to cover the answers. If you can still see the answers underneath, fold the paper in half. Test yourself again, writing your answers on the folded sheet. Continue until you answer more than 80% of the questions correctly. Of course, you can set your own target – some students will be happy only when they can score 100%!

7 File away your question and answer sheets for later use.

8 Continue to use this revision process until you have a full set of revision sheets.

9 In the last few days before the examination, your question and answer sheets should be invaluable for last-minute consolidation of your facts.

The advantage of this revision method is based firmly on *you* phrasing the questions to which you will already know the answer. Therefore, only a short example of the technique is given on the next page.

Example of a revision sheet

The example given on p. xiv is based on the first page of the first topic in this Revision Guide: "Cell Structure and Organisation".

Sample revision sheet

1	What word is used for organisms containing only one cell?	**unicellular**
2	Give an example of a one-celled organism.	**a bacterium**
3	What word is used for organisms made of many cells?	**multicellular**
4	What structure controls the passage of substances into and out of a cell?	**cell membrane**
5	In what state must all chemicals be before they can enter or leave a cell?	**in solution**
6	What is the jelly-like substance where chemical reactions occur in a cell?	**cytoplasm**
7	What is the correct term for the chemical reactions in a cell?	**metabolic reactions**
8	Where in a cell are chromosomes found?	**the nucleus**
9	What do chromosomes possess?	**genes**
10	Of what chemical are chromosomes made?	**DNA**
11	During which process does each chromosome form an exact replica of itself?	**mitosis**
12	What makes up protoplasm?	**cytoplasm + nucleus**
13	What is the space in the centre of a plant cell?	**vacuole**
14	What does this space contain?	**cell sap**
15	What is the name of the box in which a plant cell is contained?	**cell wall**
16	What chemical is this box made of?	**cellulose**
17	Name the green structures in photosynthesising cells.	**chloroplasts**
18	What pigment do they contain?	**chlorophyll**
19	Identify the following structures:	

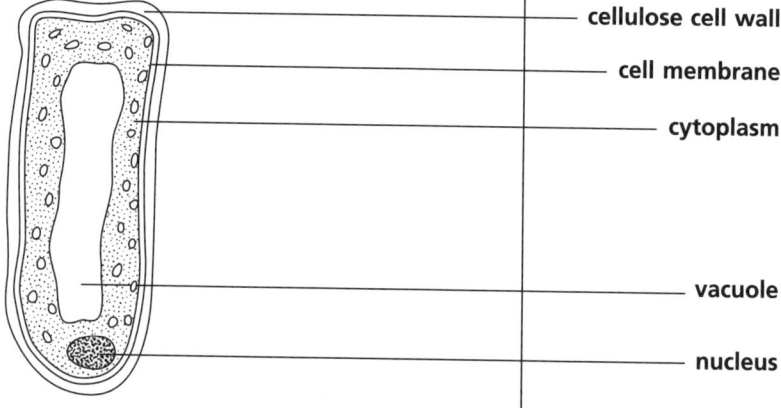

Effective revision and time management

Read the text of this book *carefully*, one section at a time. Concentrate on every sentence, making sure you understand what you have read. It is so easy to get to the bottom of a page in a book and realise that your mind was elsewhere as you were reading it. If that happens, be honest with yourself. Go back to the top of the page and start again.

As the examination approaches and more time is spent revising, it is a good idea to set aside a certain time each day for revision – do not allow yourself to be persuaded to do anything else during that time.

Work on your own with no distractions around you. Some people say they can work better listening to music. If you do, keep the music quiet – at least it may shut out other distractions!

You may find it helpful to draw up a revision calendar. Divide a sheet of paper up into squares, with one square for each day in the period before the examination. Then divide the syllabus into the same number of parts as there are days. Allocate one part of the syllabus for every day on your calendar. In this way you will know exactly what you are going to revise on each day. Your day's revision will not be complete until you have revised everything on your calendar for that day.

Some people are able to concentrate longer than others, but it is important to take a break from your work, preferably at the same time each day. When you stop, set yourself a time to start again, and *stick to it*.

Finally, good luck with your revision. This method can work. I know, because it did for me!

TOPIC 1
Cell Structure and Organisation

The basic unit of life is the **cell**. The simplest living organisms have *one* cell only. These organisms are described as UNICELLULAR.

BACTERIA (singular: 'bacterium') are examples of unicellular organisms.

Most other living organisms have many cells, and are described as MULTICELLULAR.

All cells have the following structural features in common:

(i) A CELL MEMBRANE which *controls* the passage of substances into and out of the cell. One of the most important of those substances is **water**. All other substances passing through the cell membrane are **in solution**.

(ii) CYTOPLASM – a jelly-like substance in which the chemical reactions of the cell (metabolic reactions) take place. The cytoplasm also contains:

(iii) The NUCLEUS. This contains a number of CHROMOSOMES made of the chemical DNA. Chromosomes possess genes which are responsible for programming the cytoplasm to manufacture particular proteins. When a cell divides, it does so by a process called MITOSIS during which each chromosome forms an exact replica of itself. The two cells formed are identical to each other, and to the original cell.

The cytoplasm *and* the nucleus make up the PROTOPLASM.

Plant cells have the following **additional** structures:

(i) A (large, central) VACUOLE – a space containing **cell sap**, a solution made up mostly of sugars. The vacuole is sometimes called the 'sap vacuole'. It is separated from the cytoplasm by the vacuolar membrane. Plant cells undergoing cell division do *not* have a vacuole.

(ii) The CELL WALL – a 'box' made of cellulose that encloses the cell.

If the cell is involved in the process of PHOTOSYNTHESIS, it also contains:

(iii) CHLOROPLASTS – small bodies lying in the cytoplasm. They are green in colour because they contain the pigment CHLOROPHYLL.

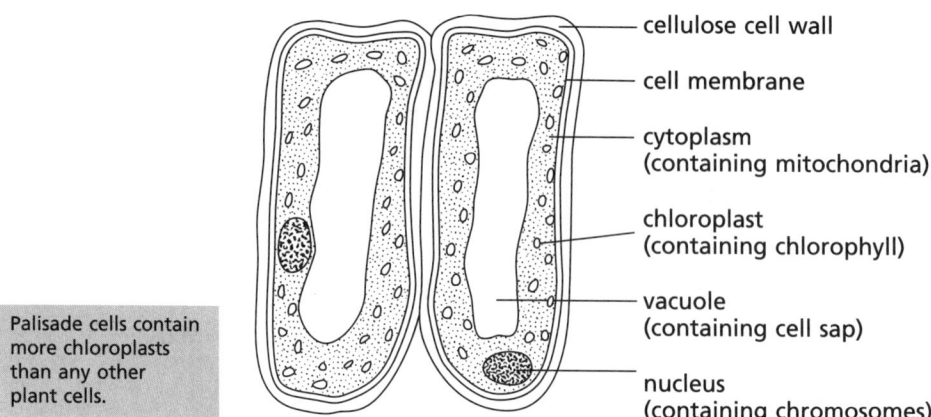

Palisade cells contain more chloroplasts than any other plant cells.

Fig. 1 Palisade mesophyll cells from a leaf

Note: The cell membrane in plants fits tightly against the cell wall, and is often difficult to see.

Similarities and differences between plant and animal cells are shown in the table below:

	Animal cell	Plant cell
Similarities	cell membrane cytoplasm nucleus	
Differences	no sap vacuole no cell wall no chloroplasts around 10–20 μm across	sap vacuole cell wall may have chloroplasts around 40–100 μm across

(1 μm = $\frac{1}{1000}$ mm)

Investigation 1.1

To observe animal cells
1. Cut a cube of fresh liver, in section, approximately 1.5 cm square.
2. Remove some cells from the cube of liver by scraping one of the cut surfaces with the end of a spatula (the end of a teaspoon would do).
3. Transfer the cells to a clean microscope slide. Add one drop of methylene blue (a suitable stain for animal cells) and one drop of glycerol (glycerine).
4. Stir the cells, stain and glycerol together and leave for 30 seconds. (This time can be adjusted according to the depth of staining required.)
5. Carefully place a clean, dry cover slip over the preparation, then wrap a filter paper around the slide and cover slip.
6. Place the slide on a bench and press hard with your thumb on the filter paper over the cover slip. The filter paper should absorb any surplus stain and glycerol, and the slide is then ready for viewing with a microscope (medium to high power).

continued page 3

CELL STRUCTURE AND ORGANISATION 3

You should be able to see these structures:

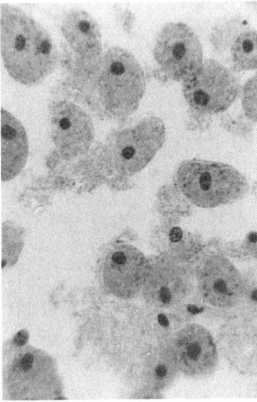

Fig. 2a Stained liver cells

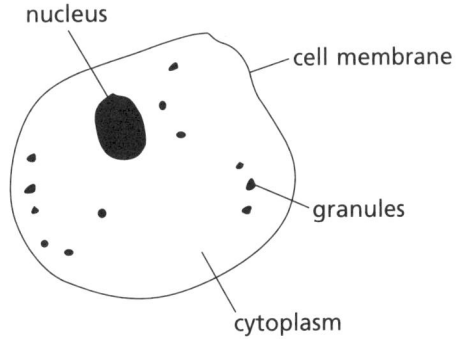

Fig. 2b Animal cell (liver)

Investigation 1.2

To observe plant cells
1 Peel off the dry outer leaves of an onion bulb.
2 Remove one of the fleshy layers beneath.
3 Using forceps or your fingers, peel away the very thin, skin-like covering (epidermis) of the layer you have removed.
4 Place three drops of dilute IODINE SOLUTION on a clean, dry microscope slide. (Iodine solution is a suitable, temporary stain for plant cells.)
5 Transfer a small piece of the epidermis (a 50–75 mm square is large enough) to the iodine solution. Make sure it lies flat and is completely covered by the iodine solution.
6 Carefully place a glass cover slip on top of the preparation and remove any excess liquid with a piece of filter paper.
7 Transfer the slide to a microscope for viewing. The onion cells are large, so it may not be necessary to use the high power of your microscope.

You should be able to see these structures:

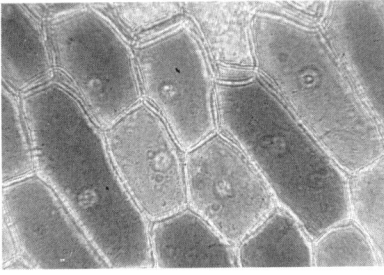

Fig. 3a Onion cells

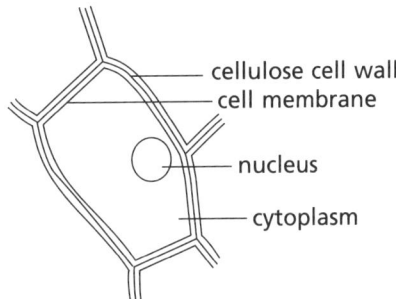

Fig. 3b Leaf epidermal cell from an onion bulb

TOPIC 2

Specialised Cells, Tissues and Organs

In UNICELLULAR organisms, one cell must be able to carry out *all* the functions of a living organism. In MULTICELLULAR organisms, cells are usually modified to carry out *one* main function. The appearance of the cell will vary depending on what that main function is.

There is a relationship between the structure of a cell and its function.

The following are examples of this relationship.

A   Root hair cell

Function

The **absorption of water and mineral ions** (salts) from the soil.

How it is adapted to this function

The outer part of its cell wall (i.e. the part in direct contact with the soil) is in the form of a long, tubular extension (the **root hair**).

This root hair:

(i)   is able to form very close contact with the water film surrounding many soil particles

(ii) greatly **increases the surface area of the cell** available for uptake of water and ions.

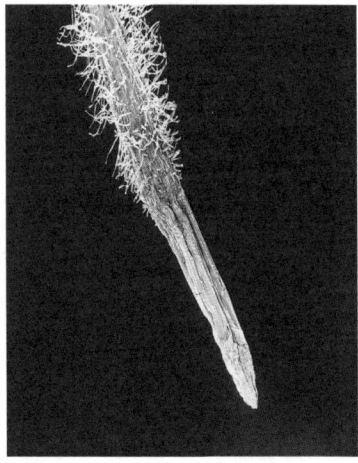

Fig. 4a   A root tip showing root hairs

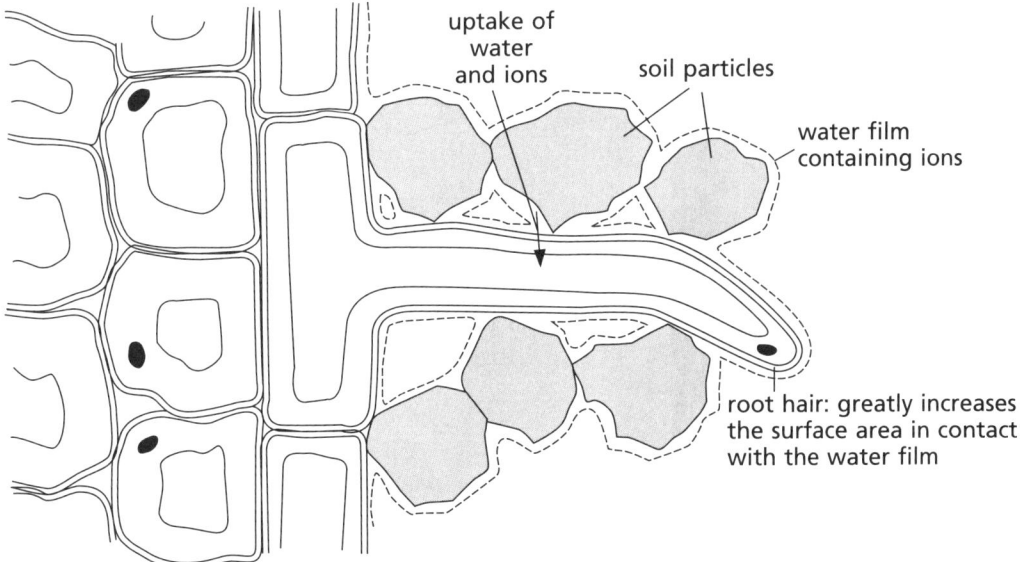

Fig. 4b A root hair cell

B Xylem vessels

Functions

(i) To **conduct water and ions** (dissolved salts) from the roots to the stem, leaves, flowers and fruits.

(ii) To **provide support** for the parts of the plant above the ground.

How they are adapted to these functions

(i) Conduction

XYLEM VESSELS are long narrow tubes, stretching from the roots, through the stem, to the leaves. They are stacked end-to-end like drain pipes.

(ii) Support

 (a) The walls of xylem vessels are strengthened by the chemical LIGNIN. As the lignin in the walls builds up, it eventually kills the xylem vessels. There is therefore no layer of cytoplasm to restrict the flow of water and dissolved salts.

 (b) Xylem vessels are part of the VASCULAR BUNDLES which run through the stems of plants like steel reinforcements in concrete pillars. They help to resist bending strains caused by the wind.

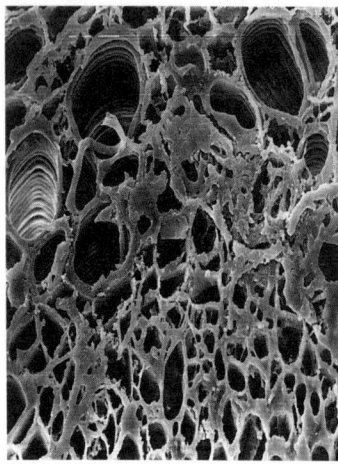

Fig. 5a Xylem tissue in a plant stem. The walls are made of lignin.

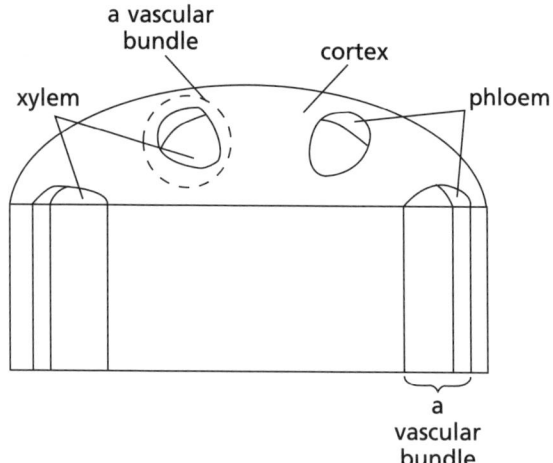

Fig. 5b A section of plant stem cut to show the arrangement of tissues in vascular bundles

C Red blood cells

Function

To **carry oxygen** around the body.

How they are adapted to this function

(i) The cytoplasm in red blood cells contains the pigment HAEMOGLOBIN. Haemoglobin combines with oxygen in the lungs to become OXYHAEMOGLOBIN.

(ii) The cells are **small** (7 μm × 2 μm) and there are **many** of them, so they have a **very large surface area** for oxygen absorption.

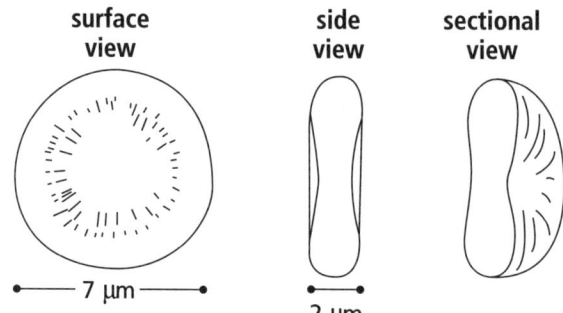

Fig. 6 Red blood cells

(iii) They have a **biconcave** shape, making their surface area for absorption even larger.

(iv) They are **flexible**, allowing them to be pushed easily through small blood vessels (capillaries).

D   Muscle cells

Function

To cause **movement** when they **contract**. (Contraction brings about a decrease in length of the cell. Muscles can do work *only* when they contract, *never* when they relax.)

How they are adapted to this function

(i) They are **long** and thin, allowing many to work side-by-side for greater force, or to form a contractile network.

(ii) Each cell (or 'fibre') contains many smaller **fibrils** – each capable of contracting.

(iii) Their cytoplasm contains many **mitochondria** (visible only with an electron microscope) which are responsible for releasing **energy** within a cell and necessary here to bring about contraction.

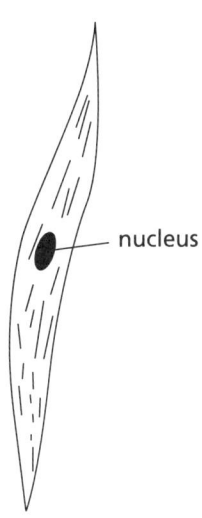

Fig. 7   A muscle cell

How cells combine to improve their efficiency

One cell working on its own would achieve very little in an individual plant or animal, so we usually find many similar cells lying side-by-side and working together, performing the same function.

Definition

Many similar cells working together and performing the same function are called a TISSUE.

Examples of tissues:
(i) xylem tissue in the vascular bundles of a plant
(ii) muscular tissue in the intestine wall of an animal.

Different types of tissue often work together to achieve a combined function.

> **Definition**

Several tissues working together to produce a particular function form an ORGAN.

Examples of organs:

(i) the leaf of a plant – an organ for the manufacture of carbohydrates during photosynthesis

(ii) the eye of an animal – the organ of sight.

Several different organs may be necessary in order to carry out a particular function.

> **Definition**

A collection of different organs working together to perform a particular function is called an ORGAN SYSTEM.

Examples of organ systems:

(i) the sepals, petals, stamens and carpels (i.e. the flowers) of a plant – for reproduction

(ii) the heart, arteries, veins and capillaries in an animal, i.e. the circulatory system.

> **Definition**

An ORGANISM is a collection of organ systems working together.

The increasing order of cell organisation found within any living organism is:

cell → tissues → organs → organ systems → organism

TOPIC 3: Diffusion and Osmosis

For plants and animals to stay alive, chemicals must be able to move easily:
(i)   from one part of a cell to another
(ii) into and out of a cell
(iii) from one cell to another.

It is an advantage to the plant or animal if this chemical movement does not require effort, or more correctly, 'expenditure of energy'. As long as there is no obstruction, chemical molecules carry out this process by DIFFUSION.

Before diffusion can occur, there must be a CONCENTRATION GRADIENT of the molecules – a region of (relatively) **high** concentration next to a region of (relatively) **low** concentration.

Definition

Diffusion is the movement of molecules from a region of higher concentration to a region of lower concentration, down a concentration gradient.

Examples of diffusion in plants

(i) The movement of **carbon dioxide** during photosynthesis. Carbon dioxide, in solution, moves **from the water film** surrounding the mesophyll cells inside a leaf, **to the chloroplasts** in the leaf.

(ii) The movement of **water vapour** during transpiration. Water vapour moves **from the water film** surrounding the mesophyll cells inside a leaf, **through the intercellular spaces** of the leaf, and **out through the stomata**.

Examples of diffusion in animals

(i) The movement of **oxygen** into the blood for respiration. Oxygen is dissolved in the moisture lining the air sacs of the lungs (ALVEOLI), then moves **through the walls of the alveoli** into the blood.

(ii) The movement of **carbon dioxide** into the blood. Carbon dioxide, in solution, moves **from the cells**, through tissue fluid, **into the blood** in capillaries.

Understanding the processes of diffusion and osmosis

A The movement of molecules by diffusion

1   Suppose a container is divided into two sections using a piece of cloth.

2   A **dilute** sugar solution, which contains a lot of water, is poured into one side of the container. A **concentrated** sugar solution, which contains less water, is poured into the other. The container is left to stand for a few minutes.

3   When checked, the concentration of the solution has changed on both sides of the container. Each side has the **same concentration** of water and sugar.

By diffusion, both the water molecules and the sugar molecules moved down their respective concentration gradients, until both sides were at the same concentration. The pores in the cloth **did not obstruct** the movement of the molecules in either direction.

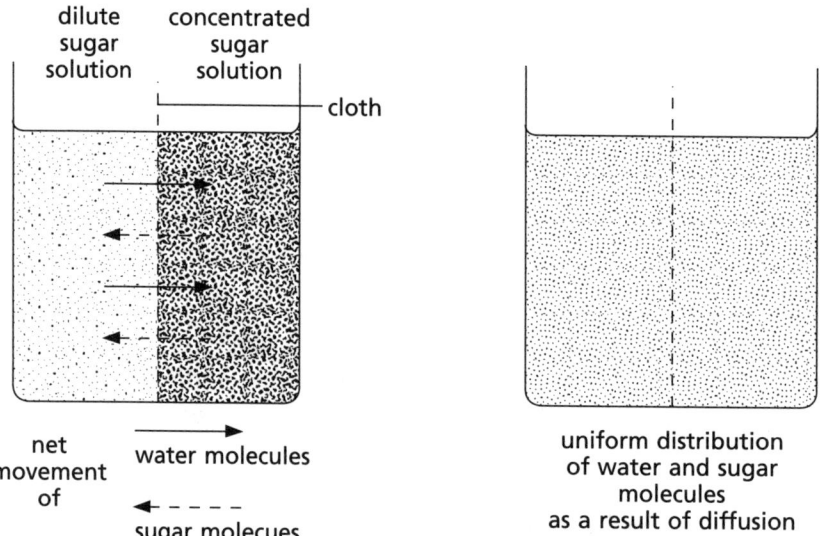

Fig. 8 The process of diffusion

B The movement of molecules by osmosis

1   Suppose a container is divided into two sections using a **membrane** with microscopic holes.

2   The same **dilute** sugar solution is poured into one side, and **concentrated** sugar solution is poured into the other. Again, the container is left to stand for a few minutes.

3   When checked, the dilute solution has **lost water molecules**, thus becoming more concentrated, while the concentrated solution has **gained water molecules** and become more dilute.

The microscopic holes of the membrane were so small that they allowed the passage of water molecules but *not* the sugar molecules. The water molecules diffused down their concentration gradient, while the sugar molecules stayed where they were.

This **specialised** case of diffusion is called OSMOSIS, and the separating membrane is described as **partially permeable**.

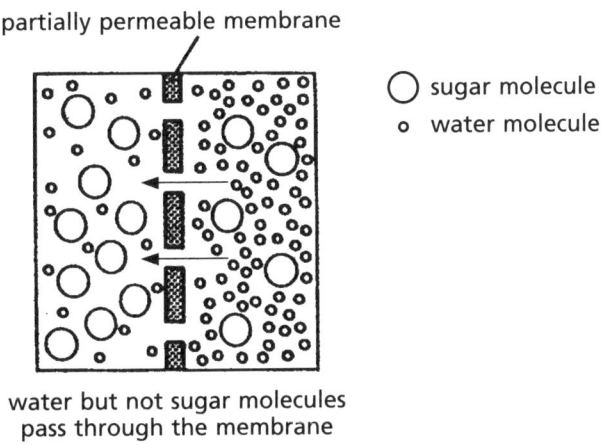

Fig. 9   Osmosis
(Reproduced by permission of the University of Cambridge Local Examinations Syndicate)

Dilute solutions, which have a relatively large number of water molecules, are said to have a HIGH WATER POTENTIAL.

Concentrated solutions, with fewer water molecules, are said to have a LOW WATER POTENTIAL.

Definition

Osmosis can be defined as the passage of water molecules from a region of high water potential, to a region of lower water potential, through a partially permeable membrane.

How water is taken up by a plant

Simple diffusion

1. The cell wall of a root hair cell is made of cellulose, a **completely permeable** substance.

2. The cell wall **does not obstruct** the passage of water into the root hair cell.

3. Where the walls of neighbouring cells **touch**, water can pass into the root by simple diffusion – **through** the cellulose of the cell walls (the 'cell wall' pathway).

Osmosis

1. *All* cell membranes are **partially permeable**.

2. The cell sap of root hair cells has a relatively **low** water potential.

3. Soil water has a relatively **high** water potential.

4. Water molecules will move into the vacuole of root hairs by **osmosis** (the 'vacuolar' pathway).

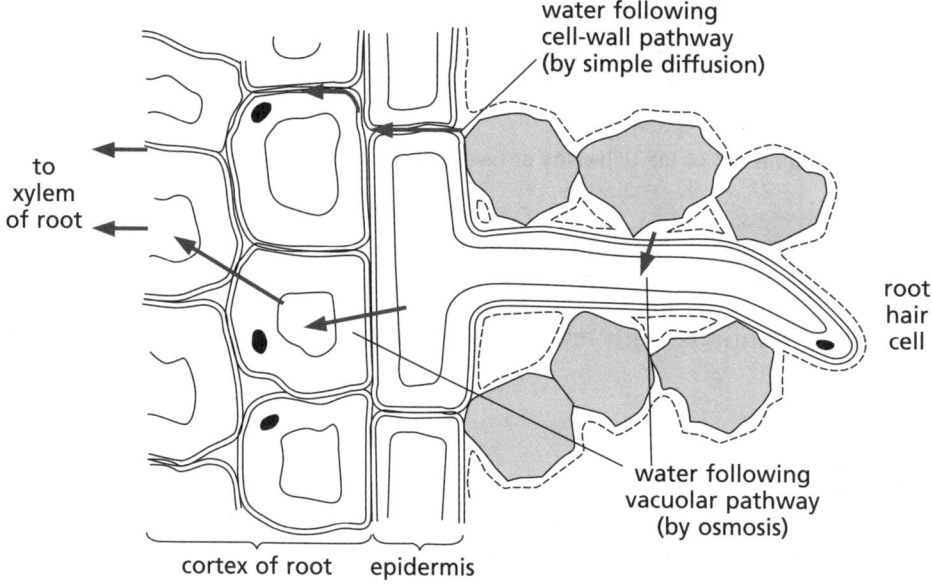

Fig. 10　How water is taken up by a plant

When water molecules enter a root hair cell, they **increase** the water potential of that cell. **Osmosis** then causes the water to move from the root hair cell to the next cell, closer to the centre of the root. The water molecules move like this from cell to cell until they reach the **xylem vessels** in the centre of the root, where they are transported away to the stem.

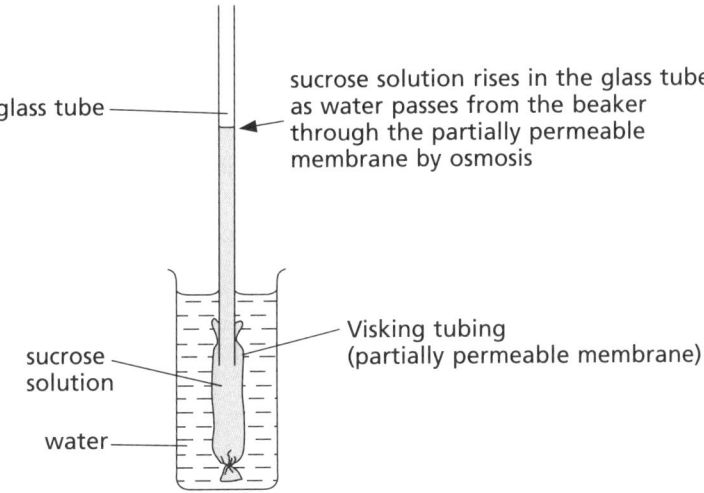

Fig. 11 A demonstration of osmosis using an artificial partially permeable membrane
(Reproduced by permission of the University of Cambridge Local Examinations Syndicate)

The effect of osmosis on plant and animal cells

A The *intake* of water by osmosis

Water enters **plant (root) cells** by osmosis, because the water potential of soil water is usually higher than the water potential of a plant's cell sap. As water enters the plant cell, the vacuole increases in volume. It presses the cytoplasmic lining of the cell against the flexible, box-like cell wall. This pressure is called TURGOR pressure, and helps to make plant cells firm.

Turgor, or turgidity, in plant cells helps:

(i)   to keep **stems upright**

(ii) to keep **leaves flat** so they can better absorb sunlight.

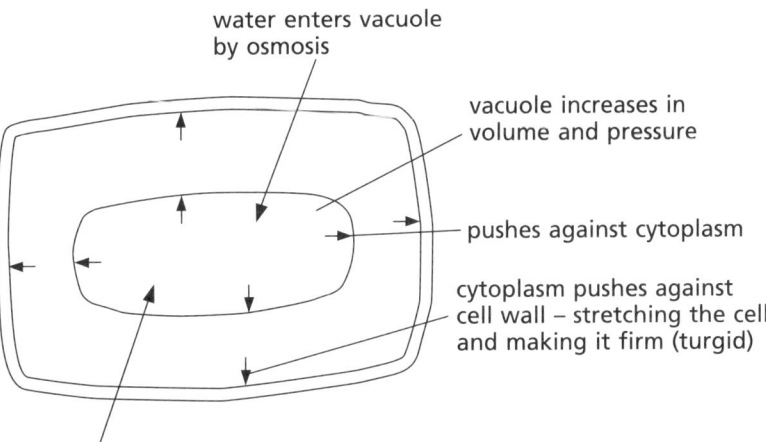

Fig. 12 Plant cell in water

Turgor resulting from osmosis can be demonstrated using a tightly-tied bag made of Visking tube (an artificial partially permeable membrane) filled with sugar solution, and placed in water for 20 minutes.

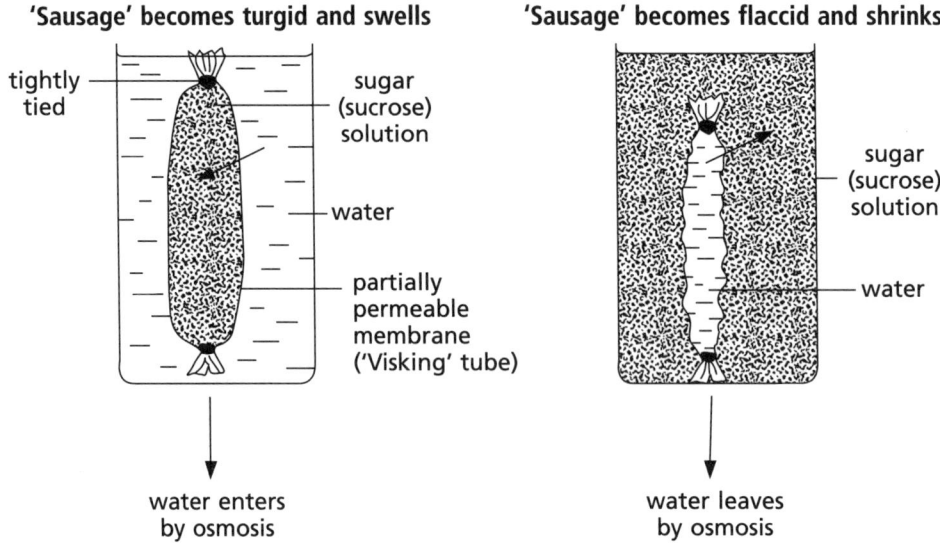

Fig. 13 Demonstration of how osmosis can affect turgidity

The water potential inside most **animal cells** is often the same as the solution in which the cells are naturally bathed (see the section on kidney function, p. 75). There is little movement of water by osmosis into or out of the cell.

However, if a red blood cell is placed in a solution with a relatively high water potential, it starts to take in water by osmosis. Since there is **no cell wall** to resist the increased pressure that results, the cell **bursts**.

B The *loss* of water by osmosis

Plant cells placed in a solution of relatively low water potential lose water from their vacuoles. The cells lose their turgor because the cytoplasm is no longer being forced against the cell wall. They become FLACCID. If the cells remain in the solution of lower water potential, so much water will be drawn from the vacuole that the cytoplasm will pull away from the cell wall. This condition is called PLASMOLYSIS.

DIFFUSION AND OSMOSIS 15

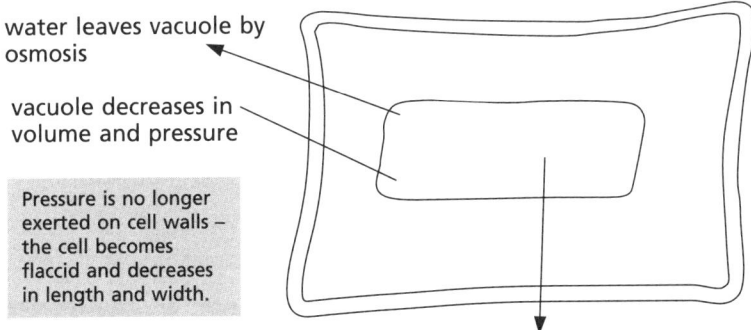

Fig. 14a Plant cell in concentrated sugar solution (flaccid)

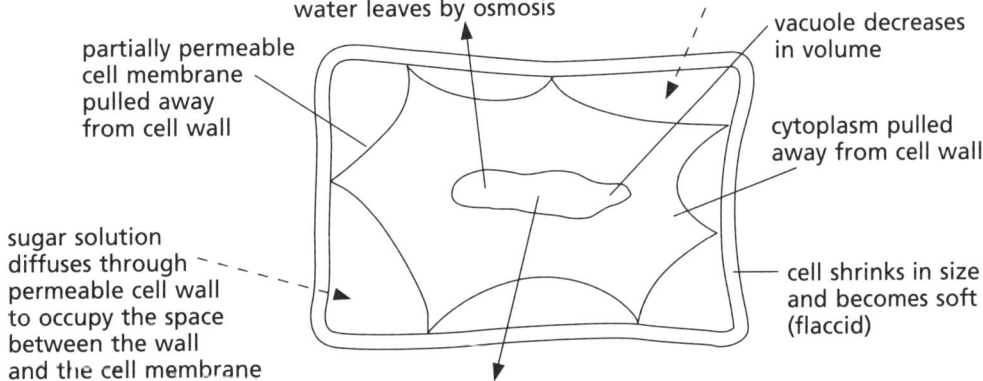

Fig. 14b Plant cell in concentrated sugar solution (plasmolysed)

Animal cells placed in solutions of lower water potential lose their shape and turgidity as water moves out of their cytoplasm. A red blood cell shrinks in size and its cell membrane becomes unevenly creased ('crenated').

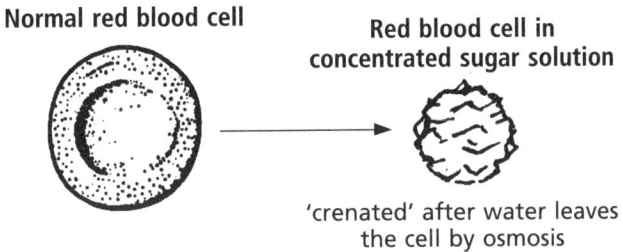

Fig. 15 The effect of placing a red blood cell in a concentrated sugar solution
(Reproduced by permission of the University of Cambridge Local Examinations Syndicate)

Active transport

Both plant and animal cells need a range of chemical molecules, other than water, for their metabolism. But these molecules may already be in a higher concentration inside the cell than outside it. In this case, the cell uses a process called ACTIVE TRANSPORT, where energy* is used to move chemicals from an area of lower concentration to an area of higher concentration.

Definition

Active transport is an energy*-consuming process where substances are transported against a concentration gradient.

*The energy required by the cell is provided by the chemical reaction of RESPIRATION. Respiration takes place in all living cells.

Examples of active transport

(i) In **plant roots**, when the **ions** needed for a plant's metabolism may be in very short supply in the soil water. Ions are absorbed by root hair cells by active transport (see p. 4).

(ii) In the **small intestine** of an **animal**, when digested food (such as **glucose**) is absorbed by the cells of the **villi** by active transport (see p. 47).

TOPIC 4

Enzymes

CATALYSTS are particular chemicals that can affect **how quickly** chemical reactions occur. Only **very small amounts** of catalysts are needed to do their job. They are not used up or changed by the reactions they effect, which means they can go on working, continuously catalysing the same reaction, so long as the reactant molecules (the SUBSTRATE molecules) are present. Catalysts usually **speed up** chemical reactions.

The chemical reactions occurring within the cytoplasm of cells are also under the control of catalysts – **biological** catalysts called ENZYMES. Special properties of enzymes are:

(i) They are all **protein** molecules.

(ii) They are made in the cytoplasm under instruction from genes on the chromosomes in the nucleus.

(iii) Each enzyme works at its fastest rate at one particular **temperature**. This is known as its OPTIMUM temperature. For most enzymes in a mammal's body, the optimum temperature is around 37°C. As the temperature rises towards 37°C, the rate of enzyme activity speeds up. If the temperature rises above the optimum, the rate of activity begins to slow down. At around 60°C, the enzyme is **destroyed** or '**denatured**' (*not* 'killed' – it was never alive). The rate of the reaction falls to (almost) 0.

(iv) Each enzyme works at its fastest rate at one particular **pH**. This is known as its OPTIMUM pH. If the pH level falls either side of the optimum, the rate of enzyme activity gradually decreases. For most enzymes in a mammal's body, the optimum is pH 7, or slightly above. However, the optimum for each enzyme depends on where it is found in the body. For example, the enzyme PROTEASE found in the stomach, where it is highly acidic, is most effective at the low pH 1.5.

Remember: pH is a measure of the degree of acidity or alkalinity. A pH of 7 is neutral, below 7 is acidic and above 7 is alkaline.

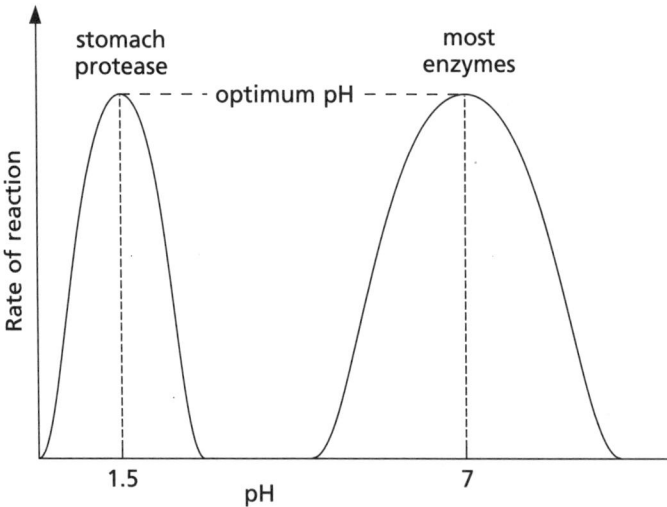

Fig. 16 The effect of pH on the rate of an enzyme-controlled reaction

How enzymes work – the 'lock and key' hypothesis

The job of an enzyme (e.g. those used in digestion) is often to break down a large molecule (the **substrate** molecule) into smaller molecules (the PRODUCT). The 'lock and key' hypothesis suggests how this may be achieved.

Each enzyme is a molecule with a **specific shape**. On part of its surface is the ACTIVE SITE (the '**lock**') – a section where its substrate molecule (the '**key**') fits *exactly*. When the substrate molecule is in position in the active site, the enzyme slightly stresses (or 'bends') the substrate, splitting it into two product molecules. The product molecules drift away from the enzyme molecule, leaving its active site free to operate again.

By including a molecule of water in this process, the newly exposed ends of the product molecules are 'sealed' so they will not re-join. This type of enzyme-controlled reaction, common in digestion, is known as HYDROLYSIS.

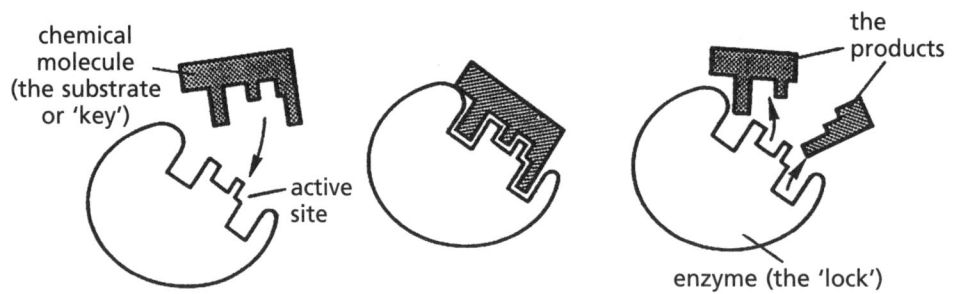

Fig. 17 The 'lock and key' hypothesis of enzyme action
(Reproduced by permission of the University of Cambridge Local Examinations Syndicate)

The 'lock and key' hypothesis explains enzyme action because:

(i) Only the correct enzyme–substrate combination can work.

(ii) Higher temperatures make the enzyme and substrate molecules move more quickly. This also means the substrate molecules **enter** the active site of the enzyme, and the product molecules **leave** the active site of the enzyme, more quickly.

(iii) Extreme heat causes the atoms of the enzyme molecule to move about so violently that they change position relative to one another. This changes the shape of the active site, and the enzyme stops doing its job.

(iv) Changes in pH may alter the shape of large molecules like proteins. If that protein is an enzyme, the shape of the active site may be changed, and the enzyme will work less efficiently.

TOPIC 5

Nutrition

Every living organism depends on nutrition – the taking in of food, and the use of that food – for survival.

Chemical structure of nutrients

CARBOHYDRATES, FATS and PROTEINS are three of the most important classes of foods. Their chemical structure is described below.

Carbohydrates

Carbohydrates are organic chemicals containing only the elements **carbon**, **hydrogen** and **oxygen**. The ratio of **hydrogen** atoms to **oxygen** atoms in a carbohydrate molecule is always 2 : 1 (as in water – hence carbo'hydrate').

Carbohydrates with **large** molecules, such as STARCH and GLYCOGEN, are **insoluble**. (A starch 'solution' is really a starch 'suspension'.)

Carbohydrates with larger molecules are made by the linking together of molecules of simple sugar.

Smaller carbohydrate molecules are **soluble**, and occur as:

(i) **complex** sugars, such as **maltose** and **sucrose** (table sugar), all with the formula $C_{12}H_{22}O_{11}$, or

(ii) **simple** sugars, such as **glucose** or **fructose**, with the formula $C_6H_{12}O_6$.

Fats (or 'oils' if they are liquid at 20°C)

Fats are also organic chemicals containing only the elements **carbon**, **hydrogen** and **oxygen**. However, the ratio of hydrogen to oxygen in the fat molecule is very much higher than 2 : 1.

Fats are formed by the joining of a GLYCEROL molecule with FATTY ACID molecules. They are all **insoluble** in water.

Proteins

Proteins also contain the elements **carbon**, **hydrogen** and **oxygen**, and **nitrogen as well**. Often proteins contain other elements such as **sulphur** and **phosphorus**.

They are large, **usually insoluble** molecules which are built up from simple, soluble units known as AMINO ACIDS.

Fig. 18 Amino acids linking to form a protein molecule (each different symbol represents one of the 22 different amino acids)

Up to 100 amino acids linked together (by chemical bonds called **peptide bonds**) form a polypeptide. Polypeptides link together to form a protein.

Tests to show the presence of carbohydrates, fats and proteins

A Carbohydrates

	Chemical ('reagent') used	How test is carried out	Result
Starch	IODINE SOLUTION	Put a few drops on the substance to be tested.	**Blue/black** colour if starch is present (**brown** if starch is absent).
*Maltose and *Glucose	BENEDICT'S SOLUTION	Add a few drops to a **solution** of the substance to be tested and heat in a water bath at 90°C.	**Red, orange yellow** or **green** if either of the sugars is present (**blue** if not).

*Benedict's solution does not distinguish between maltose (a complex sugar) and glucose (a simple sugar). When they react with Benedict's solution, both sugars work as chemicals known as 'reducing agents'. They belong to a group of sugars referred to as REDUCING SUGARS, all of which react in this way.

B Fats (The ethanol emulsion test)

Reagent used	How test is carried out	Result
ETHANOL	A dried† sample of the substance to be tested is mixed with ethanol. This mixture is poured into a test-tube of water.	The water turns **cloudy** if fat is present. The water remains clear if it is not.

†This test is more reliable if a dried sample is used. If it is not possible to dry the sample, the ethanol drained from it may already be cloudy, indicating the presence of a fat.

C Proteins (The biuret test)

Reagent used	How test is carried out	Result
BIURET SOLUTIONS	Add equal volumes of biuret solution 1‡ and 2 to the substance to be tested	A **purple** colour indicates that protein is present (**blue** if it is absent).

‡Biuret 1 contains sodium hydroxide, which is harmful to the skin. Make sure you use the proper safety precautions.

Sources and functions of nutrients

The three classes of food described above are some of the **seven** important constituents of our diet. The seven are:

1. Carbohydrates
2. Fats
3. Proteins
4. Vitamins
5. Mineral salts
6. Fibre (or roughage)
7. Water.

The main sources of these seven constituents, and why they are important in our diets are shown in the table on p. 23.

Deficiency diseases

If Vitamin C, Vitamin D, calcium or iron (indicated in the table on p. 23 with *) are lacking in a person's diet, then the individual will suffer from a DEFICIENCY DISEASE. The diseases are described below and on p. 24.

Diet lacking in Vitamin C

Symptoms include bleeding gums and wounds that do not heal properly. This disease is called SCURVY. In extreme cases, anaemia (lack of blood) and heart failure may occur.

Diet lacking in Vitamin D

If children do not have enough Vitamin D in their diet, their growing bones become soft, causing bow-legs or knock-knees. This disease is called RICKETS. If older people lack Vitamin D in their diet, their bones are more likely to fracture.

Constituent	Source	Importance
Carbohydrates		Carbohydrate molecules contain **energy** which is **released** in cells as the molecules are broken down during **respiration**.
starch	potatoes beans and peas yams cassava cereals	
sugars	honey sugar cane fruit	
Fats	fatty meat dairy foods egg yolk nuts avocadoes	Fat molecules contain more **energy** than carbohydrates and are stored in the skin and around the kidneys.
Proteins	meat peas and beans fish egg white peanuts	Proteins are used for **growth** and **repair**. Muscle is largely protein.
Vitamins		
C* (ascorbic acid)	citrus fruit (fresh) cabbage	For healthy **gums** and skin repair.
D* (calciferol)	fish liver egg yolk the action of sun on the skin	For the uptake of **calcium** from the gut and for strong **teeth** and **bone** formation.
Mineral salts		
Calcium*	flour milk	For healthy **bones** and **teeth**, for **muscle** action and blood clotting.
Iron*	liver red meat spinach	For **haemoglobin** – the **oxygen-carrying** pigment in red blood cells.
Fibre	fruit vegetables nuts	Forms bulk in the intestines. This gives the muscles of peristalsis something to push against, preventing constipation. Fibre also reduces the amount of fat absorption and reduces the risk of bowel cancer.
Water	drinks all food	Water is the **solvent** for chemicals in the body. It is the medium for all chemical reactions. It is used to cool the body and makes up about 68% of body weight.

Diet lacking in calcium

If a person lacks calcium in their diet, their bones become brittle and do not form properly. They suffer symptoms similar to those for lack of Vitamin D, and their growth is stunted.

Diet lacking in iron

A low level of iron in a diet leads to a lack of haemoglobin, which is necessary for carrying oxygen around the body. The person will not have enough energy. They will suffer from ANAEMIA. In severe cases, IRON DEFICIENCY leads to coma and death.

TOPIC 6: Plant Nutrition

Green plants are described as AUTOTROPHIC ('auto' = self, 'trophic' = feeding). They use small molecules around them (**carbon dioxide** from the **air**, and **water** from the **soil**) to build **large organic molecules** of **glucose** (a carbohydrate). This process occurs during the chemical reaction known as PHOTOSYNTHESIS.

Photosynthesis

Energy is needed to link the carbon dioxide and water molecules which are used to make carbohydrate. This energy is provided by **sunlight**. Sunlight is **trapped** in a plant by **chlorophyll**. Chlorophyll is a green-coloured chemical that contains **magnesium**. It is found within the *chloroplasts* of cells, where photosynthesis takes place.

Through the process of photosynthesis, light energy becomes 'locked away' within the carbohydrate molecule as **chemical energy**. This process is represented by the following equation:

$$\text{carbon dioxide} + \text{water} \xrightarrow[\text{chlorophyll}]{\text{light energy}} \text{carbohydrate} + \text{oxygen}$$

$$6CO_2 + 6H_2O \longrightarrow C_6H_{12}O_6 \text{ (glucose)} + 6O_2$$

Photosynthesis is therefore a process in which light energy is converted into chemical energy.

If a living organism breaks down the carbohydrate molecule during a metabolic process, the energy is released. Before being broken down, the molecule is often stored by the organism.

The first carbohydrate made during photosynthesis is glucose. Glucose is a simple sugar and is **soluble**. It increases the concentration of the cytoplasm in the cell, which slows down the rate at which enzymes in the cell work. Glucose is therefore usually converted to the INSOLUBLE carbohydrate, STARCH.

Starch is first stored in the **chloroplasts** within the photosynthesising cells. It is then converted to **sucrose** to be carried to the **storage organs** of a plant (see the section on translocation, p. 50). Here, sucrose is converted back to starch. The tuber of a potato is an example of a plant's storage organ.

The importance of photosynthesis to the living universe

Almost all forms of life rely on the chemical energy found in carbohydrate, the product of photosynthesis. Plants may convert this carbohydrate into protein or fat before it is passed on.

The oxygen produced by photosynthesis is essential for the respiration of most life forms. Photosynthesis also uses up the carbon dioxide released by respiration, converting it into carbohydrate (see the section on the carbon cycle, p. 105).

What does a plant need to photosynthesise?

We can use experiments to show that carbon dioxide, light energy and chlorophyll are necessary for the process of photosynthesis. It is difficult to show that water is necessary for photosynthesis, because the removal of water from a plant may have serious effects on other functions of the plant, not just on photosynthesis. The following experiments use potted plants; varieties such as *Pelargonium*, a member of the geranium family, or *Coleus* may be used, depending on what plants are available.

Things to remember when performing experiments

The importance of a control

In the first three experiments given below, a **comparison** is made between a leaf (or part of a leaf) which is able to function **with** all the requirements for photosynthesis, and a leaf (or part of one) where *one* of the requirements is missing. In this way, the results of the experiment are shown to be **valid**.

The apparatus and materials which provide this comparison make up the CONTROL to the experiment. Wherever possible, *all* biological experiments should have a control.

Experimental error

To reduce error, each of the experiments below should be **repeated** several times, if possible. An *average* of the results should then be taken.

PLANT NUTRITION

Investigation 6.1

To show that carbon dioxide is necessary for photosynthesis

Apparatus
- two well-watered **de-starched*** potted plants (e.g. *Pelargonium* or *Coleus*)
- polythene bag to fit over one of the pots
- cotton (to tie the polythene bag over the pot and around the stem)
- a large piece of flat glass
- two bell jars
- petroleum jelly (Vaseline)
- a small beaker containing concentrated sodium hydroxide (follow the safety precautions when handling)

*Before the experiment, the plants should be kept in a dark place (e.g. a cupboard) for 24–48 hours, so that any starch present in their leaves has been used up. This is important because these types of plants immediately turn any glucose they make during photosynthesis into starch, and we will be testing the leaves after the experiment to see if any starch is present. We must therefore make sure there is no starch present before we begin the experiment.

Method
Set up the experiment as follows:

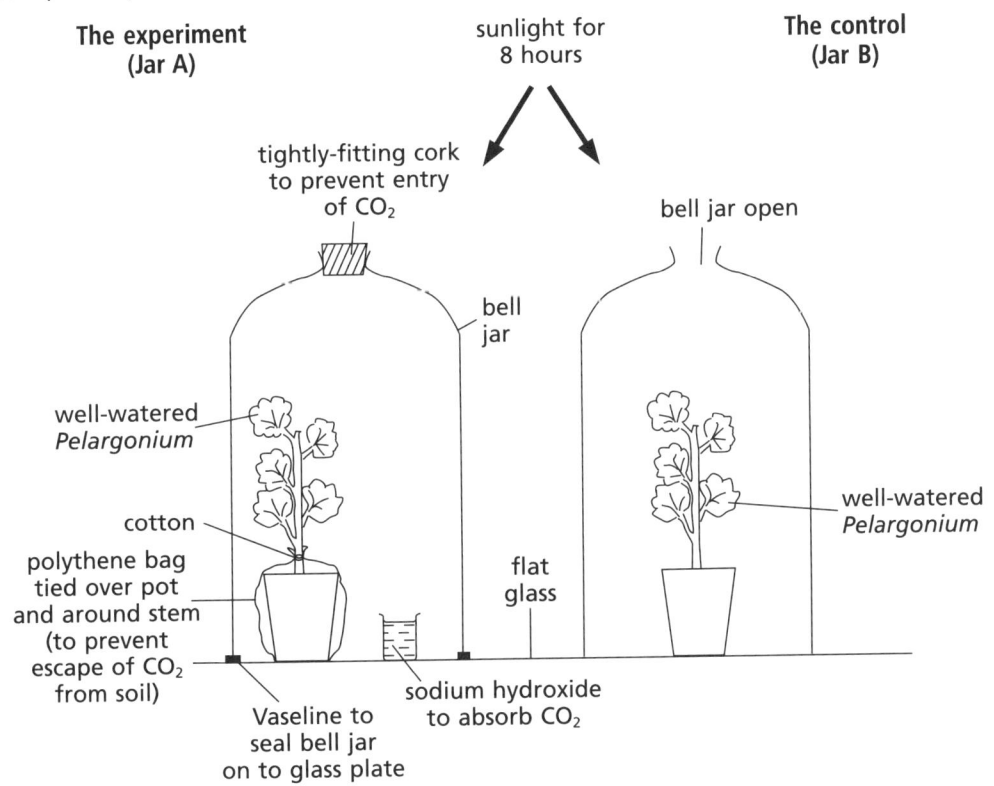

The experiment (Jar A) — sunlight for 8 hours — **The control (Jar B)**

- tightly-fitting cork to prevent entry of CO_2
- bell jar
- bell jar open
- well-watered *Pelargonium*
- cotton
- polythene bag tied over pot and around stem (to prevent escape of CO_2 from soil)
- Vaseline to seal bell jar on to glass plate
- sodium hydroxide to absorb CO_2
- flat glass
- well-watered *Pelargonium*

Fig. 19 Experiment to show carbon dioxide is necessary for photosynthesis

The two plants are left side-by-side in sunlight. After about **eight** hours, a leaf is taken from each plant and tested for the presence of **starch** as shown on the next page.

The starch test: to show the presence of starch in a leaf
1 Transfer the leaf to a beaker of **boiling water** for about **one** minute.
2 **Turn off the Bunsen burner.**
3 Transfer the leaf to a large test-tube which is half-full of **methylated spirits** (meths).
4 Place the test-tube (with the leaf in the meths) into the recently-boiled water, and allow the heat of the water to bring the meths to the boil. The chlorophyll is removed from the leaf, but the leaf becomes brittle.
5 Remove the leaf from the meths, and rinse it in the hot water. This will soften the leaf.
6 Spread the leaf on a white tile and add **iodine solution**.
7 If starch is present, the leaf will turn **blue/black**. If not, it will stain **brown**.

Results
If this procedure is carried out on the two leaves from Jar A and Jar B, the results should be as follows:
Leaf from Jar A stains brown. There is no starch present.
Leaf from Jar B stains blue/black. Starch is present.

Conclusion
Conditions in the two jars were identical, except that only Jar B contained carbon dioxide. Carbon dioxide is necessary for photosynthesis.

Investigation 6.2

To show that light is necessary for photosynthesis
Apparatus
- a well-watered, de-starched, potted plant (e.g. *Pelargonium* or *Coleus*)
- a cork cut into two pieces
- a pin

Method
The apparatus is set up as shown in Fig. 20.

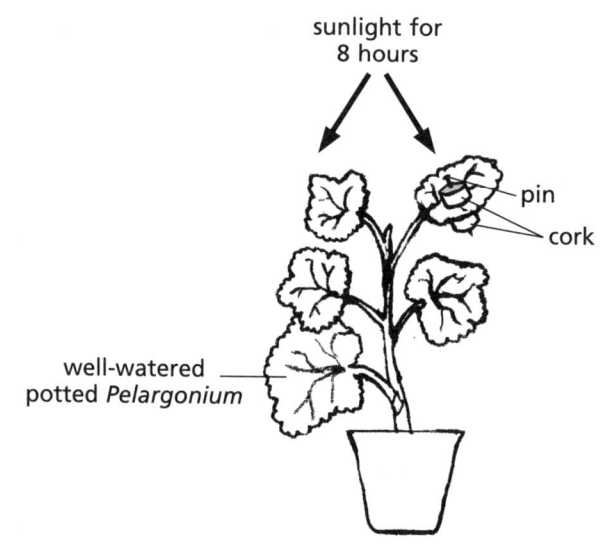

Fig. 20 Experiment to show that light is necessary for photosynthesis

The experiment is left in sunlight for eight hours.
The cork is removed from the leaf, and the starch test is carried out on the leaf (see Investigation 6.1, pp. 27-28).

Results
Where the cork covered the leaf, the leaf stains **brown**. The rest of the leaf stains **blue/black**.

Conclusion
Starch is produced only in areas of the leaf where light is able to reach. Light is necessary for photosynthesis.

Investigation 6.3

To show that chlorophyll is necessary for photosynthesis
Apparatus • a potted plant (e.g. *Pelargonium* or *Coleus*) that is well-watered, de-starched and **variegated**

Note: A 'variegated' plant has leaves one part of which are green (where chlorophyll is present) and the rest contains no chlorophyll (and is, therefore, often white).

Method
Leave the plant in sunlight for eight hours. Remove one leaf and carry out the starch test (see Investigation 6.1, pp. 27-28).

Results

Before starch test

white (no chlorophyll)

green (containing chlorophyll)

After starch test

brown (no starch present)

blue/black (starch present)

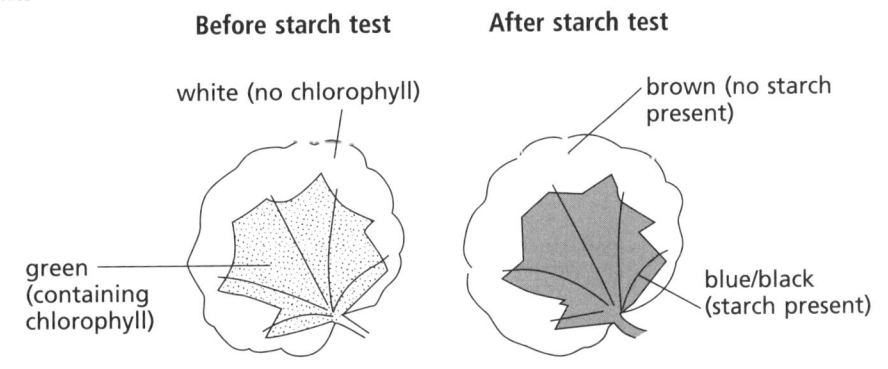

Fig. 21 Experiment to show that chlorophyll is necessary for photosynthesis

Conclusion
Starch is made only in areas of the leaf where chlorophyll is present. Chlorophyll is necessary for photosynthesis.

Waste product of photosynthesis

After carrying out the three experiments described above, we can deduce that carbohydrate (starch) is produced when a plant has access to carbon dioxide, sunlight and chlorophyll.

However, there is also a **waste product** of the process. This can be shown if a water plant is allowed to photosynthesise in the laboratory. Water plants such as *Elodea* or *Hydrilla* may be used for these investigations.

Investigation 6.4

To show that oxygen is given off during photosynthesis

Apparatus
- large beaker
- short-stemmed funnel
- two thick coins (to act as funnel supports)
- sodium hydrogencarbonate powder (to supply carbon dioxide to the plant)
- test-tube
- water plant (e.g. *Elodea* or *Hydrilla*)

Method
Set up the apparatus as shown in the diagram below. Leave it for two days in a place where it will receive sunlight.

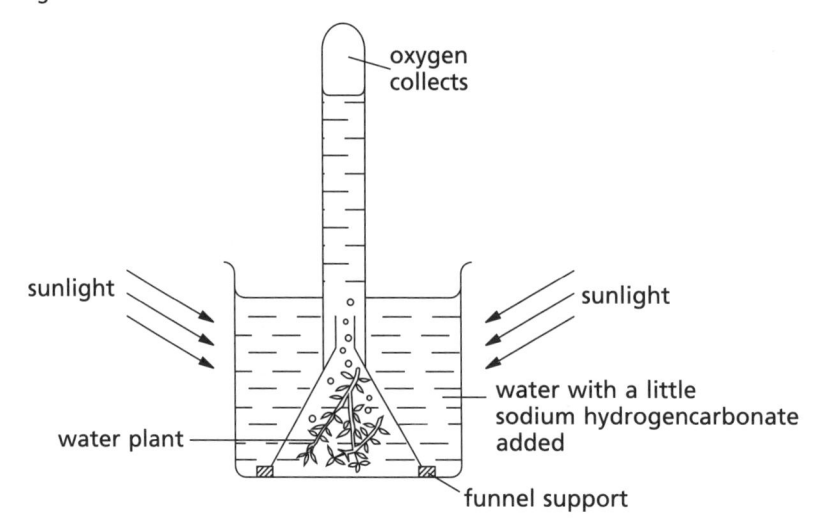

Fig. 22 Experiment to show that oxygen is given off during photosynthesis
(Reproduced by permission of the University of Cambridge Local Examinations Syndicate)

Results
A gas collects at the top of the test tube which is found to **re-light a glowing splint**.

Conclusion
Only oxygen has the power to re-light a glowing splint, so oxygen has been released during photosynthesis.

The **Control** for this experiment is to set up the same experiment in a dark cupboard, for the same length of time. No gas collects in the test tube.

The rate of photosynthesis

We can now look at a plant's **rate** of photosynthesis, that is, how quickly it photosynthesises. This rate changes if we vary the levels of certain elements: light, carbon dioxide and temperature. We can demonstrate this in experiments by measuring the release of oxygen by a water plant.

Investigation 6.5

To show the effect of varying light intensity on the rate of photosynthesis

Apparatus
- a large test-tube
- a bench lamp
- a length of stem from a water plant (e.g. *Elodea* or *Hydrilla*)
- a timer

Method
The apparatus is set up as shown in Fig. 22. It is better to carry out this experiment in a darkened room so that the only source of light reaching the plant is the bench lamp.

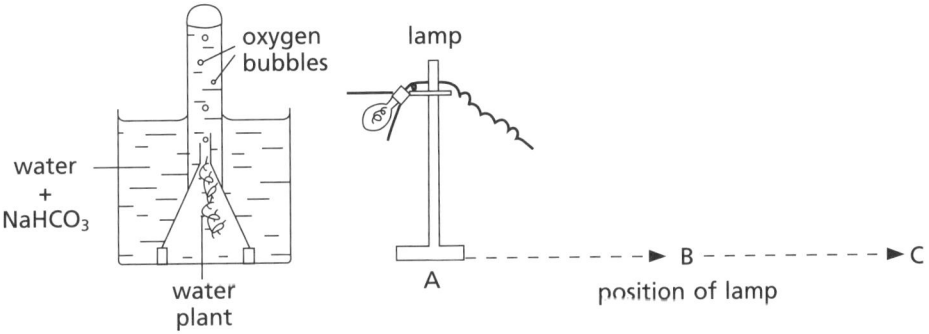

Fig. 23 Experiment to show the effect of varying light intensity on photosynthesis

As the water plant photosynthesises, bubbles are released from the cut end of the stem. Place the bench lamp at position A. Leave the plant for about 10 minutes – this allows the plant time to adjust to the conditions. Count the number of bubbles released by the plant for a measured period of time (e.g. 3 minutes). Record the results.
Move the lamp to position B. Again leave the plant for 10 minutes, then count the bubbles released by the plant for the same length of time and record the results.
Move the lamp to position C, and repeat the procedure.

Results
As the lamp is moved further away from the plant, the intensity of light reaching the plant decreases. As the light intensity decreases, so does the number of bubbles released by the cut stem over the same period of time.

Conclusion
The rate of photosynthesis decreases with decreased light intensity.

Investigation 6.6

To show the effect of varying the carbon dioxide concentration on the rate of photosynthesis

Apparatus
- a large test-tube
- a bench lamp
- a length of stem from a water plant (e.g. *Elodea* or *Hydrilla*)
- a timer
- sodium hydrogencarbonate powder

Method

When sodium hydrogencarbonate dissolves in water, it supplies the water with carbon dioxide:

$$NaHCO_3 \longrightarrow NaOH + CO_2$$

Immerse the length of stem in a test-tube filled with tap water. The water should be at room temperature. Leave it for about 20 minutes so the plant stem can adjust to the conditions. Place a bench lamp about 25 cm away and direct it at the plant. Count the number of bubbles released by the stem over a period of 3 minutes, and record the results.

Carefully weigh out 0.25 g of sodium hydrogencarbonate and add it to the water in the test-tube. Gently shake the tube to dissolve the powder, then leave for 20 minutes. Again, place the bench lamp about 25 cm away from the plant, and count the number of bubbles released over 3 minutes. Repeat this process twice, adding a further 0.25 g of hydrogencarbonate each time.

Results

More carbon dioxide becomes available to the plant as more sodium hydrogencarbonate is added to the water. As the amount of carbon dioxide increases, so does the number of bubbles released by the stem, measured over the same period of time.

Conclusion

As the amount of carbon dioxide available to the plant increases, so does the amount of carbon dioxide released from it. The increased amounts of available carbon dioxide therefore increase the rate of photosynthesis.

Investigation 6.7

To show the effect of varying the temperature on the rate of photosynthesis

Apparatus
- a large test-tube
- a bench lamp
- a length of stem from a water plant (e.g. *Elodea* or *Hydrilla*)
- a large beaker
- a timer
- a thermometer

Method

Set up the apparatus as in Investigation 6.6, but with the test-tube in a large beaker of water (a water bath). The temperature of the water bath is the only factor in this experiment that is altered. Lower the temperature of the water bath by adding ice, then leave the plant for 20–30 minutes to adjust to the conditions. Count the number of bubbles released by the cut stem over a period of 3 minutes and record the results.

Raise the temperature of the water bath above room temperature by adding warm water. Again, give the plant time to adjust (20–30 minutes). Check the thermometer regularly to make sure the temperature is maintained, adding warm water if necessary. Count the number of bubbles released over 3 minutes and record the results.

> **Results**
> The warmer the temperature (up to around 45°C) the more bubbles are released over the same period of time.
>
> **Conclusion**
> The warmer the temperature (up to about 45°) the faster the rate of photosynthesis.

Limiting factors

The availability of light, carbon dioxide, water and a suitable temperature all affect the rate of photosynthesis. However, the rate of photosynthesis in a plant depends on which one of these factors is in **shortest supply**. That particular factor will limit the rate of photosynthesis, even when all others may be ideal (or 'optimum'). Light, carbon dioxide, water and temperature are therefore LIMITING FACTORS.

How plants obtain raw materials

Roots

Roots absorb the **water** necessary for photosynthesis **from the soil**. Water is carried from the soil to the leaves (see section on transpiration, p. 52).

A few millimetres behind the tip of every root, and extending also for a few millimetres, lies the **region of root hairs**. The many root hair cells provide a very **large surface area** for the uptake of water (and of ions) from the soil. The earlier section on osmosis (see pp. 9–16) explains how water is absorbed by the root hair cells.

Leaves

In most plants, the leaves:
(i)   absorb carbon dioxide from the air
(ii) absorb sunlight energy
(iii) manufacture carbohydrate
(iv) release the waste product, oxygen.

Most of a plant's photosynthesis takes place in the leaves. Leaves are **organs** containing several different TISSUES. Cells within these tissues are adapted to perform a particular function as efficiently as possible.

Leaf structure

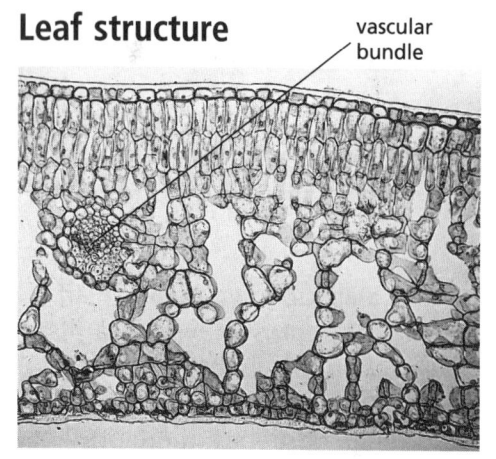

Fig. 24a Transverse section of a dicotyledonous leaf: whole leaf including the vascular bundle of a small vein

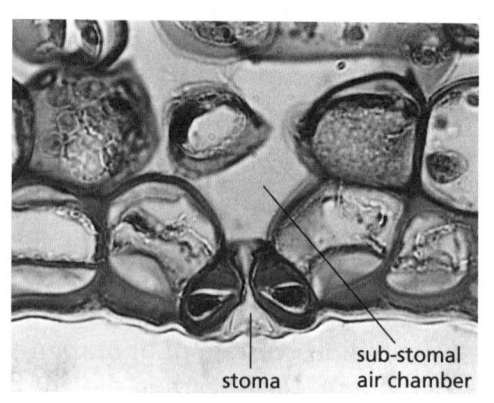

Fig. 24b Transverse section of a dicotyledonous leaf: stoma and sub-stomal air chamber

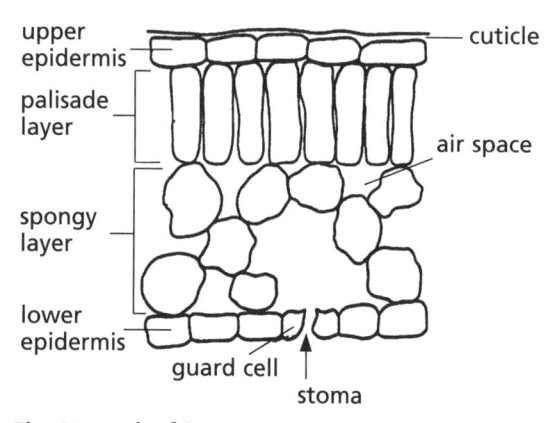

Fig. 25a A leaf in transverse (cross-section) to show a stoma

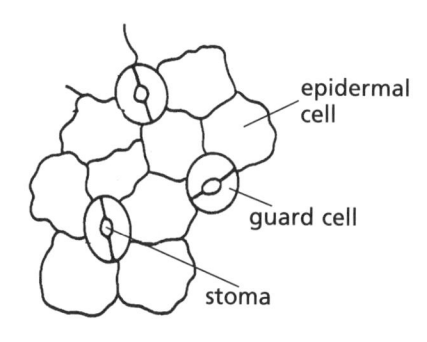

Fig. 25b Stomata on the undersurface of a leaf

How a leaf is adapted for photosynthesis

Structure	Features	Functional adaptations
Cuticle	Waxy non-cellular covering to help **protect** the leaf.	• **waterproof** • **transparent** to allow light to enter
Upper epidermis	A single **layer** of cells that secretes the cuticle.	• **no** chloroplasts, so allowing light to reach the cells beneath
Chloroplasts	Where photosynthesis takes place inside cells.	• contain **chlorophyll** • large surface area for uptake of carbon dioxide

continued page 35

Structure	Features	Functional adaptations
		• usually convert glucose to starch and store it temporarily
• in dim light, may move nearer to the illuminated surface of the cell
Mesophyll cells	**Palisade** and **spongy cells** (see below).	• walls have enormous surface area for GASEOUS EXCHANGE – they absorb carbon dioxide and release oxygen during photosynthesis
Palisade cells	Usually one layer of closely-packed, long cells. The first cells to receive light.	• contain largest number of **chloroplasts**. These are the most active cells in photosynthesis.
• walls are coated with a water film
Spongy cells	They:
• carry out some photosynthesis
• allow gases to freely **diffuse** throughout the leaf.	• fewer chloroplasts than palisade cells
• loosely packed with many air ('intercellular') spaces between them
• walls are coated with a water film
Veins (vascular bundles)	Contain xylem and phloem tissues (see below).	
Xylem tissue	Strengthens the leaf, helps to **resist tearing. Transports** water and ions to the leaf.	• They are dead cells, end-on-end, functioning like long drainpipes.
Phloem tissue	**Transports** dissolved sugar (sucrose) mostly away from the leaf. Transports amino acids to and from leaf.	
Lower epidermis	Layer of cells that forms the lower protective boundary to the leaf.	• may be coated with a thin waxy cuticle
• cells **do not** contain chloroplasts **except** the **guard cells**
Guard cells	Specialised epidermal cells. Control the opening and closing of the stoma between them. See Figs. 26a and 26b on p. 36.	• occur in **pairs**
• control the stoma as a result of their degree of turgidity (see the section on osmosis, pp. 9–16)

continued page 36

Structure	Features	Functional adaptations
Stoma (plural 'stomata')	Pores that allow: • **carbon dioxide** to enter the leaf for photosynthesis • **oxygen** to leave the leaf during photosynthesis • some exchange of these gases **in the opposite direction** in low light intensities when the plant is respiring faster than it is photosynthesising. Stomata also allow **water vapour** (a gas) to leave a leaf during **transpiration.**	

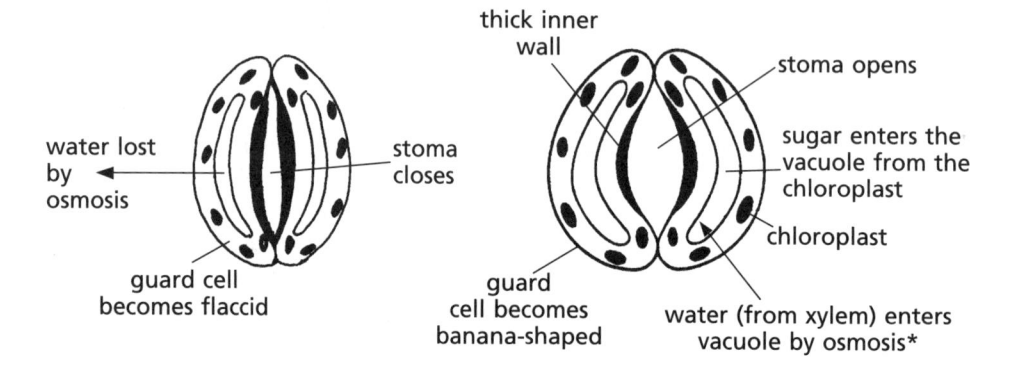

Fig. 26a How guard cells control the size of a stoma in the dark

Fig. 26b How guard cells control the size of a stoma in the light

*The guard cell becomes turgid, but the thicker inner wall does not stretch as much as the outer thinner one.

(Reproduced by permission of the University of Cambridge Local Examinations Syndicate)

How a leaf is involved in the process of photosynthesis

1 Carbon dioxide **diffuses down** a **concentration gradient** from the atmosphere, through the STOMATA, into the leaf.

2 Carbon dioxide diffuses freely throughout the leaf in the intercellular spaces.

3 Carbon dioxide DISSOLVES in the film of water which surrounds the mesophyll cells. The water is delivered to the leaf in the xylem of the vascular bundles.

4 Carbon dioxide diffuses in solution into the mesophyll cells and passes to the chloroplasts, where photosynthesis occurs.

5 Sugar made by photosynthesis is carried away ('translocated') from the leaf in the phloem of the vascular bundles.

6 Oxygen diffuses from the mesophyll cells into the intercellular spaces and out through the stomata, **across** a concentration gradient into the atmosphere.

Mineral nutrition in a plant

The importance of nitrogen-containing ions

Living organisms need PROTEINS for growth and repair. Plants have to manufacture ('synthesise') their own proteins. To do this, they convert their carbohydrates into amino acids, then link the amino acids together to form proteins.

Nitrogen is another element plants need to be able to convert carbohydrate into amino acid. Plants absorb nitrogen, as the NITRATE ION (NO_3^-), **from the soil** through root hairs. Nitrogen makes up about 79% of the atmosphere, but plants cannot make direct use of it in this form.

Investigation 6.8

To show the effects of a lack of nitrogen on the growth of a plant

Apparatus
- two small cuttings or seedlings
- two containers
- cotton wool
- black paper or black polythene
- culture solutions (available from suppliers)

Method
Two seedlings (e.g. sorghum), or small cuttings with the same number of leaves are selected from a quick-growing plant and held in the top of two containers (A and B) using cotton wool, as shown in Fig. 27.

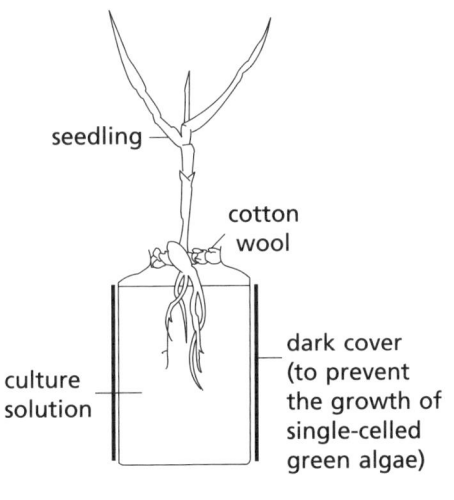

Fig. 27

> Container A contains a '**complete culture solution**', i.e. a solution comprising all the necessary salts* dissolved in distilled water (*supplying the following ions: potassium, calcium, magnesium, iron, nitrate, sulphate and phosphate). A complete culture solution can be made by dissolving 1 g calcium nitrate, 0.25 g each of potassium nitrate, magnesium sulphate and potassium phosphate, and a trace of ferric chloride in 1 litre of distilled water.
>
> Container B contains a similar solution, but lacking in **nitrate** ions. (Use calcium and potassium chlorides instead of nitrates when making up the solution.)
>
> The two containers are left in light and at a suitable temperature. It is advisable to blow air into the solutions each day, using a small glass tube.
>
> **Results**
> Container A (the **Control**): Seedling grows tall and healthy, with vigorous root growth.
>
> Container B: Seedling fails to grow, leaves begin to die and root system fails to develop.
>
> **Conclusion**
> Nitrogen (present in nitrates) is needed for the healthy growth of plants.

The importance of magnesium ions

MAGNESIUM IONS, like nitrates and other ions, are absorbed from the soil through the root hairs. Magnesium is the central atom in a **chlorophyll** molecule.

The use of nitrogen-containing ions in agriculture

Normally, plants obtain their nitrates from decaying organic materials in the soil. However, agricultural land often lacks this organic matter. To increase the amount of nitrates available to crops, a farmer may add **artificial** nitrogen-containing fertilisers (e.g. nitrate or ammonium salts, which soil bacteria will convert into nitrates – see the section on the nitrogen cycle, p. 106). The fertiliser boosts the growth of the crop, and the farmer can get a quick and high yield.

The dangers of the overuse of artificial fertilisers

Although better crops are produced by using artificial fertilisers, there is a danger that the readily soluble nitrates will be washed into streams, rivers and lakes. This can cause:

(i) An **abundant growth of water plants** (EUTROPHICATION).

(ii) When these plants eventually die, they are decayed by **bacteria** which **use up the oxygen** in the water resulting in the **death** of the water animals such as **fish**.

(iii) If this water is used as drinking water by humans, the high levels of nitrate may lead to **cancer** of the stomach.

TOPIC 7: Animal Nutrition

Plants manufacture their own food (they are **autotrophic**). Animals cannot, so they obtain their food requirements 'second-hand' either by eating plants, or by eating other animals which have eaten plants. Animals are HETEROTROPHIC ('hetero' = other, 'trophic' = feeding).

The constituents of an animal's diet are listed on p. 23. However, for the animal to be **healthy**, its diet must contain these constituents in their **correct amounts**. A diet which has the correct amount of each constituent is called a BALANCED DIET.

A balanced diet is different for each person, and depends on their lifestyle, age and sex.

Type of person	Special requirements	Reason
Child	protein carbohydrate calcium	for growth for energy for bones and teeth
Active adult	carbohydrate protein	for energy to build muscles
Pregnant woman	iron salts calcium protein	for blood for baby's bones for making baby's cells

The (basal) metabolic rate of males is higher than that of females. If a man and a woman are involved in identical activities, the man will therefore require **more energy** from his diet.

Fats provide the greatest amount of energy per unit mass – just over twice as much as carbohydrates and proteins. For this reason, an individual who eats a diet rich in fats is likely to become **obese** (overweight). The amount of energy contained within the foods they consume is much larger than the energy they use up.

Problems caused by an unbalanced diet

A person's diet may be unsuitable for healthy growth for two main reasons:

A The **balance** of constituents is incorrect – leading to **malnutrition**.
B There is **insufficient quantity** – leading to **starvation**.

A **Malnutrition**

Constipation, **heart disease** and **obesity** are three of the most important effects of malnutrition.

Constipation is a result of **insufficient fibre** in the diet (see the section on nutrients, p. 23). A diet lacking in fibre may, over several years, lead to bowel cancer.

Heart disease can occur when animal fats and cholesterol form deposits called ATHEROMA on the walls of the CORONARY ARTERY, the vessel that carries blood to the heart muscle. Atheroma narrows the artery and restricts blood flow, decreasing oxygen supply to the heart muscle. In severe cases, the artery may become blocked, leading to a cardiac arrest (heart attack).

Atheroma decreases the bore (diameter) of the arteries and thus can lead to high blood pressure, which increases the risk of heart disease.

Obesity is associated with high blood pressure and **heart disease**. It is often the result of eating too much animal fat, and the heart has to work harder to move the body's excess weight. Obesity may also lead to **diabetes**, **stress on joints**, and **social rejection**.

B Starvation

Starvation results in very restricted growth and development, particularly of muscles, leading to weakness. Resistance to disease is severely reduced, and death eventually follows.

Starvation is often the result of **famine**, a lack of adequate amounts of food to support the population. Famine may result from one or many of the following:

- poverty
- overpopulation
- drought
- flooding
- crop failure due to disease
- poor farming techniques
- war/political instability.

The world produces enough food to sustain the current population. However, some areas overproduce, while others do not produce enough. The cost of transporting the food to where it is required is often too high for those who need it.

Overpopulation may be controlled through education and the availability of birth control methods.

Poor farming techniques often worsen the effects of natural events, like drought and flood. Education on improved farming practices, and an understanding of the effects of deforestation and land clearing, may ease these problems (see the section on the effects of human activity on the ecosystem, pp. 113–114).

Biological research is developing disease-resistant crops, and improved methods of disease control.

The human alimentary canal

Human (heterotrophic) nutrition involves **four** basic stages:

1. Ingestion — taking food into the digestive system — 'eating'.
2. Digestion — (i) mechanical — chopping and grinding food with teeth and muscular churning of the food, as in the stomach
   — (ii) chemical — breaking large insoluble molecules into small, soluble ones (using enzymes).
3. Absorption — taking digested food into the bloodstream.
4. Assimilation — using the absorbed food in metabolic processes.

Any food which cannot be digested or absorbed is passed out of the alimentary canal during **egestion**.

The main regions of the human alimentary canal are shown in Fig. 28.

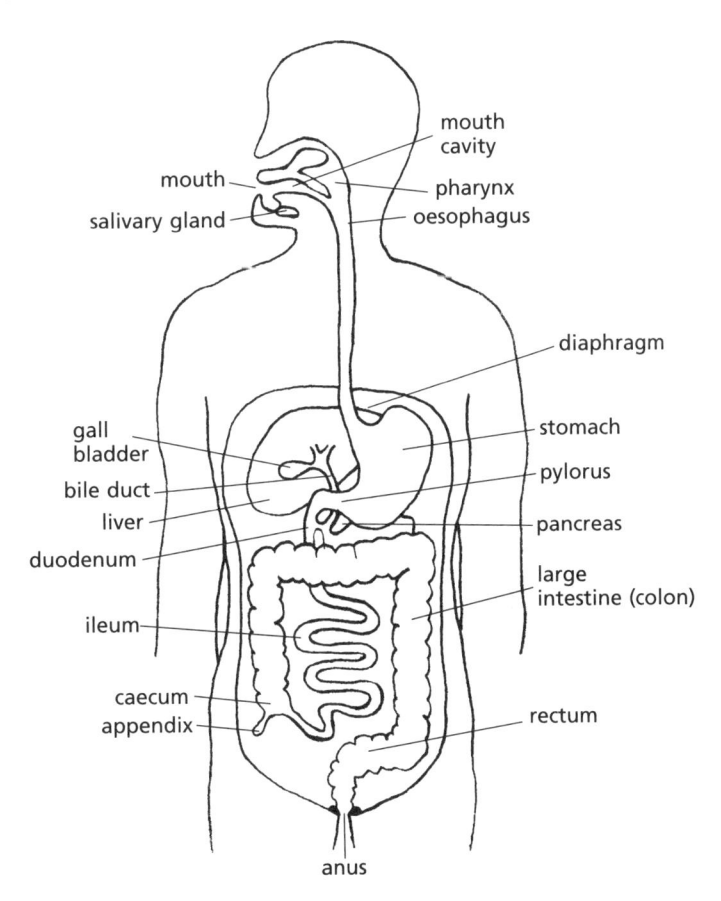

Fig. 28 The human alimentary canal and associated organs

The functions of the main regions of the alimentary canal

Mouth

This is the opening through which food is ingested into the **buccal cavity** (or mouth cavity). The buccal cavity processes the food as follows:

1 **Teeth** mechanically digest the food (see p. 45).

2 **Salivary glands** secrete a solution (**saliva**) of the enzyme **amylase** to digest starch, and the protein **mucin**. Mucin is sticky, so it binds the food together and lubricates it.

3 The **tongue** rolls the food into balls or boli (singular: 'bolus') and pushes them to the back of the buccal (mouth) cavity for swallowing.

Oesophagus

The oesophagus is a muscular tube connecting the mouth cavity and the stomach. Waves of muscle contractions, called PERISTALSIS, travel down the oesophagus, steadily pushing each bolus towards the stomach.

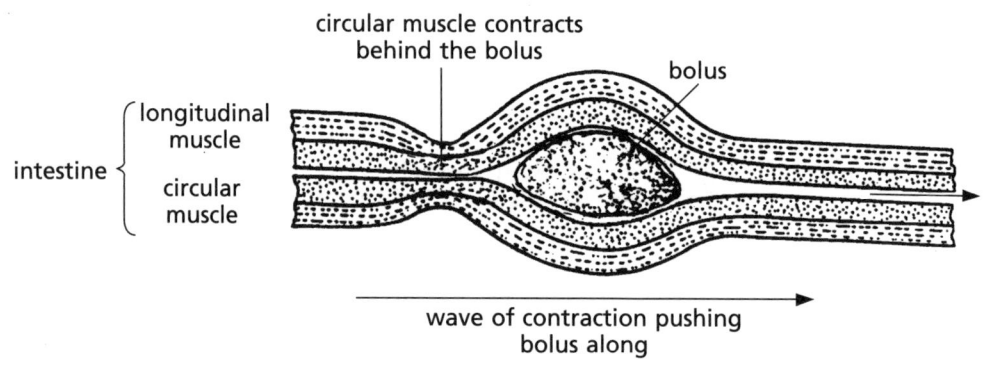

Fig. 29 Peristalsis
(Reproduced by permission of the University of Cambridge Local Examinations Syndicate)

Stomach

The stomach is a muscular bag which churns the food for up to four hours. The stomach wall secretes **gastric juice** which contains:

(i) The enzyme **protease** for starting the digestion of **proteins**, changing them to POLYPEPTIDES.

(ii) **Hydrochloric acid** to:
 – provide the correct pH for protease to work
 – kill potentially harmful bacteria in food.

(iii) The enzyme RENNIN to clot protein in milk (in children only).

After treatment in the stomach, the food is in the form of soup-like 'chyme'. It passes through a ring of muscle called the **pylorus** or **pyloric sphincter**, which relaxes to allow the food to enter the duodenum.

Duodenum

The duodenum is a tube about 30 cm long which:

(i) Receives **bile** via the bile duct, from the liver.

(ii) Receives **pancreatic juice** from the pancreas, through the pancreatic duct.

(iii) Releases a digestive juice from its walls. This **intestinal juice** contains **protease** and the enzyme **lipase**, for fat digestion.

Pancreas

The pancreas lies between the stomach and the duodenum. It secretes **pancreatic juice**, which it passes to the duodenum to help in digestion (as well as releasing the hormone insulin – see p. 88). Pancreatic juice contains the following enzymes:

(i) AMYLASE for digesting starch

(ii) PROTEASE for digesting protein

(iii) LIPASE for digesting fat.

The amylase from the pancreas completes the job started by the amylase in the buccal cavity, changing any remaining **starch** to **maltose** sugar.

The protease changes any remaining **proteins** to **polypeptides**. Unlike the acid stomach contents, where protease starts the digestion of protein, the contents of the duodenum are very slightly alkaline. The alkaline bile from the liver neutralises the stomach's hydrochloric acid.

Bile breaks up, or *'emulsifies'*, fats into small droplets, which greatly increases their surface area. Lipase can then work on them far more quickly, changing **fats** into **fatty acids** and **glycerol**.

Liver

The liver is the largest internal organ and is called the 'chemical factory' of the body. Like the pancreas, it is not technically part of the alimentary canal, but its function of producing **bile** is closely associated with digestion. Bile is a greenish-coloured fluid. It is **alkaline** due to the salts it contains, and is stored in the **gall bladder** before it is passed into the duodenum. Its functions are:

(i) to neutralise acidic chyme from the stomach

(ii) to emulsify fat.

Large food molecules are almost ready for absorption. But first, enzymes in the intestinal juice change maltose into **glucose** by the enzyme maltase, and polypeptides into **amino acids**.

Ileum

The ileum is the region where the **absorption** of digested food takes place. To increase its efficiency, its **surface area is increased** in the following ways:

(i)   it is about seven metres long (in a person)
(ii) its walls are folded ('pleated') longitudinally
(iii) its walls have millions of microscopic finger-like projections called VILLI (see p. 47).

Colon

The colon absorbs water, salts and vitamins. For more effective absorption, its walls are folded (transversely, or cross-ways, this time) to increase its surface area. Infections of the colon lead to diarrhoea.

Food is moved steadily along the duodenum, ileum and colon by **peristalsis** (which also occurs in the oesophagus). The indigestible fibre forms the bulk against which the muscles of the intestines can push.

Rectum

The rectum is a muscular storage chamber where the undigested food (**faeces**) is held and moulded before being pushed out through the anus during **egestion**.

Anus

The anus is the exit to the alimentary canal. It is closed by a ring of muscle (the anal sphincter) which is relaxed during egestion (or 'defaecation').

Summary of chemical digestion in the alimentary canal

Name of food	Where digested	Enzyme involved	Product
(Carbohydrates)			
Starch	buccal cavity	amylase	maltose
Starch	duodenum	amylase (from pancreas)	maltose
Maltose	duodenum	maltase	glucose
Proteins	stomach	protease	polypeptides
Proteins	duodenum	protease (from pancreas)	polypeptides
Polypeptides	duodenum	protease	amino acids
Fats	duodenum	lipase (from pancreas and intestinal juice)	fatty acids and glycerol

The need for chemical digestion

Most foods contain insoluble starch, protein and fat. These **large, insoluble molecules** cannot be absorbed into the blood stream, so they need to be broken down into **small, soluble** and **absorbable** (diffusible) ones. **Glucose**, **amino acids**, **fatty acids** and **glycerol** are the smallest forms of their 'parent' molecules.

Teeth and the part they play in mechanical digestion

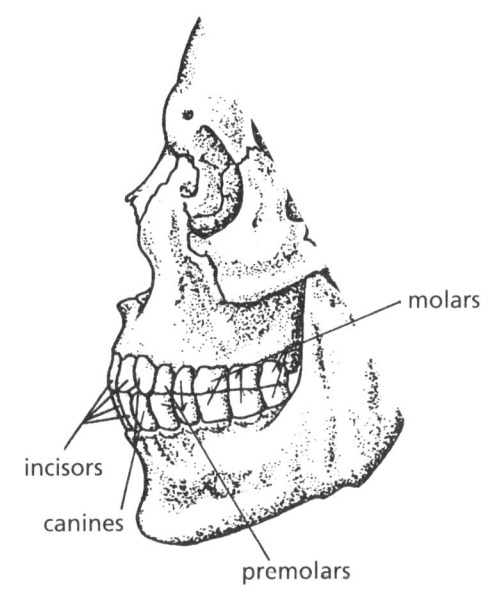

Fig. 30 Human teeth
(Reproduced by permission of the University of Cambridge Local Examinations Syndicate)

A person has **two** sets of teeth in their lifetime. The first set (called MILK TEETH) last for around 10–12 years, then they are pushed out by the **permanent** teeth. There is only one permanent set of **molar** teeth – there are no 'milk molars'.

In the permanent set, there are four types of tooth. The number of each type of tooth, shown below, is expressed as 'per quarter-jaw'. A quarter-jaw is one half of the top jaw, or one half of the bottom jaw.

Incisors

There are **two** incisors in the front of each quarter-jaw. They are sharp, spade-like teeth for **biting and cutting** food. They are single-rooted.

Canines

There is **one** canine per quarter-jaw. They are shaped like a cone, are sharp and used for **biting and cutting** food. They are single-rooted.

Pre-molars

There are **two** pre-molars per quarter-jaw. The surface of each tooth has two projections ('cusps') which are used for **crushing and grinding** food. They are double-rooted teeth.

Molars

There are **three** molars per quarter-jaw. The tooth surface is square with four cusps, or points, for **crushing and grinding** food. They are double-rooted teeth. The third molars – wisdom teeth – do not usually appear until a person is at least 17 years old.

Therefore, the function of teeth in mechanical digestion is to **bite**, **cut**, **crush** and **grind** food (also loosely called 'chewing').

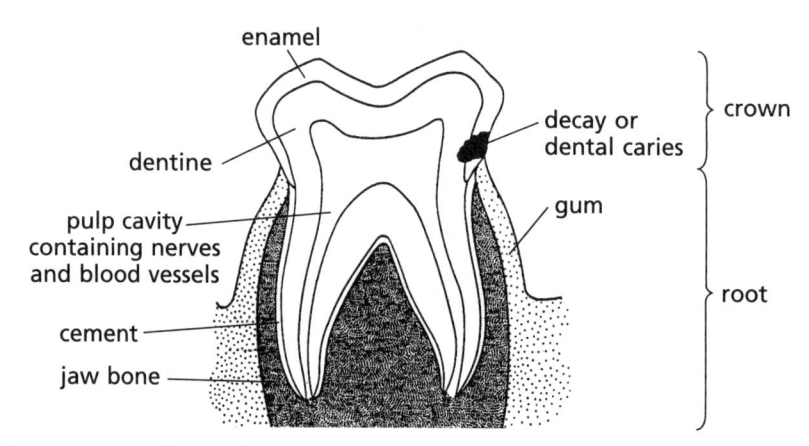

Fig. 31 The structure of a (molar) tooth
(Reproduced by permission of the University of Cambridge Local Examinations Syndicate)

The importance of proper tooth care

If teeth are not properly cared for, they may suffer from **dental caries** (or **dental decay**).

Decay process

1. Food (particularly food containing sugar) becomes stuck between the teeth.

2. **Bacteria** settle in the sugary deposits, using them for their own metabolism.

3. The bacteria excrete **acids** which dissolve the outer non-living covering (**enamel**) of the tooth.

4. A **cavity** develops, in which more sugary deposits collect. More bacteria settle, excreting more acids. The size of the cavity increases.

5 Eventually, the decay reaches the **living** parts of the tooth. The first area affected is the dentine, where there are nerve endings. The tooth begins to ache. Then the decay reaches the pulp cavity – leading to an abscess (a painful swelling filled with pus).

Tartar

If you do not clean your teeth, a mixture of food, saliva, cheek cells and bacteria collects at the neck of the tooth (where it enters the gum). This deposit is called **tartar**. The acids released by the bacteria damage the enamel of the tooth in that region, and cause **gum disease**.

Plaque

If not removed, tartar hardens to form **plaque**. Plaque forms a solid barrier, so bacteria trapped between it and the tooth can decay the tooth without interference.

How to care for teeth

(i) Do not eat sweet or starchy foods before going to bed. Saliva flow stops when we are asleep and prevents the sugar from being washed away. It is better to eat a raw, crunchy food, such as a carrot.

(ii) Brush teeth last thing at night, and first thing in the morning. Careful brushing removes plaque.

(iii) Use dental floss regularly to remove fragments of food from between the teeth.

(iv) Use a toothpaste which:
 – contains fluoride to strengthen the tooth enamel
 – contains a bactericide (to kill bacteria)
 – is alkaline, to neutralise acids released by the bacteria.

(v) Visit the dentist regularly for an examination, and have treatment if required.

The absorption and assimilation of food

Villi

The villi of the ileum are specially adapted for the process of food absorption. They:

(i) are extremely **numerous** – increasing the internal surface area of the ileum

(ii) are very **thin-walled** (one cell thick)

(iii) contain **blood capillaries** just beneath their walls
(iv) contain special structures (**lacteals**) for absorbing fatty acids and glycerol
(v) are able to **move** to bring themselves into close contact with food.

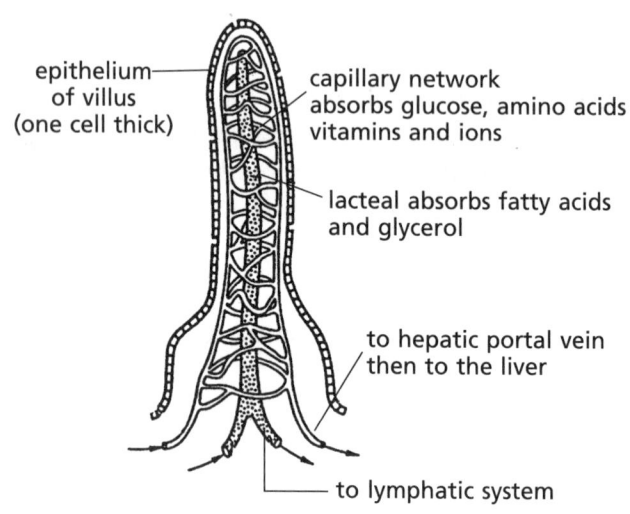

Fig. 32 A villus
(Reproduced by permission of the University of Cambridge Local Examinations Syndicate)

Amino acids and glucose, after absorption by the blood capillaries in the villi, are carried **directly** to the **liver** for the first stage of their treatment in the body. They are carried by a blood vessel called the **hepatic portal vein**.

Fats, after entering the lacteals in the villi, travel in the LYMPHATIC SYSTEM. They by-pass the liver and enter the circulatory system at a vein in the neck.

Assimilation

The main food substances, absorbed as small soluble molecules, must now be built up into the larger molecules needed by the body.

Glucose (and any other simple sugars which can be absorbed by the villi) may be used as it is, as a substrate for RESPIRATION to release energy. However, after a meal, there is more glucose available than is needed immediately. It needs to be **stored**. For this purpose, it is built up into a large insoluble molecule called **glycogen** (similar to starch). It is stored in the cells of the **liver** and **muscles**. The uptake of glucose and its conversion to glycogen is controlled by the hormone **insulin**, secreted by the pancreas.

Amino acids are used in cells for building up **proteins** as the cells **grow**, and also for making special proteins such as **enzymes**. Amino acids and proteins are **never stored**. Any **excess** amino acids are broken down in the **liver** by a process called DEAMINATION.

Two separate molecules are produced as a result of deamination:

(i)   A **carbohydrate** which can be changed to glycogen and stored.

(ii) UREA, a **nitrogenous** waste product (i.e. one which contains nitrogen), which passes in the blood from the liver to the kidneys for excretion in **urine**.

The role of the liver in glucose and amino acid metabolism

The liver is involved in the **regulation of blood glucose levels**. It is involved in changing glucose to glycogen, and storing glycogen when blood glucose levels are high. It also re-converts glycogen to glucose, and releases the glucose into the blood when blood glucose levels are low. The liver also removes excess amino acids from the blood by deamination.

Another major function of the liver is DETOXIFICATION, the removal and breakdown of poisons (**toxins**) from the blood. One of these toxins is **alcohol**. Although the liver is able to remove small quantities of alcohol, even on a regular basis, frequent high levels of alcohol in the blood can eventually lead to **liver disease** ('cirrhosis').

Fat metabolism

The liver does not play a major part in fat metabolism. Once in the blood, **fatty acids** and **glycerol** re-combine to form tiny fat droplets. Fats at body temperature are in liquid form, so the word LIPID is used to cover both fats and oils.

Lipids are stored in special storage cells in the skin ('adipose' tissue), and around the kidneys.

Fat is a good insulator, or protector, against **physical damage** and **low temperature**, and is a very efficient **energy store**. But fat is also heavy, and can lead to obesity.

TOPIC 8

Transport in Flowering Plants

The transport system of flowering plants has to provide:

(i) A way of carrying **water and ions from the roots to the leaves**.

(ii) A way of carrying **sugars and amino acids from the leaves** to other parts of the plant while it is photosynthesising.

(iii) If necessary, a way of carrying **sugars and amino acids from storage organs to the leaves** when it is not photosynthesising.

Vascular bundles contain the following tissues for transport:

(i) XYLEM for carrying **water and ions** (*Remember* 'Water in the XYlem – WXY').

(ii) PHLOEM for carrying **sugar and amino acids** (*Remember* 'PHloem carries PHood'!).

The movement of sugar and amino acids around a plant is called TRANSLOCATION.

The positions occupied by xylem and phloem in the vascular bundles of roots, stems and leaves in a typical dicotyledonous plant are shown in Fig. 33.

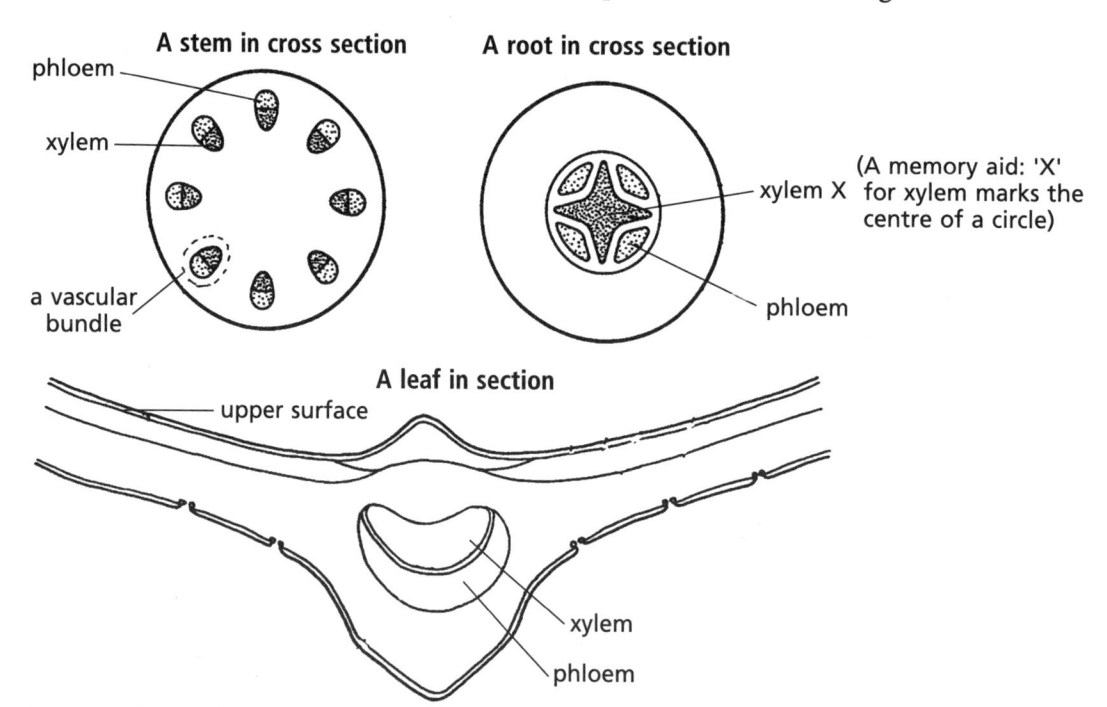

Fig. 33 The position of xylem and phloem in a stem, root and leaf
(Reproduced by permission of the University of Cambridge Local Examinations Syndicate)

Xylem vessels are long tubes. They are held open by walls **strengthened** by the chemical **lignin**. Wood is lignified xylem vessels. Thus xylem vessels also:

(i) help **support** the stem and photosynthesising tissues of the leaf

(ii) resist forces on the roots which might pull the plant out of the ground.

Investigation 8.1

To show that water travels up a stem in the xylem

Apparatus
- a beaker
- food colouring
- a soft-stemmed dicotyledonous plant (e.g. a broad bean, or balsam)

Method
Cut the plant stem about 1 cm above the root. Place the stem in water containing food colouring and leave it, as shown in Fig. 34, for about six hours.
Remove the stem from the beaker and carefully cut it through at 2–3 cm from its base.

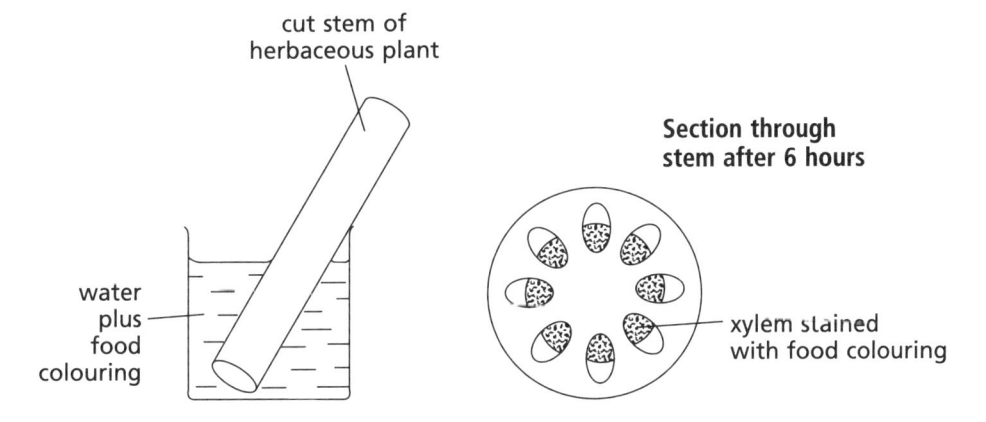

Fig. 34 Demonstration that water travels in the xylem of a stem
(Reproduced by permission of the University of Cambridge Local Examinations Syndicate)

Results
The vascular bundles will have been stained by the food colouring. Using a razor blade, *carefully* cut a very thin section from the stem, and view it under a microscope. It will be seen that the coloured region of the vascular bundle is in the position occupied by the xylem.

The path taken by water through a plant

Three forces cause water to rise up a plant. They are:

A ROOT PRESSURE
B CAPILLARITY
C TRANSPIRATION PULL.

A Root pressure

In the section on osmosis (see pp. 9–16) we saw how water enters **root hairs**. Osmosis and diffusion also carry water across the root to the vascular bundle of the stem. This causes a pressure (called 'root pressure'), forcing water into the xylem, and pushing it along the root towards the stem.

B Capillarity

Once in the xylem of the stem, water is carried upwards by a second force, called 'capillarity'. Capillarity is the movement of liquids upward through very narrow tubes. This force can be demonstrated by dipping the end of very narrow capillary tubing in water. Xylem vessels have a microscopic bore (diameter), which can be responsible for carrying water 20 cm or more up a plant.

C Transpiration pull

The third force is a result of the evaporation of water from the mesophyll cells of the leaf, and the removal of the water vapour through the stomata of the leaf. This process is called **transpiration**. It creates the force known as 'transpiration pull'. Water is drawn up to the leaf to replace the water that has been lost.

Transpiration pull, in particular, relies on the fact that water molecules are attracted to one another and are not pulled apart as they move up the plant. These forces of **molecular cohesion** ensure that a continuous stream of water and ions travels up the plant. This is known as the **transpiration stream**.

Transpiration

Definition

Transpiration is the loss of water vapour from the stomata.

Transpiration takes place in the following way:

1. Water leaves the xylem vessels in the leaf and forms a water film on the walls of the mesophyll cells inside the leaf. This water film is for **dissolving carbon dioxide** for use during photosynthesis.

2. Water from the water film evaporates into the intercellular (leaf) spaces – greatly increasing the humidity of the air inside the leaf.

3. There is now a greater concentration of water vapour molecules inside the leaf than in the atmosphere outside, so the water vapour **diffuses** out through the **stomata** into the atmosphere.

Transpiration occurs as long as the stomata are open for the uptake of carbon dioxide. If the transpiration rate **exceeds** the rate that water can be absorbed from the soil, then water starts to be lost from the plant's cells. The cells **lose their turgidity**, and the plant begins to WILT.

Conditions affecting the rate of transpiration

The atmospheric conditions which affect the rate of evaporation of water, also affect the rate of transpiration.

Transpiration speeded up by	Transpiration slowed down by
dry air	humid air
high temperature	low temperature
moving air (wind)	still air
bright light*	dim light*

*These conditions do not affect the rate of evaporation, but affect the size of the stomata through which the water vapour passes.

Although transpiration can lead to wilting, it also has the following **advantages**:

(i) It maintains a constant supply of **ions** to the leaves.

(ii) It brings **water** to the mesophyll cells for **photosynthesis**.

(iii) It helps to supply **water** to all cells for **metabolic processes** and for **turgidity**.

(iv) It helps to **cool** leaves – important in very hot climates.

TOPIC 9: Transport in Human Beings

The term 'transport system', in humans, refers to the **circulatory system**. Like the transport system in flowering plants, it is made up of a system of tubes. Unlike flowering plants, there is a **pump** and a system of **valves** to ensure that the liquid (**blood**) within the tubes flows through them in only **one direction**.

Dual circulation

During **one** complete circulation of the human (mammalian) body, blood travels **twice** through the heart:

1. Blood arrives at the heart from the other organs of the body, then travels to the **lungs**.
2. From the lungs, blood travels back to the heart, then to the other **organs** of the body.

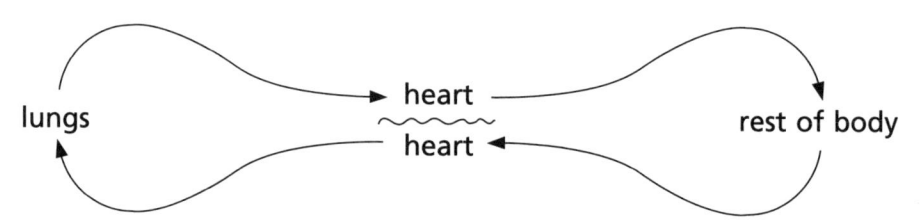

As shown above, the heart is completely divided into two halves so it can play its part in the dual circulation.

Blood needs to travel only a short distance from the heart to reach the lungs, which lie either side of the heart. Blood has to travel much further to reach other parts of the body, such as the toes. Blood leaving the heart in the **lesser** circulation (to the lungs) is not therefore under as much pressure as it is in the **greater** circulation. (Blood must always be able to reach the tissues of the fingertips, even when the arms are raised.)

The main blood vessels of the body

Blood always **leaves** the heart in ARTERIES. These vessels have thick muscular walls, and can withstand the high pressure of the blood. A large artery is called an **aorta**; a small one is called an **arteriole**.

Blood **returns** to the heart, under much lower pressure, in thinner-walled vessels called VEINS. A large vein is a **vena cava**; a small one is a **venule**.

Blood passes from arterioles to venules through microscopic blood vessels called CAPILLARIES.

Figure 35 shows the names of the blood vessels associated with some of the main organs of the body.

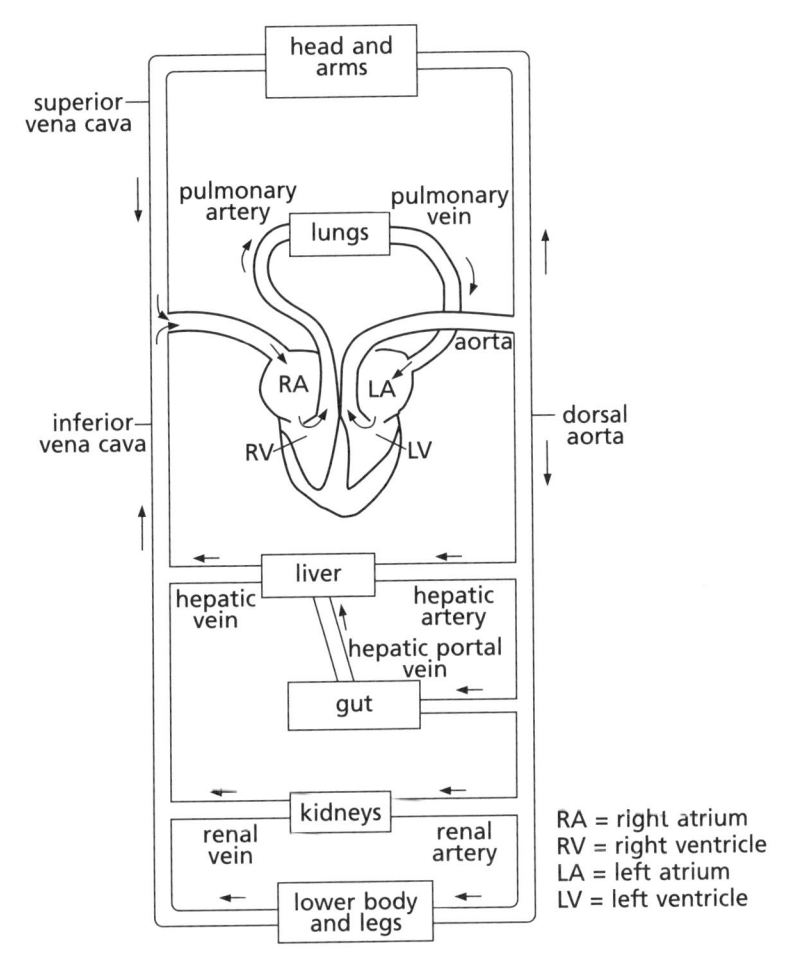

Fig. 35 The mammalian circulatory system

The heart and how it functions

Important facts about the heart:

(i)   It is a **muscular pump**.

(ii) It is made of special muscle (**cardiac** muscle) which has the ability to **contract rhythmically** (even without stimulation).

(iii) It never tires or suffers from cramp.

(iv) It beats about 70 times per minute in the average adult at rest.

(v)   It has **four** chambers, all with similar volumes when full – **two** ATRIA 'on top' (in mammals which walk upright) of **two** VENTRICLES.

(vi) Atria (singular: 'atrium') have thin walls and receive the blood.

(vii) Ventricles have **thick** muscular walls to pump the blood out of the heart under pressure. The **left** ventricle has the thickest walls, to send blood round the body.

(viii) A system of **valves** ensures **one-way flow** of blood through the heart (see Fig. 36).

(ix) A wave of contraction (called **systole**) passes over the heart from atria to ventricles. It forces blood from the atria into the ventricles, then forces blood out of the ventricles. As the ventricles contract, the mitral and tricuspid valves are slammed shut causing the 'lubb' sound of the heartbeat.

(x) The heart muscle then relaxes (**diastole**). As the ventricles relax, the semi-lunar valves close to stop blood being drawn back into the ventricles. The closing of the valves causes the 'dupp' sound. There is then a pause before the next cycle of systole-diastole (or 'lubb-dupp' of the heart).

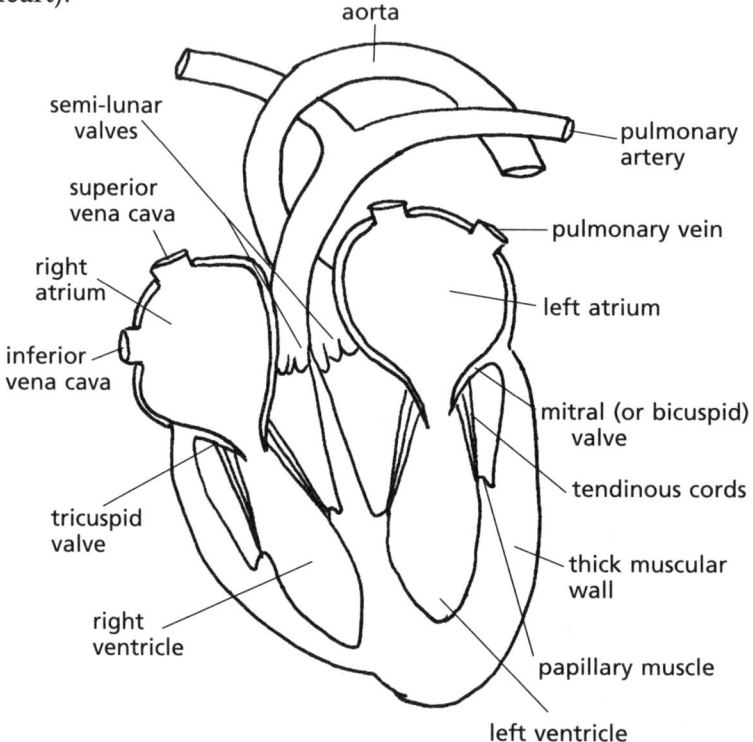

Fig. 36 The mammalian heart

Each beat of the heart creates a surge of pressure in the arteries, called the **pulse**.

There is no such surge in the veins, where blood flows smoothly under much lower pressure. Veins, however, have **semi-lunar valves** which ensure that blood continues to flow back towards the heart. Otherwise, veins rely on the movement of nearby muscles (e.g. the calf muscles of the leg) to 'massage' the blood from one set of semi-lunar valves to the next.

A comparison of the three types of blood vessel

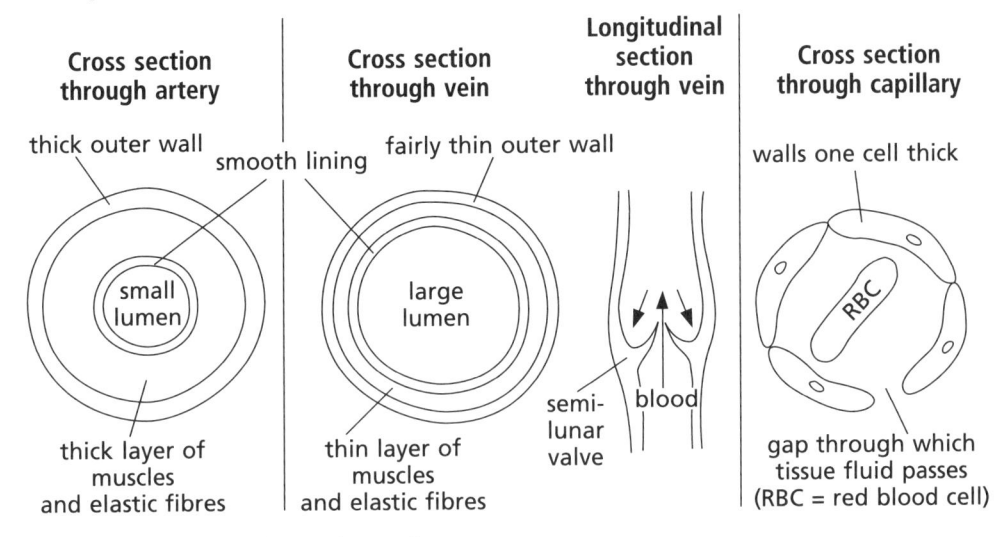

Cross section through artery — thick outer wall, smooth lining, small lumen, thick layer of muscles and elastic fibres

Cross section through vein — fairly thin outer wall, large lumen, thin layer of muscles and elastic fibres

Longitudinal section through vein — semi-lunar valve, blood

Cross section through capillary — walls one cell thick, RBC, gap through which tissue fluid passes (RBC = red blood cell)

Fig. 37 A comparison of blood vessels

Differences between arteries, veins and capillaries

Arteries	Veins	Capillaries
Take blood *from* the heart	Take blood *to* the heart	Take blood from arteries to veins
Blood under high pressure	Blood under low pressure	Pressure rises then gradually falls as blood flows from arteries to veins
Blood flows in pulses	No pulse	Pulse gradually disappears
Thick muscular walls Small lumen	Thinner walls Large lumen	Walls are one cell thick, leaky* and red blood cells travel in single file
No semi-lunar valves	Semi-lunar valves	**No** semi-lunar valves
Carry oxygenated blood (except pulmonary artery)	Carry deoxygenated blood (except pulmonary vein)	Blood slowly loses its oxygen

*Blood plasma (except its proteins) + white blood cells and platelets (*not* red blood cells) escape through these gaps in the capillary walls. They form a fluid called TISSUE FLUID.

The pulse beat in an artery can be located by gently pressing on the wrist at the base of the thumb using your middle and index fingers.

The pulse is usually expressed as the number of heartbeats per minute. One easy method of measuring pulse rate is to count the number of beats in a short period of time – say 15 seconds – then calculate the rate per minute.

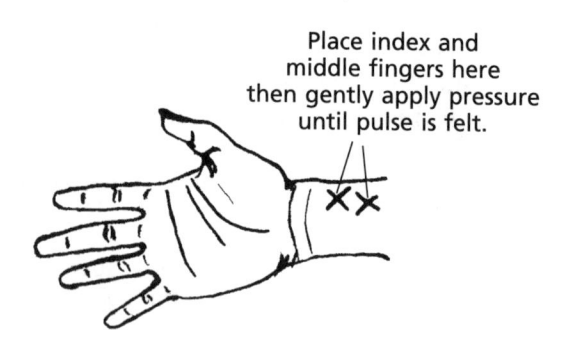

Place index and middle fingers here then gently apply pressure until pulse is felt.

Fig. 38 Counting the pulse

Investigation 9.1

To show the effect of physical activity on pulse rate

Method
The number of pulse beats per minute is counted in a person at rest. This is done three times, and each result is recorded. The **average** number of pulse beats per minute is calculated.
About five minutes of exercise is performed (e.g. running, or stepping on and off a stair step).
The number of pulse beats in 10 seconds is counted and recorded. After 20 seconds, the number of beats is again counted over a 10-second period.
The process is continued for 10 minutes.
Each recorded number is multiplied by 6 to obtain the rate per minute.
The results can be used to draw a graph to show how the rate of heartbeat gradually returns to normal after exercise. The fitter the subject, the quicker the pulse rate returns to normal.

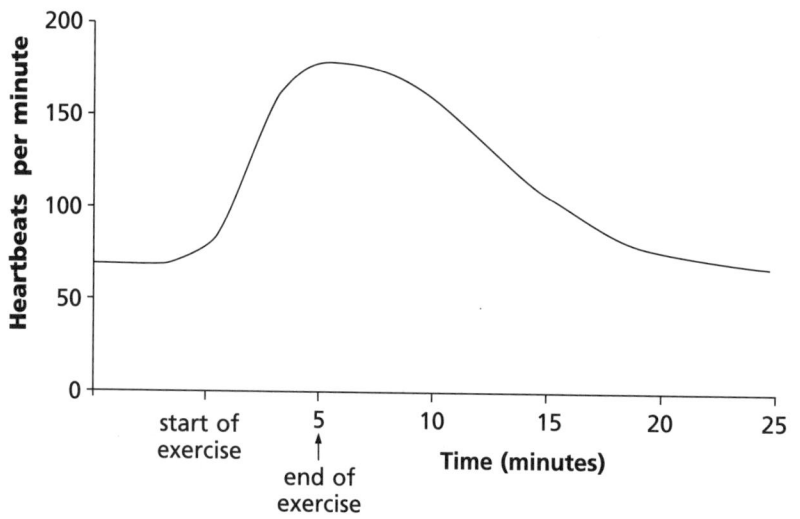

Fig. 39 The effect of exercise on pulse rate

Heart disease

Diet is important for a healthy heart (see the section on diet and heart disease, p. 40), but, like all muscles, the heart benefits from **exercise**.

The harmful effects of **atheroma** on the **coronary artery** are described on p. 40. The heart may also be affected by cigarette smoking. **Carbon monoxide** in cigarette smoke encourages the build up of atheroma, and **nicotine** increases the tendency for **blood to clot**. The coronary artery may therefore not supply enough blood to the heart muscle.

People who lead **stressful** lives are also at risk of heart disease. Stress causes the release of raised levels of the hormone ADRENALINE, which constricts artery walls. In this way, stress adds to existing problems of partially blocked arteries.

To decrease the risk of heart disease:

(i) restrict the intake of animal fats and cholesterol

(ii) avoid obesity

(iii) do not smoke

(iv) settle for a less stressful lifestyle

(v) take regular exercise.

Blood: features and functions of the main components

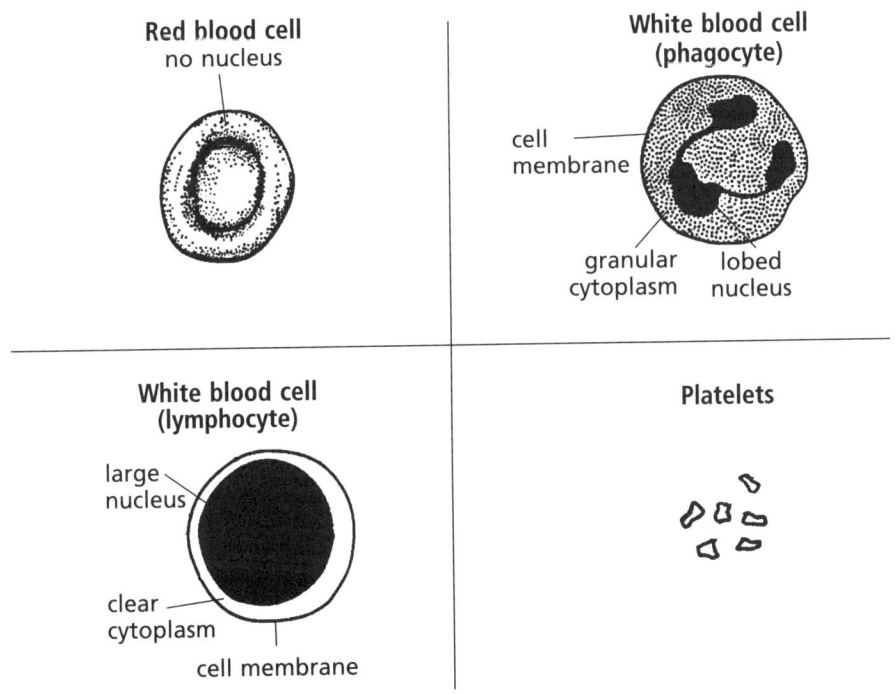

Fig. 40 Blood
(Reproduced by permission of the University of Cambridge Local Examinations Syndicate)

Red blood cells (RBCs)

Structure

(i) **Biconcave discs**.

(ii) Extremely small (2 μm × 7 μm) (1 μm = $\frac{1}{1000}$ mm).

(iii) **No nucleus**.

(iv) Live for only **120 days**.

(v) Made in the bone marrow.

(vi) Destroyed in the liver.

(vii) Cytoplasm contains the red **iron**-containing protein called **haemoglobin**.

(viii) Flexible, so they can pass through the very narrow capillaries.

(ix) There are 4,000,000–5,000,000 RBCs per mm^3 of blood.

Their microscopic size, biconcave shape and very large numbers provide an **enormous surface area** for the function given below.

Function

The **uptake** and **carriage** of **oxygen**, by the haemoglobin in the form of OXYHAEMOGLOBIN.

White blood cells

There are two types of white blood cells:

A PHAGOCYTES
B LYMPHOCYTES.

A Phagocytes

Structure

(i) About 10 μm in diameter.

(ii) A **lobed nucleus**.

(iii) Made in the bone marrow.

(iv) Capable of movement ('amoeboid' movement), and can squeeze out of capillaries.

(v) There are about 5,000 per mm^3 of blood.

Function

They carry out PHAGOCYTOSIS. That is, they **ingest** potentially harmful **bacteria**, to prevent or overcome infection.

B   Lymphocytes

Structure

(i)   About 10 μm in diameter.

(ii)   A **large round nucleus** occupying almost all of the cell.

(iii)   Made in **lymph nodes**.

(iv)   There are about 2,000 per mm³ of blood.

Function

They produce ANTIBODIES which 'stick' to bacteria and clump them together ready for being ingested by phagocytes. Some antibodies are in the form of ANTITOXINS. Antitoxins neutralise poisons (toxins) in the blood which have been released by invading bacteria.

Antibodies are **specific** to the organism against which they are produced. They may stay in the blood only for a few weeks, or for a lifetime. If they stay for a lifetime, they give life-long immunity against the effects of that particular disease-causing agent (or **pathogen**).

Tissue rejection

Our immune system is unable to distinguish between possibly harmful protein (e.g. a pathogenic bacterium) and potentially useful 'foreign' protein (e.g. a transplanted heart or kidney). There is always a danger of TISSUE REJECTION when a transplant operation is carried out. There is less chance of rejection if the protein structure in the transplanted organ is similar to the proteins of the recipient. Organs from a (close) relative are far less likely to be rejected because the protein types are similar.

Platelets

Structure

(i)   Fragments of cells.

(ii)   Made in bone marrow.

(iii)   There are 250,000 per mm³ of blood.

Function

PLATELETS play a part in **blood clotting** and help to block holes in damaged capillary walls.

Plasma

Structure

(i) Pale yellow watery fluid.

(ii) Contains the following materials **in solution**:
- digested foods (**amino acids, glucose**)
- vitamins
- ions (salts)
- excretory materials (**urea, carbon dioxide**)
- hormones
- plasma (or 'blood') proteins (e.g. antibodies, and FIBRINOGEN*)

and also:
- fat droplets (in suspension)
- heat
- red and white blood cells and platelets.

Function

The PLASMA carries all materials from where they are absorbed or produced to the parts of the body where they are needed or excreted. For example, plasma carries carbon dioxide from the cells of the body to the lungs.

***Fibrinogen** is a soluble protein. When it comes in contact with enzymes released by damaged cells, it is converted into an **insoluble, stringy** protein called FIBRIN. This forms a mesh which traps blood cells and becomes a CLOT– preventing the entry of bacteria. The clot dries and hardens to form a SCAB, which covers the wound until the skin beneath has repaired.

How substances in the capillaries reach the cells of the body

Capillaries leak, so some – but not all – of the materials in plasma can escape. All blood cells, except phagocytes, are too large to leave the capillaries. By their own effort, phagocytes are able to squeeze out between the cells in the capillary walls. Most plasma protein molecules are too large to pass out of the capillaries. All the smaller molecules in solution pass out to bathe the cells in **tissue fluid** (see also p. 57).

Tissue fluid = blood **without** red blood cells, plasma proteins and some white blood cells.

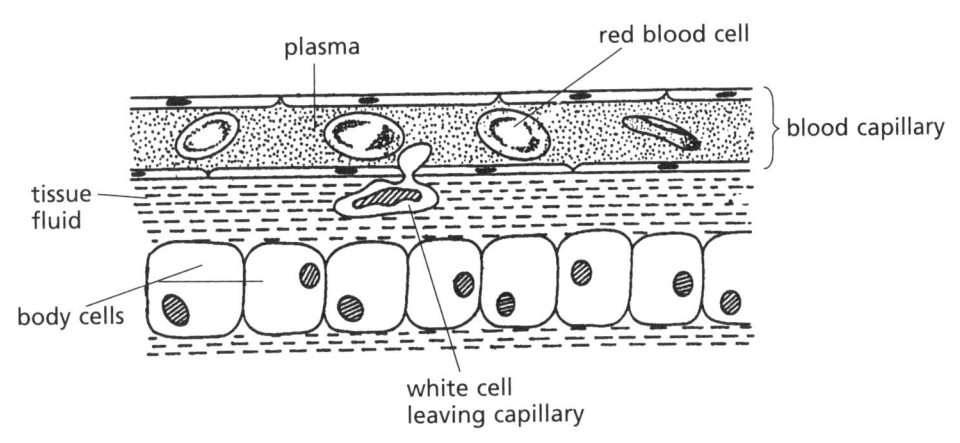

Fig. 41 The relationship between blood, tissue fluid and body cells
(Reproduced by permission of the University of Cambridge Local Examinations Syndicate)

TOPIC 10: Respiration

> **Definition**
>
> Respiration is a characteristic of all living organisms. It is the release (not 'production') of energy from food substances in all living cells. The food substance involved is usually glucose.

There are **two** forms of respiration:

A Aerobic respiration

This is the **release** of **relatively large** amounts of energy by using **oxygen** to break down foodstuffs (i.e. by 'oxidising' them).

AEROBIC RESPIRATION usually takes the form of the **oxidation of glucose** in the cytoplasm of living cells. The process is controlled by **enzymes**. It unlocks the chemical energy in the glucose molecule, releasing it for metabolic activities, and releasing also the waste products **carbon dioxide** and **water**.

$$C_6H_{12}O_6 + 6O_2 \longrightarrow 6CO_2 + 6H_2O + \text{energy released*}$$

(glucose) (oxygen)   (carbon dioxide) (water)

*16.1 kJ/g glucose

The energy that is released may be used in the following ways:

(i) for **muscle contraction** (bringing about movement and locomotion)

(ii) to help link together amino acids in order to **manufacture proteins** (such as enzymes and proteins used for growth and repair)

(iii) for **cell division**

(iv) for **active transport** of chemicals through cell membranes (e.g. the uptake of glucose through the villus walls)

(v) conversion into **electrical** energy in the form of **impulses** along nerve cells

(vi) conversion into **heat** energy to **maintain a constant body temperature**.

B Anaerobic respiration

This is a form of respiration in which **relatively small** amounts of energy are released by the breakdown of food substances **in the absence** of oxygen.

ANAEROBIC RESPIRATION is the process by which **yeast** cells break down **glucose** during **fermentation**. The product is **ethanol** ('alcohol').

$$C_6H_{12}O_6 \longrightarrow 2C_2H_5OH + 2CO_2 + \text{some* energy released}$$

(glucose)   (ethanol)   (carbon dioxide)

*1.17 kJ/g glucose

Less energy is released than in aerobic respiration because the alcohol molecule is relatively large and still contains a considerable amount of chemical energy.

In the human body

Anaerobic respiration also occurs in the **human body** – especially in **muscles**. It happens when there is not enough oxygen reaching the cells to convert all the glucose into carbon dioxide and water. Instead, the glucose is partially broken down, without oxygen, to **lactic acid**, with only a limited amount of energy being released.

glucose   ⟶   lactic acid + some* energy released

*0.83 kJ/g glucose

The circulatory system carries the lactic acid away from the muscle to the liver, where it is oxidised to carbon dioxide and water. But this happens **after the period of exercise has finished**. The oxygen being used for this process is said to be used to pay off the **oxygen debt**.

If the circulation is inefficient, high levels of lactic acid in the muscles may lead to **cramp**.

Gaseous exchange in man

Oxygen enters the blood from the lungs. **Breathing** is a muscular, pumping action that takes in air from the atmosphere and moves it to the lungs. Breathing in (INSPIRATION) is responsible for presenting air with its oxygen to the surfaces in the lungs where gaseous exchange will take place. EXPIRATION pushes the air, now containing waste carbon dioxide, back into the atmosphere (breathing out).

The differences between inspired and expired air

Inspired air	Expired air
20% oxygen	16% oxygen
0.04% carbon dioxide	4% carbon dioxide
relatively dry	saturated
at air temperature	at body temperature
relatively dirty	relatively clean

Practical demonstrations can show these differences.

Demonstration 10.1

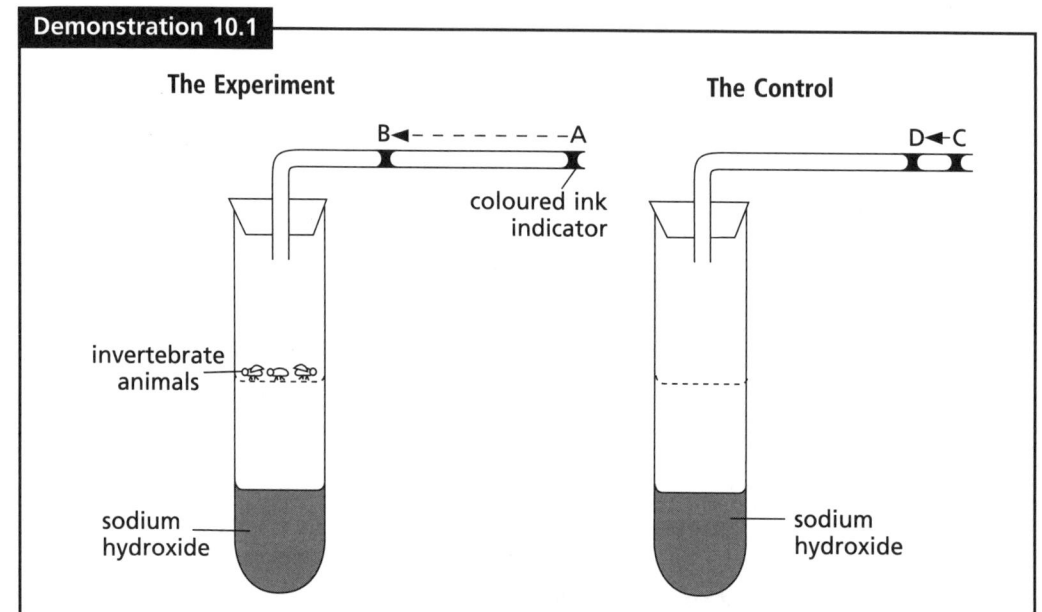

Fig. 42a Experiment to show that animals use oxygen during respiration

The experiment
For each molecule of oxygen taken in by the animals, a molecule of carbon dioxide is given out. The molecule dissolves in the sodium hydroxide, decreasing the volume within the apparatus. The indicator thus moves from **A** to **B**.
Note: When all the oxygen in the tube has been used up, the total volume inside the apparatus would have decreased by 20%.

The control
In the same period of time, the only carbon dioxide to dissolve in the sodium hydroxide is that already in the air. The indicator moves only from **C** to **D**.

Demonstration 10.2

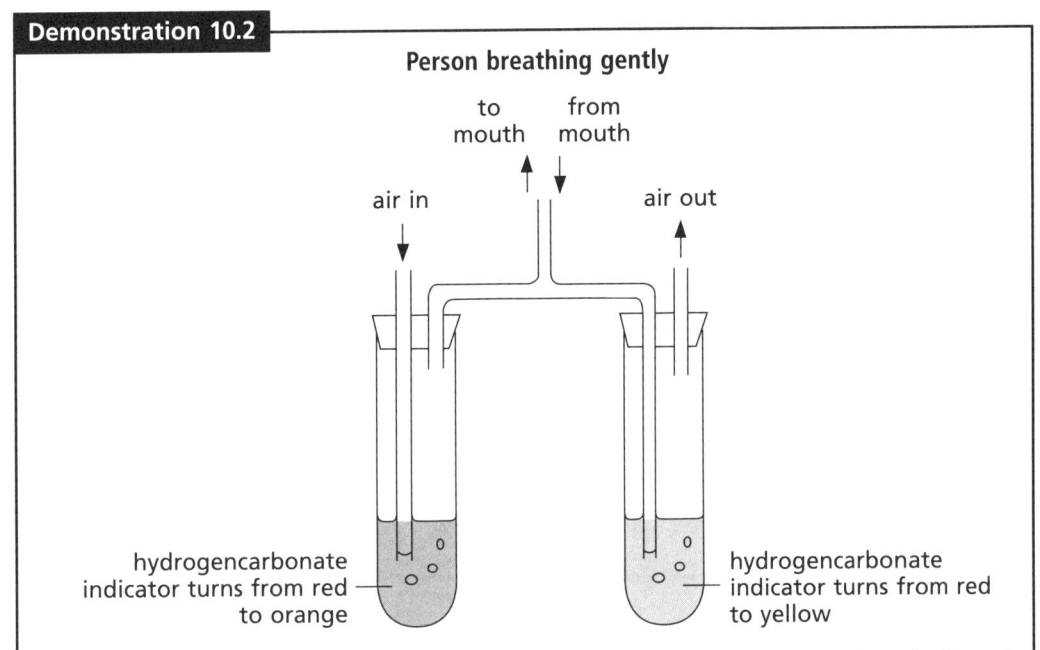

Fig. 42b Experiment to show that air breathed out contains more carbon dioxide than air breathed in

(Left tube: air in — hydrogencarbonate indicator turns from red to orange. Right tube: air out — hydrogencarbonate indicator turns from red to yellow. Person breathing gently: to mouth / from mouth.)

Demonstration 10.3

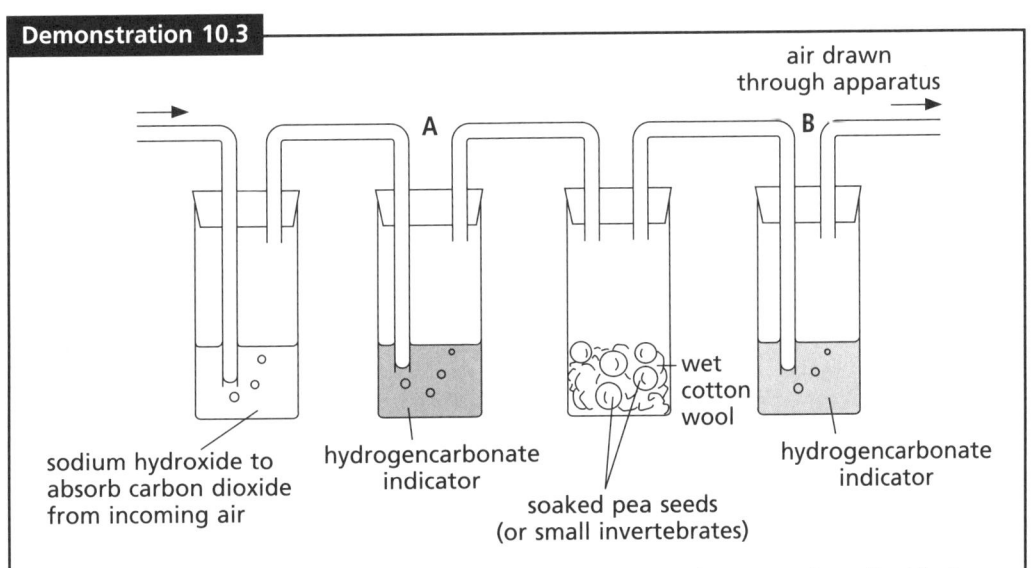

Fig. 42c Experiment to demonstrate that living organisms give out carbon dioxide from respiration

(Apparatus from left to right: sodium hydroxide to absorb carbon dioxide from incoming air; hydrogencarbonate indicator (A); soaked pea seeds (or small invertebrates) with wet cotton wool; hydrogencarbonate indicator (B); air drawn through apparatus.)

A   The hydrogencarbonate indicator remains red, showing that no carbon dioxide is passing on to the next tube.

B   The hydrogencarbonate indicator changes from red to yellow, showing that carbon dioxide is present. The carbon dioxide is evolved by the respiring peas.

Depending on the need for oxygen in the body (and the need to remove waste carbon dioxide), the **rate** and **depth** of breathing may vary.

More oxygen is used, and more carbon dioxide is released, when we are active. This can be demonstrated in the following way.

Investigation 10.1

To show the effect of exercise on the rate of breathing
Count the number of breaths taken in one minute by a person at rest (it is easier to count someone else's breathing rate than it is to count your own). Do this **three** times and take an average (around 15 breaths per minute).
The person should then perform five minutes of exercise (as in Demonstration 9.1, see p. 58). Using the same procedure as in Demonstration 9.1, count the number of breaths in a 10-second period every 30 seconds for 10 minutes.
Calculate the rate per minute, and plot a graph of breathing rate against time.

Investigation 10.2

To show the effect of regular exercise on the depth of breathing
Regular exercise can affect the volume of air a person is able to inspire, then expire, in one deep breath. This can be demonstrated by using the simple **respirometer** shown below.

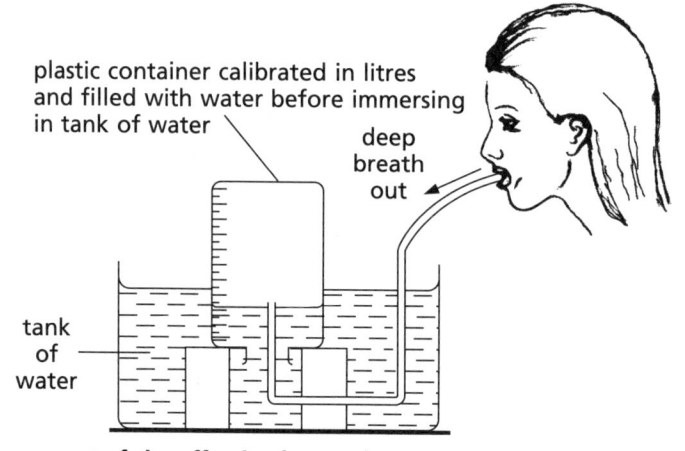

Fig. 43 Measurement of the effective lung volume

Organise a group of athletes and a group of non-athletes to breathe in as far as they can, then breathe out through the rubber tube as far as they can. Measure the volume of water expelled from the container by each person.
Calculate the **average** volume per person for the athletes, and the average volume for the non-athletes. Compare the results.
Athletes should be able to exhale a greater volume of air (and thus, be able to breathe more deeply).

The **immediate** effect of exercise on the depth of breathing may be successfully demonstrated only with a commercial respirometer. A person breathes in and out through a tube connected to a piece of electronic equipment which measures the depth and the frequency of breathing. The respirometer produces a graph of the results.

If a person measured the depth and rate of their breathing before a period of exercise, then every 30 seconds after exercise, the results would be similar to the graph shown below.

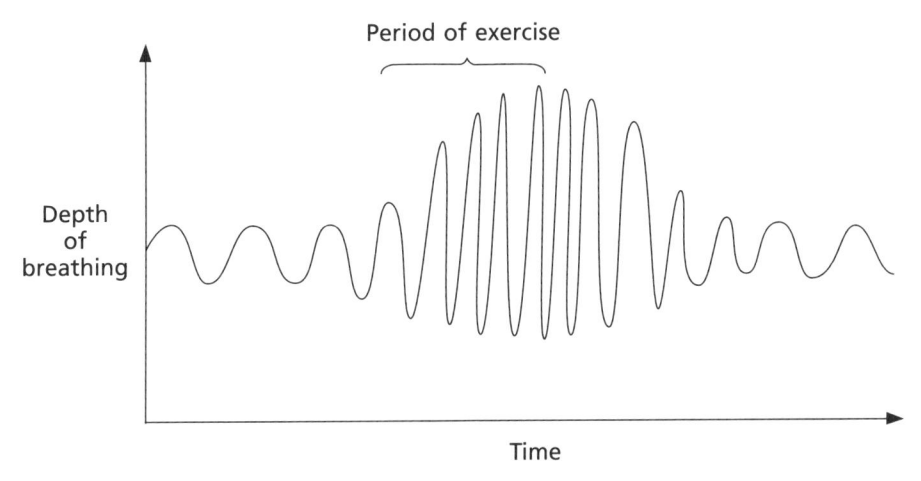

Fig. 44 The effect of exercise on breathing rate and depth

The structure of the respiratory organs

A pair of **lungs** lie in the airtight **thoracic** ('chest') **cavity**, as shown in the diagram on p. 70.

During breathing, the lungs are inflated and deflated by the action of muscles which help to form the thorax. They are:

(i)   the **intercostal** muscles (between the ribs)
(ii) the muscles of the **diaphragm**. The diaphragm is a sheet of muscle lying below the lungs, separating them from the abdomen. It is curved upwards (towards the lungs) like a dome.

These muscles work to alter the **volume** of the thoracic cavity, which, in turn, alters the **pressure** within the thoracic cavity.

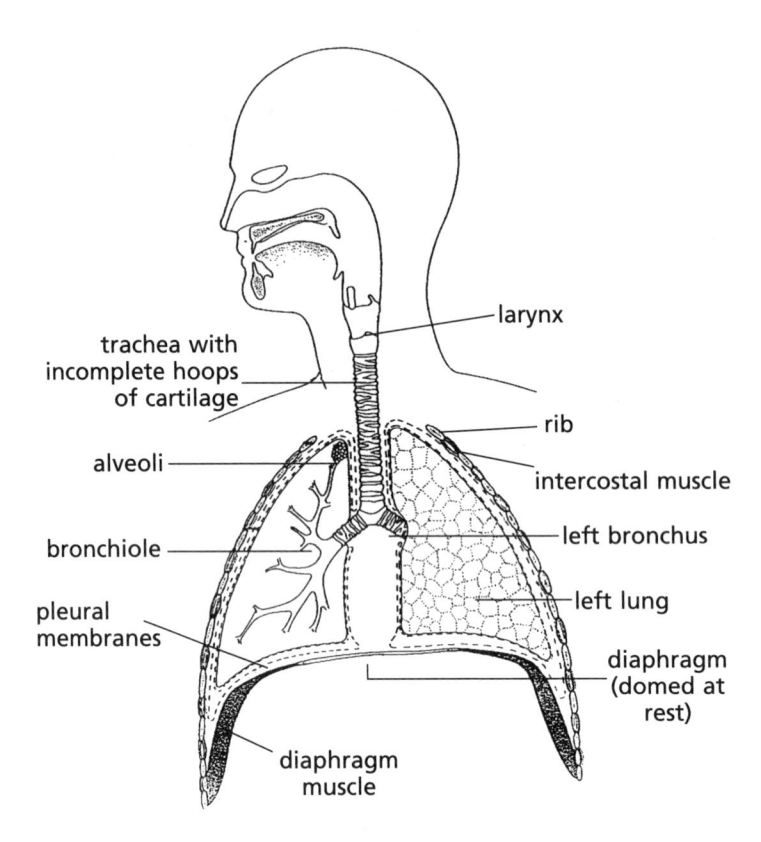

Fig. 45 The respiratory organs
(Reproduced by permission of the University of Cambridge Local Examinations Syndicate)

During inspiration

1 The (external) **intercostal muscles contract**. This causes the ribs to swing **up** and **out** – increasing the volume of the thorax ('front' to 'back').

2 The muscles of the **diaphragm contract**, pulling it **flat** – further increasing the volume of the thorax (this time 'top' to 'bottom').

The resulting increase in volume of the thorax **decreases its pressure**.

The only connection between the thorax and the higher pressure of the outside atmosphere is via the mouth and nose. Air from the atmosphere is **forced** towards the region of lower pressure. It passes through the mouth and nose, down the **trachea**, through the **bronchi and bronchioles** and into the **alveoli**. Gaseous exchange occurs.

During expiration

1 The (external) **intercostal muscles relax** – the ribs swing **down** and **in**.

2 The **diaphragm muscles relax** and the diaphragm **domes upwards** again.

These actions **decrease** the volume of the thoracic cavity, **increasing** its pressure. Air is **forced** back out into the atmosphere.

There are also smaller **internal** intercostal muscles. They **relax** during inspiration and **contract** during **expiration** to help provide some force to the action.

How alveoli are adapted for the process of gaseous exchange

(i) The millions of alveoli provide a **large surface area** for gaseous exchange.

(ii) The walls of the alveoli are covered with a layer of **water** to dissolve the gases.

(iii) The walls are only **one cell thick** for quick and easy **diffusion** of gases in solution.

(iv) They are richly supplied with **capillaries** for rapid transport of the gases.

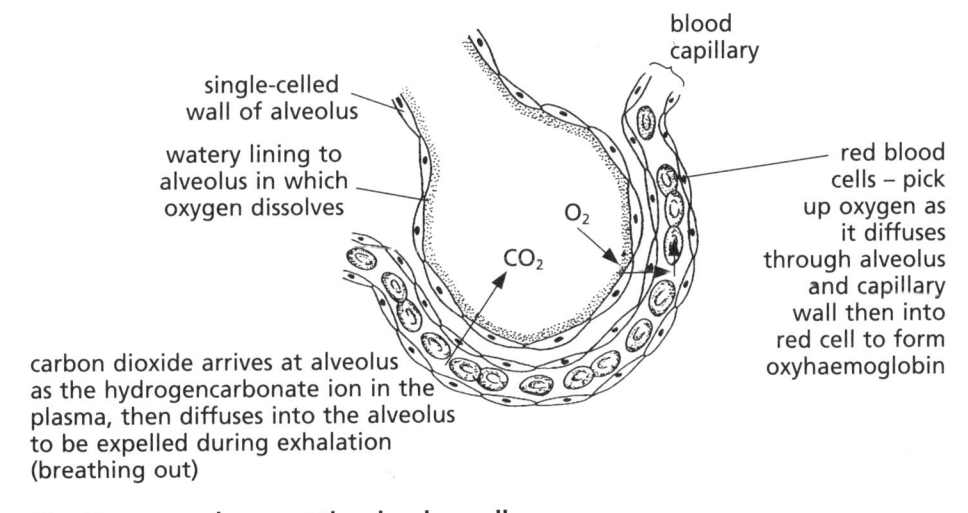

Fig. 46 Gaseous exchange at the alveolus wall
(Reproduced by permission of the University of Cambridge Local Examinations Syndicate)

The effect of respiratory diseases on the process of gaseous exchange

Chronic bronchitis

Bronchitis is an inflammation of the airways ('chronic' means extending over a long period of time). It leads to an overproduction of mucus, which tends to block the bronchi and bronchioles. This makes breathing difficult, and decreases the efficiency of the gaseous exchange process. Less oxygen reaches the blood, which affects organs such as the heart and the brain, and the extremities. It also causes a distressing cough.

Emphysema

Emphysema is a condition often associated with chronic bronchitis. The walls of the alveoli become stretched and lose their elasticity. They do not empty properly, creating a build-up of carbon dioxide in the lungs. The patient suffers from breathlessness, and decreased efficiency of heart, brain etc. through too much carbon dioxide (and insufficient oxygen) in the blood.

Lung cancer

Cells in the lungs begin to divide uncontrollably, forming thickened tissues through which gases cannot pass, and which may block airways. Unless treated early, lung cancer is likely to be a fatal condition.

TOPIC 11

Support, Movement and Locomotion

Support refers to the skeleton and its role in holding up the body structure and giving it shape.

Movement refers to the change in the position of one part of the body in relation to another part.

Locomotion refers to the movement of the entire body from one place to another.

In most animals movement and locomotion could not occur without the **contraction** of **muscles**. Muscles provide the necessary **force**. The bones of the **skeleton**, to which the muscles are attached, operate as **levers**. They also support the body clear of the ground.

The arrangement of bones in a limb is illustrated by the human **arm** (a **mammalian forelimb**).

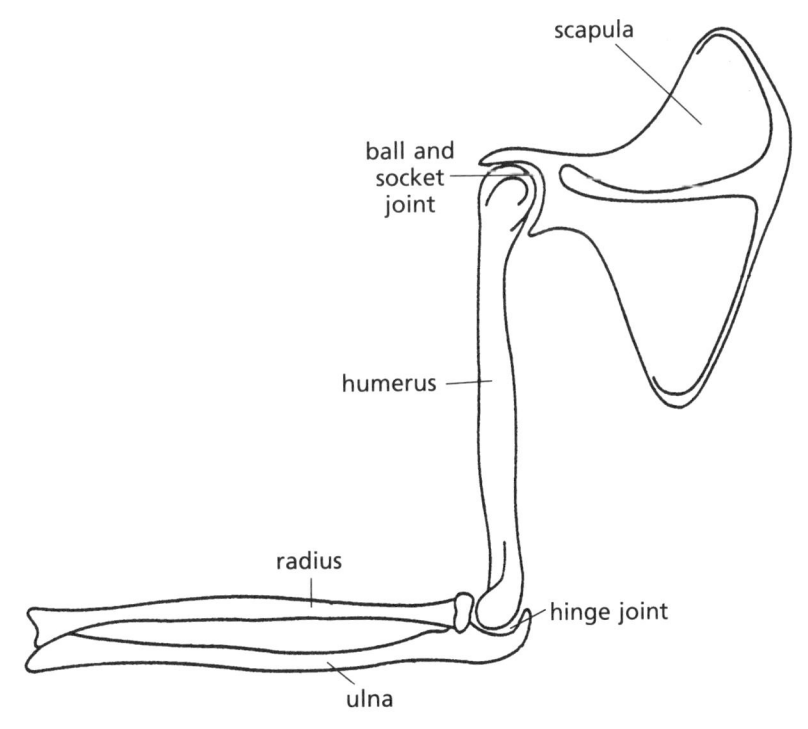

Fig. 47 Bones of the arm
(Reproduced by permission of the University of Cambridge Local Examinations Syndicate)

Some bones are strongly fused together to provide protection (as in the skull). But most bones are able to move freely on one another in order to permit movement. The **two** main types of joint which allow this movement are seen in the arm:

(i) The BALL AND SOCKET JOINT at the shoulder which allows free movement in **many planes** (though not quite 'all-round' movement).

(ii) The HINGE JOINT at the elbow which allows movement in **one plane only**.

How muscles move bones at a joint

Muscles work in the following way:

(i) They can **pull** but never push.

(ii) They pull **only** when they **contract**.

(iii) When they contract, they **decrease** in length.

(iv) When returning to their original length, they **relax** (*not* 'expand').

(v) They are attached to bones by TENDONS which do not stretch. They are arranged in ANTAGONISTIC PAIRS, and apply their force either side of the bone they are required to move.

(vi) One muscle of the pair (the FLEXOR) **contracts** to bend the limb at the joint. As it does so, the other muscle in the pair (the EXTENSOR) **relaxes**.

(vii) The extensor contracts to straighten the limb at the joint, and as it does so, the flexor relaxes. The arrangement of the antagonistic muscles at the hinge joint of the elbow are shown below.

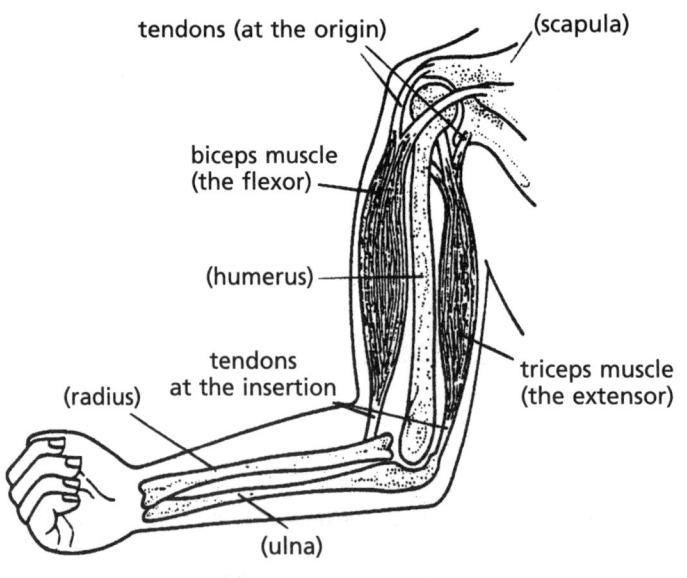

Fig. 48 The muscles of the upper arm (showing the antagonistic arrangement)
(Reproduced by permission of the University of Cambridge Local Examinations Syndicate)

TOPIC 12

Excretion

The metabolic reactions within the body are always creating waste products.

> **Definition**
>
> EXCRETION is defined as the removal of toxic materials and waste products of metabolism from organisms.

There are two main sets of excretory organs for removing metabolic waste products, the **lungs** and the **kidneys**.

Excretory organ	Material removed	Method of removal
Lungs	carbon dioxide	breathing out (expiration or exhalation)
Kidneys	urea	in urine
	toxins	in urine

Note: The sweat glands in the skin also remove small amounts of urea, as a constituent of sweat.

The removal of faeces from the alimentary canal is *not* regarded as excretion, because the fibre which makes up the faeces is not the product of a chemical reaction in the body. Instead, it is passed all the way through the intestines unaffected by enzymes. However, the pigment which colours the faeces, which comes from the chemical breakdown of red blood cells, *can* be regarded as excretory.

The kidneys

The kidneys are two brown bean-shaped organs lying dorsally (i.e. towards the back) in the abdominal cavity. They are supplied with blood via the **renal artery**. Blood returns to the rest of the circulation by the **renal vein**. The kidneys' role is to carry out **high pressure filtration** of the blood, during which **two** functions have to be achieved:

(i) The removal of **urea** and **toxins** from the blood (i.e. part of **excretion**).

(ii) The maintenance of a constant concentration of blood plasma (OSMOREGULATION).

Osmoregulation may be achieved either:

(i) by the removal (if it is in excess) or the retention of **water**, or
(ii) by the removal (if they are in excess) or the retention of **ions** (salts).

If a diabetic person has an excess of glucose in their blood, the kidneys will remove some of the glucose as well.

The materials removed from the blood by each kidney are sent down the **ureter** to the **bladder** where they are **stored**. Relaxation of the **bladder sphincter** muscle allows them to leave the body as a solution called URINE via the **urethra**.

Urine = urea + ions + toxins + water

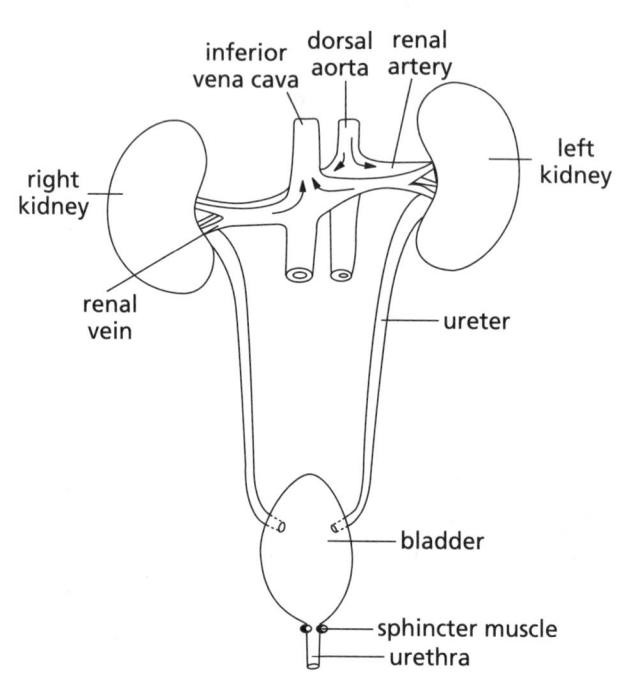

Fig. 49 The excretory organs

Kidney dialysis

If a person's kidneys stop working properly ('fail'), there will be a build-up of urea and toxins in their blood which will eventually prove fatal. A **kidney transplant** may be possible if a donor with a suitable tissue type is available. Otherwise, KIDNEY DIALYSIS may be used.

A **kidney dialysis machine** removes chemicals with **small** molecules (urea, toxins and ions) from a patient's blood, but does not allow larger molecules (such as plasma proteins) to leave the blood.

The blood is passed through **dialysis tubing**, which is placed in a **bathing** or **washing fluid**. Only the small molecules in the blood can pass from the tubing into the fluid. The fluid is continuously renewed, and washes away the substances removed from the blood. By varying the concentration of substances in the washing fluid, the amounts of those substances which leave the blood can be controlled. The concentration of plasma in the blood can also be controlled in this way. The dialysed blood is then returned to the patient.

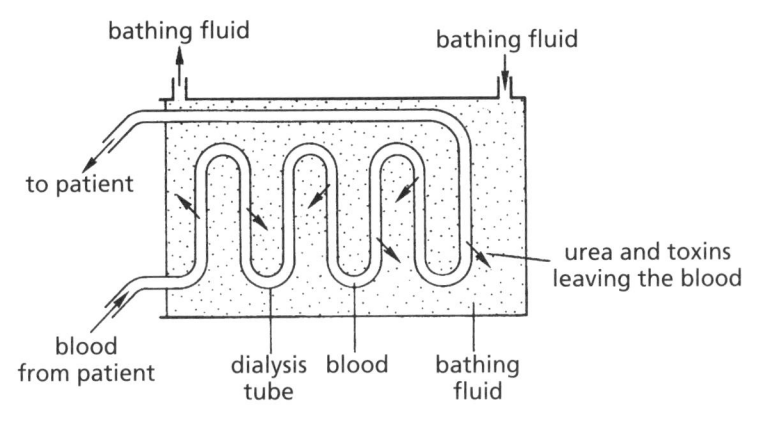

Fig. 50 How an 'artificial kidney' works
(Reproduced by permission of the University of Cambridge Local Examinations Syndicate)

TOPIC 13: Homeostasis

The body will operate most efficiently when conditions within it remain reasonably stable. As has been shown, the kidneys have the important function of keeping the blood plasma at a constant concentration. The tissue fluid bathing the body's cells is therefore always at a constant concentration. Because cell membranes are partially permeable, osmosis will ensure that the concentration *within* all cells remains constant as well. Many organs within the body play a part in maintaining constant conditions. They are described as **organs of homeostasis**.

> **Definition**
>
> **HOMEOSTASIS is defined as the maintenance of a constant internal environment.**

The skin

The skin is the largest organ of the human body. It is an important **sense organ** but also forms the barrier between the body and the external environment. It is the organ through which we may both gain and lose heat. This is particularly important in the **homeostatic** process of **temperature regulation**.

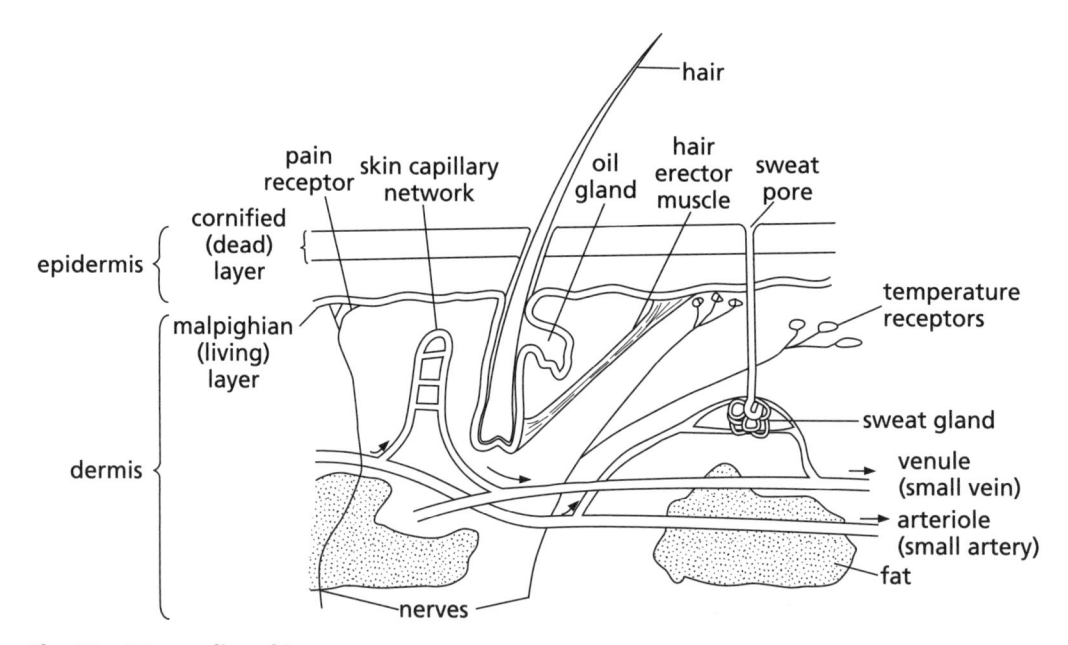

Fig. 51 Mammalian skin

The part played by the skin in temperature regulation

When the temperature of the blood rises above 37°C	When the temperature of the blood falls below 37°C
The **sweat glands** release more **sweat**.	Sweating is greatly reduced.[b]
The sweat **evaporates**.[a]	
Arterioles in the skin **dilate** (become wider as their muscular walls relax).	Arterioles in the skin **constrict** (become narrower as their muscular walls contract).
More blood is brought to the skin – blood carries heat.[a]	Less blood flows beneath the skin.[b]
	Fat in the DERMIS of the skin acts as an **insulator**.[b]

[a] More heat is lost to the environment, cooling the blood, and allowing the body temperature to return to normal. (*Note:* The person may also take cold drinks and seek shade.)
[b] Less heat is lost to the environment, allowing metabolic processes to release energy in the form of heat to help bring the body temperature back to normal.

Shivering

If the temperature of the blood falls below 37°C and the measures outlined above are inadequate, muscles in the body will start to contract and relax rhythmically, which releases heat energy. This reaction is called **shivering**.

To help raise their body temperature, a person may take warm drinks, increase the insulating layer of air around their body by wearing more clothes, and do some exercise.

Temperature receptors in the skin

As a sense organ, one of the properties of the skin is to be able to **detect temperature change in the external environment**. A change in atmospheric temperature will be detected by temperature receptors on the skin. These will start some of the temperature control mechanisms even before there is any significant change in the temperature of the blood.

Changes in the blood temperature are detected by the HYPOTHALAMUS situated on the under-side of the **brain**. This is the structure responsible for the **coordination** of all temperature control mechanisms.

The concept of control by negative feedback

To maintain a constant internal environment, it is necessary to have **receptors** ('sensors') in the body to detect when the environment fluctuates too far either side of the required state. Then there must be a mechanism to return the conditions to normal.

A system which automatically brings about a correction, regardless which side of the optimum the change has occurred, is called a NEGATIVE FEEDBACK system.

How the **regulation of body temperature** illustrates **negative feedback**:

detected by the hypothalamus in the brain

↗   ↘

rise in blood temperature   increased sweating vasodilation

↗   ↘

heat released during exercise   heat loss

↗   ↘

body temperature of 37°C   **body temperature returns to 37°C**

↘   ↗

cold environment   blood temperature rises

↘   ↗

drop in blood temperature   decreased sweating vasoconstriction shivering

↘   ↗

detected by the hypothalamus in the brain

TOPIC 14: Coordination and Response

A. Nervous coordination in human beings

The various organs of the body must work in coordination if an organism is to survive effectively in its environment. To achieve this, the body has a series of **receptors** which pass information about the environment to a **coordinating centre** called the CENTRAL NERVOUS SYSTEM or **CNS**. The CNS is made up of the brain and the spinal cord. After receiving the information, the CNS directs a **response** in the appropriate **effectors** (muscles or glands).

The eye

The eye is one of the most important of the receptors. It provides us with information on **dimensions**, **colours** and the **distance** of objects in our environment.

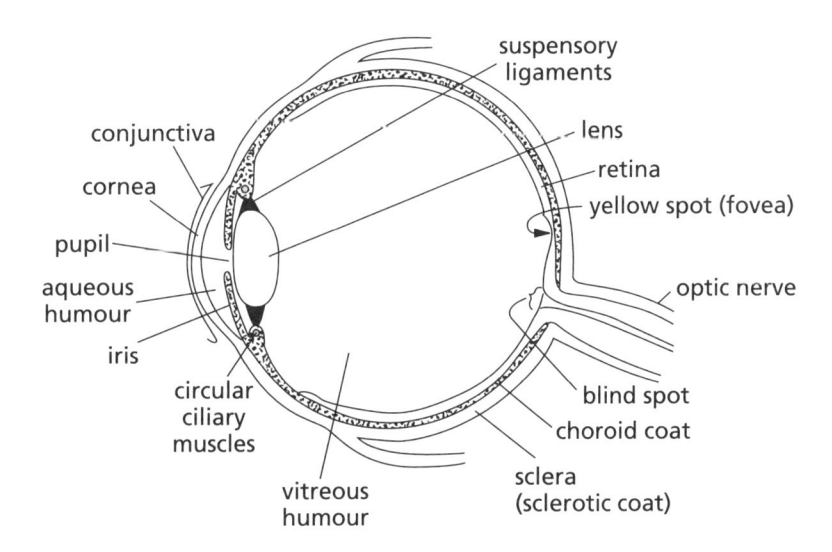

Fig. 52 The eye
(Reproduced by permission of the University of Cambridge Local Examinations Syndicate)

How the eye produces a focused image

1 **Light rays** from an object enter the transparent CORNEA.

2 The cornea 'bends' (**refracts**) the light rays in towards one another.

3 The light rays pass through the **aqueous humour** and **pupil**.

4 The **transparent, elastic** LENS is altered in shape. It is made:
   - fatter, to **decrease** its **focal length**, or
   - thinner, to **increase** its focal length.

   This is called ACCOMMODATION.

5 The relatively small amount of refraction now produced by the lens brings the rays to **focus** on the RETINA.

6 The retina contains **light-sensitive cells**:
   (i) RODS which work well when light intensity is low, and
   (ii) CONES which detect colour.

   These cells are stimulated by the light of the image, and convert the light energy into electrical energy.

7 Electrical energy, in the form of an **impulse**, travels along the **optic nerve** to the brain.

8 The brain **de-codes** the impulse to produce the sensation of sight.

Other important facts

(i) The image of objects that we are looking **directly** at (i.e. which are in the centre of our field of vision) falls on a very sensitive part of the retina called the FOVEA, or **yellow spot**. This region has far more cones than rods. Cones provide a picture with greater detail and in better colour.

(ii) There are *no* rods or cones at the point where the retina is joined to the optic nerve. Images formed on this part of the retina are *not* converted into impulses and relayed to the brain. This region is called the BLIND SPOT. We have blind spots in both of our eyes, but are not usually aware of them. Each eye records a different part of our field of view and covers the blind spot of the other.

Accommodation

The ability of the lens to change shape and focus on objects at different distances is called accommodation. This ability depends on:

(i) the **elasticity** of the lens
(ii) the existence of **ciliary** muscles which are used to alter the shape of the lens
(iii) the **suspensory ligaments** which transfer the effect of the ciliary muscles to the lens.

When viewing a near object	When viewing a distant object
The (circular) **ciliary muscles contract**, reducing their circumference.	The (circular) ciliary muscles **relax,** increasing their circumference.*
They **reduce pull** on the (elastic) **suspensory ligaments**.	The suspensory ligaments are **pulled tight.**
With less force on the lens, its elasticity allows it to become wider ('bulge') – **decreasing** its **focal length.**	The lens is stretched to become longer and thinner, **increasing** its focal length.
Rays from the near object produce a focused image on the retina.	Rays from the distant object are brought to focus on the retina.

* The pressure of the vitreous humour stretches the ciliary muscles as they relax, and causes them to pull on the suspensory ligaments.

The value of having *two* eyes

Apart from overcoming the effect of the blind spot, two eyes view the same picture from two slightly different positions. This provides vision in **three dimensions**, the ability to **judge distance** (and therefore speed), and offers animals a chance of survival even if one eye is damaged.

The 'pupil' (or iris) reflex

Bright light could seriously damage the delicate light-sensitive cells of the retina. The intensity of light falling on the retina is therefore controlled by the IRIS. It has an **antagonistic** arrangement of **circular** and **radial** muscles.

In dim light	In bright light
Light-sensitive cells in the retina detect the light intensity.	Light-sensitive cells in the retina detect the light intensity.
Impulses are sent along the optic (a **sensory**) nerve to the brain.	Impulses are sent along the optic (a **sensory**) nerve to the brain.
The brain returns impulses along a **motor** nerve to the **radial** muscles of the iris.	The brain returns impulses along a **motor** nerve to the **circular** muscles of the iris.
The radial iris muscles **contract** while the circular iris muscles **relax**.	The circular iris muscles **contract** while the radial iris muscles **relax**.
The diameter of the pupil **increases**, allowing more light to enter.	The diameter of the pupil (the hole in the centre) **decreases**, allowing less light to enter, decreasing the risk of damage to the retina.

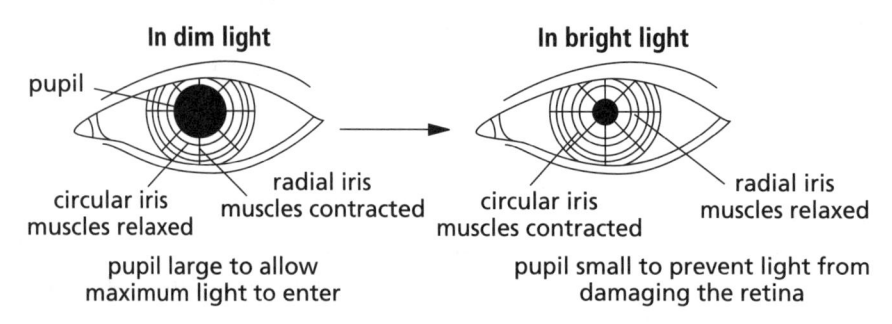

Fig. 53 Antagonistic muscles in the iris
(Reproduced by permission of the University of Cambridge Local Examinations Syndicate)

The brain and nervous system

The nervous system is made up of the central nervous system, or CNS (made up of the brain and spinal cord), and a system of **nerves**. Nerves carry impulses between receptor organs (e.g. the eyes), the CNS, and effectors (muscles or glands).

The most highly developed part of the CNS is the **brain**.

The functions of the major parts of the brain

Cerebrum

The cerebrum is in the form of two matching halves – known as the cerebral hemispheres – and is responsible for:

(i) the **coordination** of the organs of the body
(ii) the control of **voluntary** actions
(iii) the reception of **sensation**.

At the very front of the cerebrum is the region responsible for memory and morals (the '**higher mental activities**'). At the back lies the region responsible for **sight**.

Cerebellum

The cerebellum is the region of **balance** and **instinct**.

Medulla

The medulla joins the brain to the spinal cord. It controls **unconscious** activities such as heartbeat, peristalsis and breathing.

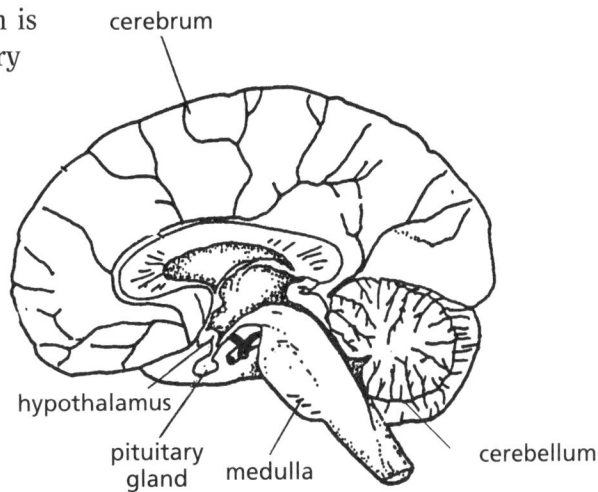

Fig. 54 The human brain
(Reproduced by permission of the University of Cambridge Local Examinations Syndicate)

Hypothalamus

The **hypothalamus** lies under the cerebrum and is the part of the brain responsible for **monitoring changes**, particularly in the blood. It may be regarded as the 'homeostat' of the body.

Pituitary gland

Situated beneath the hypothalamus, the pituitary gland is made up partly of nerve tissue. It is sometimes called the 'master' gland because it manufactures chemicals called HORMONES and releases them into the blood. These hormones control the activity of many glands and other organs throughout the body, such as those responsible for **growth** (e.g. of bones) and **development** (e.g. sexual development). Therefore, the pituitary gland has a very important part to play in **coordination**. It is regularly 'instructed' by the hypothalamus.

Spinal cord

In the same way that a series of nerves (**cranial nerves**) serve the brain, impulses are relayed to, and conducted from the spinal cord by nerves called **spinal nerves**. Spinal nerves are connected with receptors and effectors in parts of the body other than the head.

In emergency situations, the spinal cord can receive and transmit impulses to bring about rapid, often protective responses called REFLEX actions. The **central** region of the spinal cord (the **grey matter**) contains nerve cells (**relay neurones**) involved solely in this process. The outer region of the spinal cord (the **white matter**) contains nerve cells involved in either supplying sensory information to the brain, or passing impulses on to muscles which are instructed by the brain (i.e. voluntary actions).

Nerves

A nerve is like a telephone cable: it contains a large number of small 'wires' called NEURONES. Each neurone is an individual nerve **cell** with its own cytoplasm, cell membrane and nucleus.

Neurones which conduct impulses *from* sensory receptors *to* the brain or spinal cord are called **sensory neurones**.

Neurones which then direct those impulses either to other parts of the brain or to other parts of the spinal cord are called **relay neurones**.

Neurones which conduct impulses *from* the brain or spinal cord *to* effectors are called **motor** (or **efferent**) **neurones**.

Neurones are **insulated** by a fatty ('myelin') sheath. They are **long**, they **target** the **exact** area to be affected and they conduct their impulses very **quickly**. These features are vital if an action is to be taken very quickly to prevent damage, as in a **reflex action**.

Reflex action

Definition

A reflex action is a coordinated response to a specific stimulus.

In the example of the iris reflex, the brain is the part of the CNS involved, and the reflex action is called a **cranial reflex**.

When the spinal cord **alone** directs the response, the action is described as a **spinal reflex**. For example, when we quickly remove our finger from a hot object.

The sequence of events in a spinal reflex is:

1. A **stimulus** is received by the **sensory receptor** (in the example given above, the hot object provides the stimulus and the sensory receptor is located in the finger).

2. An **impulse** is generated and carried along by **sensory neurones** towards the spinal cord.

3. The sensory neurones become part of a **spinal nerve**.

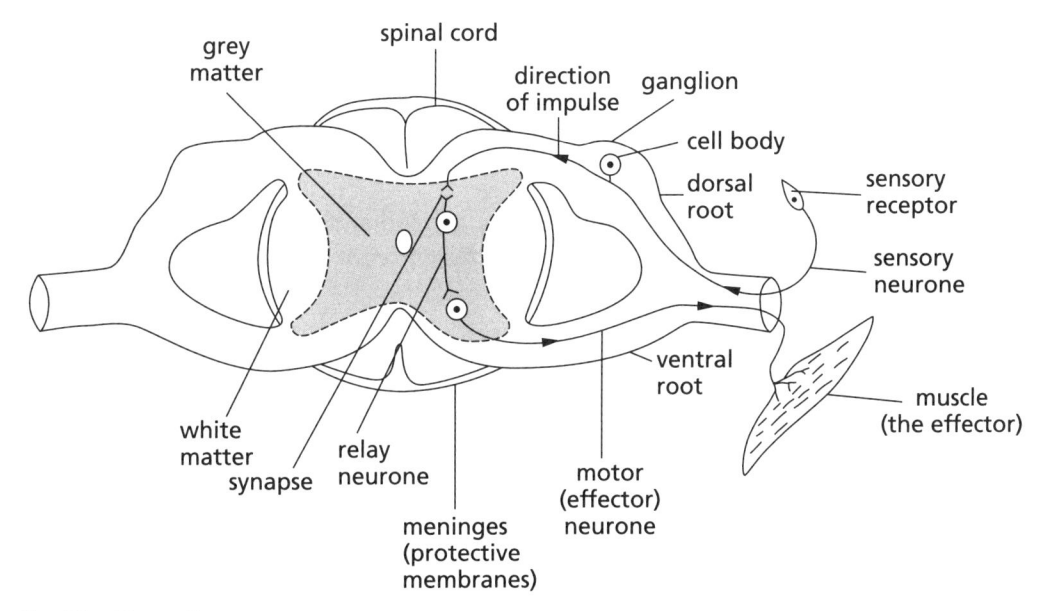

Fig. 55 The reflex arc

4   The impulse travels toward the spinal cord along the **dorsal root**. The dorsal root is part of the linking pathway between outside stimuli and the spinal nerve.

5   Impulses arrive at the nerve endings of the sensory neurone in the **grey matter** of the **spinal cord**.

6   The nerve endings release a **chemical** which **diffuses** across a gap – the SYNAPSE – between the sensory neurone and the nerve endings of a **relay neurone**. The chemical stimulates the relay neurone to produce an impulse.

7   Another synapse links the relay neurone with a **motor neurone**.

8   The impulse travels along motor neurones away from the spinal cord along the **ventral root**. The ventral root is part of the linking pathway between the spinal nerve and the effector.

9   The nerve endings of the motor neurone are applied to the **effector** (the biceps muscle in this case).

10 A **response** is produced (as the biceps muscle contracts to lift the hand clear of the stimulus).

B. Chemical coordination in human beings

Hormones

Definition

A hormone is a chemical substance, produced by a gland and carried by the blood, which alters the activity of one or more specific target organs. It is then destroyed in the liver.

Hormone molecules must be relatively **small**, **soluble** and **diffuse easily**, so they can pass quickly from the cells that make them, into (and, later, out of) blood capillaries.

The **endocrine** glands that produce hormones have no ducts (small tubes) to carry the hormones away. Instead, they pass their hormones directly into the blood. These glands are therefore described as **ductless**. The ADRENAL GLANDS and the PANCREAS are examples of endocrine glands. *Note:* Special cells in the ISLETS OF LANGERHANS in the pancreas produce a hormone, but the rest of the organ produces **digestive juice** which contains enzymes *not* hormones.

Gland	Situated	Hormone produced	Target organ	Effect of hormone
Adrenal	above the kidneys	ADRENALINE (the 'fight, fright and flight' hormone)	liver	turns glycogen into glucose to boost blood sugar levels in emergencies*
			heart	heart beats faster – more oxygen to brain and muscles
			voluntary muscles	tire less easily
Islets of Langerhans	in the pancreas	INSULIN	liver and muscles	promotes the uptake of glucose by cells
				promotes the conversion of glucose to glycogen for storage

*Some examples of emergencies are: the moments before the start of a competitive event (including an examination!), when being chased by an angry dog, or during a heated argument. Other effects of adrenaline include increasing blood pressure, diverting blood away from the intestines and towards the muscles about to be used, and increasing air flow to the lungs. All of these help to make the body work more efficiently to cope with the emergency.

Diabetes

If a person's Islet of Langerhans cells do not produce enough insulin, the level of **glucose** in their blood will **rise**. **Glucose** will be present in their **urine**. The increased concentration of their blood plasma will draw water from their cells by osmosis, making them thirsty, tired, and causing them to urinate more frequently.

If insulin production is not seriously reduced, it may be possible to treat the condition by **restricting** the person's intake of carbohydrate. In **more extreme cases**, however, the treatment will include regular **injections** of insulin. The carbohydrate intake must then be regulated to match the amount of insulin injected.

C. Chemical control of plant growth

The growth of plants is also controlled by **hormones**, often referred to as '**plant growth substances**'. They are produced by plants in minute quantities.

AUXINS make up one group of plant hormones. Auxins control:

(i) the **enlargement** of plant cells (after division), and
(ii) the **modification** of the new cell to carry out a particular function.

Herbicides

Auxins can be produced **synthetically** (that is, they can be made by humans from artificial substances), and relatively **cheaply**.

Synthetic auxins can be used as herbicides to kill weeds. When a herbicide is applied to a plant, the plant's growth rate is stimulated. But the plant does not produce the enzymes needed to break down synthetic auxins, and the plant is not able to make food material fast enough to sustain the growth rate.

Selective (hormone) weedkillers are designed to kill only certain types of plants. For example, many weeds are **broad-leaved** (dicotyledonous) plants, while cereal crops are **narrow-leaved** (monocotyledonous) plants. If a crop in a field is sprayed with a selective weedkiller, effective only on broad-leaved plants, then the broad-leaved weeds in the field will die but the narrow-leaved crop will not be harmed.

Tropisms

Plants usually respond to stimuli by changing their direction of growth in relation to the direction of the stimulus. Such growth responses are called **tropisms**.

Plants respond to the stimuli of **light** and **gravity**.

> **Definitions**
>
> Phototropism is the growth response made by part of a plant to the directional stimulus of light.
>
> Geotropism is the growth response made by part of a plant to the directional stimulus of gravity.

An explanation of tropisms

In plants, the very tip of shoots and roots (the 'apex') has cells (**receptor cells**) specialised to receive stimuli. The elongating cells which occur just beyond the region of cell division are the **effector cells**, and the link between the two are **growth hormones** called **auxins**. Auxins are manufactured at the tip of the shoot or root and pass back to the growth regions. A **differential concentration** of auxins causes a **differential growth** on that side of the shoot or root.

The response of plant shoots to one-sided light

Monocotyledonous plants (e.g. sorghum and maize) are often used to demonstrate this effect, since the shoots are covered by a sheath (the **coleoptile**) for the first three or four days of growth. This coleoptile responds to stimuli.

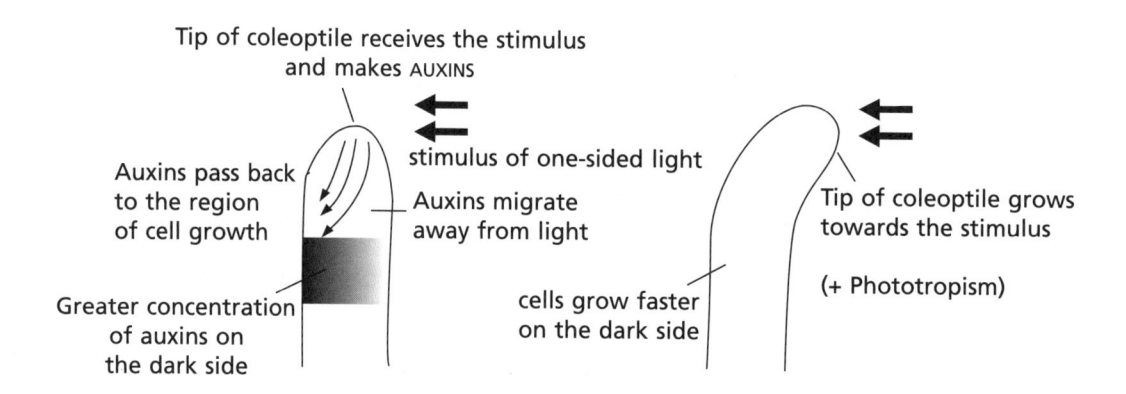

Fig. 56 Positive phototropism in a maize coleoptile

As shown in the figure, the coleoptile responds to one-sided light by **growing** (*not* 'bending') towards it. This is termed **positive** (or '+') **phototropism**. It is caused by an accumulation of auxins on the dark side of the coleoptile, since, *in shoots* auxins *increase* the rate of cell growth, causing the cells on the darker side to grow faster than those nearer the light source.

The response of plant shoots and roots to gravity

Auxins accumulate on the lower side of (horizontal) shoots and roots due to gravity. However, *auxins have the opposite effect on root cells to that on cells in shoots*. Increased concentrations **slow down** the rate of growth. Thus, a horizontal root grows downwards, displaying **positive (+) geotropism**, whilst shoots grow away from gravity, showing **negative (-) geotropism**.

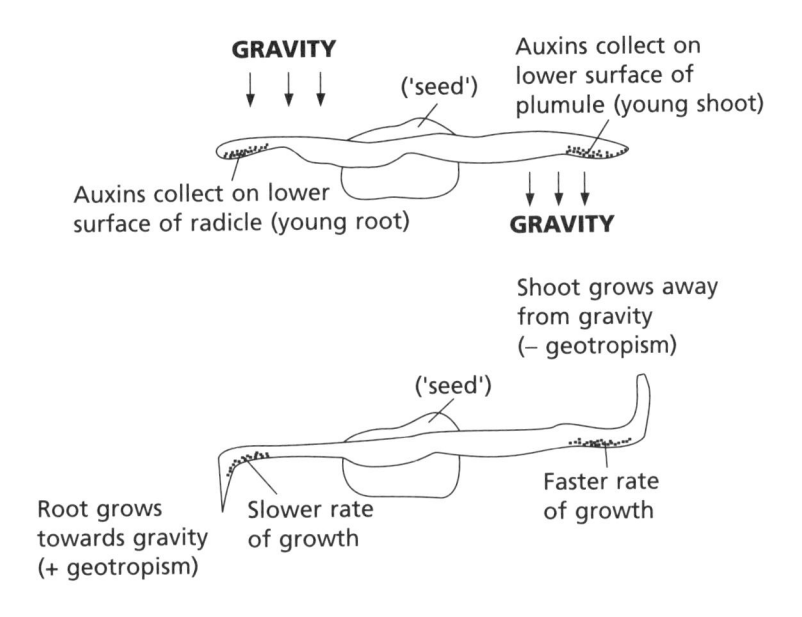

Fig. 57 Geotropism in a seedling

Tropisms are **slow**, **permanent** responses, ensuring that;
- stems and their attached leaves are best positioned to receive maximum sunlight for photosynthesis
- roots are firmly anchored in the soil where they can absorb water and mineral ions.

Taxic responses

When an animal **moves its whole body** in **response to a stimulus**, this is described as a **taxic** response. Many invertebrates show taxic responses, often as a protection against predators.

e.g. **blowfly larvae** show **negative phototaxis** (i.e. they move away from light). This may be demonstrated by covering a bench lamp with a piece of cardboard in which a vertical slit has been cut. In an otherwise darkened room, if the narrow beam of light from the bench lamp is shone on the blowfly larva, the larva will be seen to begin to move along the beam of light, away from the lamp.

TOPIC 15

The Use and Abuse of Drugs

Hormones are chemicals manufactured *by* and *within* a living organism, which have a specific effect on that organism's metabolism. Chemicals not made by the organism may be introduced into the body of the organism for a specific effect. These chemicals are called DRUGS.

> **Definition**
>
> A drug is an externally-administered substance which modifies or affects chemical reactions in the body.

Drugs may be used for **beneficial** effects:

(i) For **pain relief** (aspirin, paracetamol and morphine).

(ii) For **treatment of disease**. Diseases caused by **bacteria**, such as **syphilis**, are treated with drugs called ANTIBIOTICS. A well-known antibiotic is **penicillin**.

(iii) Drugs are also used for their **mood influencing** effect. This can be useful for treating patients with emotional disorders such as depression.

Drug abuse

If a drug is taken simply for enjoyment, often in large amounts, it can lead to **addiction**.

Heroin

Heroin is a drug which is abused in this way. It is a **powerful depressant** that has a sedative effect. It removes feelings of anxiety, and creates a sense of extreme well-being. Heroin is a drug to which the body shows TOLERANCE. This means that progressively **increased** dosages are needed to maintain (or produce) the feelings of well-being.

The person using the drug ('user') may end up in a state of **dependence**, where they crave the drug and cannot face life without it. If they cannot get further supplies, they suffer severe WITHDRAWAL SYMPTOMS, like diarrhoea, vomiting, muscular pain, shaking and hallucination.

These are signs that abuse of the drug has led to addiction. Addiction can lead the user into a life of **crime** to get money and/or regular supplies of the drug.

Heroin is a drug normally taken by injection into a vein. If several addicts use the same unsterilised needles, they are at high risk of contracting blood-borne diseases such as **hepatitis** and **AIDS**.

Alcohol

Alcohol is widely used and readily available in many societies, where it is generally regarded as a more 'socially acceptable' drug. However, it has these effects:

(i) It is a **depressant**, creating a feeling of well-being.

(ii) It **slows reaction times** (increasing the risk of accident).

(iii) When consumed in **excessive** quantities it leads to **loss of self control**. Many people under the influence of alcohol behave in a way they would be ashamed of when sober.

(iv) It also leads to **liver damage** which can eventually prove fatal.

Like heroin, alcohol is a drug of addiction. Withdrawal symptoms are not as severe as those for heroin, but a person may go to great lengths to satisfy their cravings. Often their **families suffer** as a consequence, not only from financial hardship, but also from **physical violence**, which often accompanies alcoholism.

Nicotine

Nicotine is the drug of addiction present in cigarette smoke. A person suffers (relatively) mild withdrawal symptoms if their craving for nicotine is not satisfied. This drug has the following effects:

(i) It is a **poison** which **increases** heart rate and **blood pressure**.

(ii) It may cause **blood clotting**, increasing the risk of **thrombosis** (blockage in a blood vessel). Thrombosis in the coronary artery will result in a heart 'attack'.

Other harmful components of cigarette smoke:

(i) **Tar** forms a layer over the walls of the alveoli, restricting gaseous exchange. Tar is also a **carcinogen** and prolonged exposure to it may lead to **lung cancer**.

(ii) **Carbon monoxide** is taken up, permanently, by **haemoglobin** in preference to oxygen (forming carboxyhaemoglobin). It greatly **reduces** the ability of the **blood** to carry **oxygen**.

(iii) **Irritant chemicals** in smoke cause the cells lining the bronchi and bronchioles to increase their production of **mucus**. These chemicals also **destroy the cilia** lining the trachea. Cilia sweep away the dirt in a 'moving carpet' of mucus and carry it to the throat for swallowing. The build-up of mucus is relieved only by continual coughing ('smoker's cough'). Persistent coughing may damage the walls of the alveoli, allowing them to become over-stretched. This may lead to **emphysema** (see p. 72). Irritant chemicals also cause inflammation of the bronchi (**bronchitis**) and may increase the risk of secondary bacterial infection of the bronchial walls.

(iv) A pregnant woman who smokes also **risks the health of her baby**. **Less oxygen** reaches the baby as a result of the effects of carbon monoxide, and **nicotine** can pass from mother's to baby's blood. Babies born to mothers who smoke during pregnancy have been shown to be **underweight**, perhaps less intelligent, and there is a greater risk of **miscarriage**.

(v) **Passive smoking**. Evidence now exists that breathing the smoke from other people's cigarettes can be harmful. Cigarette smoke is certainly an **irritant** to the eyes and leaves a lingering smell in clothes. Smoking is therefore increasingly becoming a **socially unacceptable** habit.

TOPIC 16

The Diversity of Organisms

Microorganisms (and their importance in biotechnology)

All organisms are collections of chemical molecules which, when working together, show what are known as the 'characteristics of life'. These are: respiration, reproduction, excretion, nutrition, sensitivity, growth, movement and a cellular structure.

MICROORGANISMS are organisms which are studied only with the aid of a microscope. Often, they are made up of one cell only (i.e. they are **unicellular**).

Viruses

VIRUSES are such simple organisms that biologists do not regard them as truly living. They have the following main characteristics:

(i) They are less than 300 nm in size – around 50 times smaller than a bacterium (1 nm, or nanometre, is one thousand millionth of a metre). They can be seen only with an **electron microscope**.

(ii) They contain **nucleic acid** (DNA or RNA).

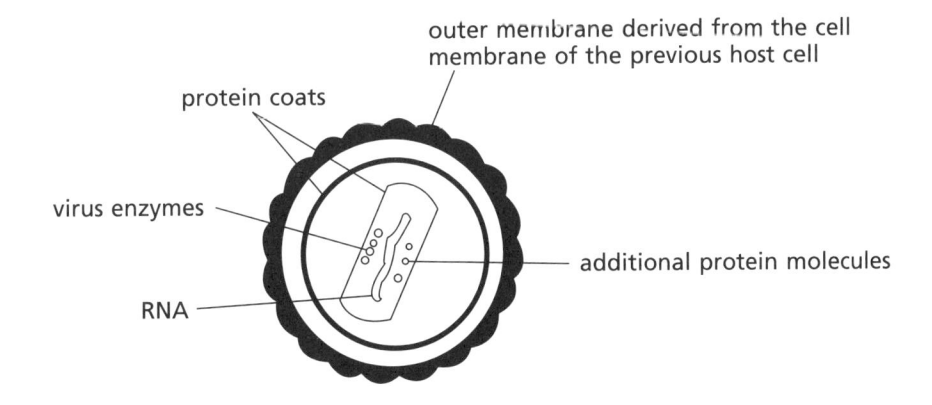

Fig. 58 A virus (the human immuno-deficiency virus: HIV)

(iii) The nucleic acid is surrounded by a coat (two, in the case of HIV) of **protein** (known as the **capsid**).

(iv) They can **reproduce only inside living** ('host') **cells**.

(v) They are **parasites**, and **cause disease** (they are **pathogenic**).
Examples of diseases caused by viruses are influenza, measles and AIDS.

(vi) Viruses are **not affected by antibiotics**.

Bacteria

Bacteria are the simplest of the (truly) living organisms. They have the following characteristics:

(i) They have a size in the range of 0.5–5 µm (1 µm = $\frac{1}{1000}$ mm).

(ii) They are **unicellular**.

(iii) They have **no true nucleus** (their DNA lies 'loose' in the cytoplasm).

(iv) They have a **cell wall**.

(v) They may be (pathogenic) PARASITES or they may be SAPROTROPHS – feeding on dead organic matter causing it to decay. Some may be involved in NITROGEN FIXATION (see the section on the nitrogen cycle, p. 106).

(vi) They are killed by **antibiotics**.

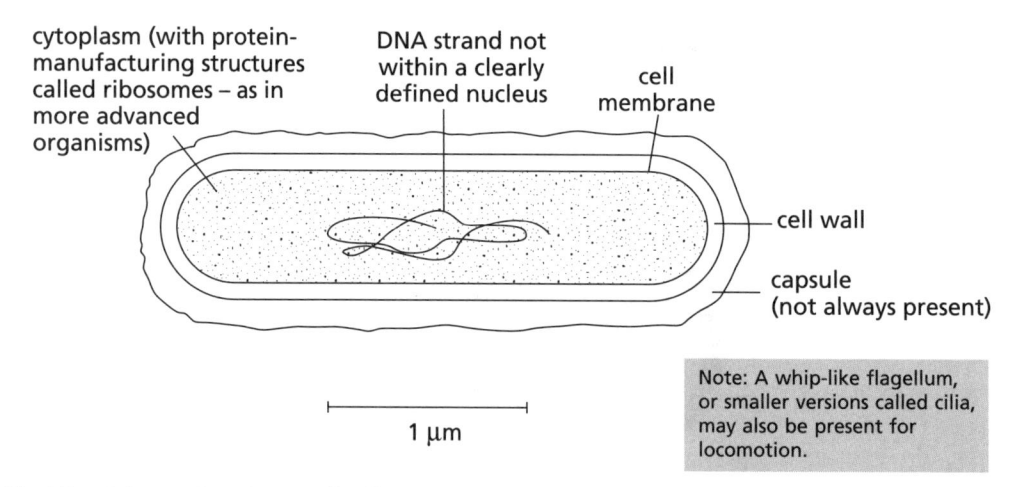

Fig. 59 A bacterium (generalised)

Fungi

FUNGI are usually much larger organisms, visible to the naked eye. They have the following characteristics:

(i) They have **no chlorophyll**, and thus have **heterotrophic** nutrition: digesting large molecules with **enzymes** and absorbing the soluble products. They are **parasites** or **saprotrophs**.

(ii) They have a 'cell' wall made of **chitin**.

(iii) They are usually made of a large number of tubular threads (**hyphae**) intertwined to form a **mycelium**.

(iv) Hyphae are not divided into individual cells. The lining of **cytoplasm** has many **nuclei** and the central space in the hyphae is a **vacuole** full of (vacuolar) sap.

(v) If they store carbohydrate, they store **glycogen**.

(vi) They reproduce by producing **spores**.

The role of microorganisms in decomposition

Many microorganisms such as bacteria and fungi feed as **saprotrophs**, using **external digestion**. They release **enzymes** onto their dead organic substrate ('food'). These enzymes are:

(i) **Protease** which digests proteins to amino acids. Amino acids are then further broken down to ammonium ions.

(ii) **Amylase** which digests starch to simple sugars.

(iii) **Lipase** which digests fats to fatty acids and glycerol.

Some of the end-products are absorbed by the microorganisms for use in their own metabolism. For example, amino acids for building up proteins during growth; sugars for energy release during respiration – with CO_2 and H_2O as waste products; fats for energy storage. Gradually, the dead matter is broken down, releasing its mineral ions which are returned to the soil for recycling as they are taken up for use by plants.

The roles of bacteria and fungi in food production

A. Bacteria and yoghurt

Milk is heated to 90°C, then cooled to between 40°C and 45°C. The correct species of bacterium (e.g. *Lactobacillus*) is added and the milk is kept at this temperature for 24–36 hours. Over this time the bacteria convert milk sugar (lactose) into **lactic acid** by **anaerobic respiration**. The acid **curdles** the milk to produce the characteristic texture and sharp flavour of yoghurt.

B. Bacteria and cheese

Milk is warmed to 40°C, inoculated with **bacteria** (e.g. *Streptococcus*) and mixed with **rennin**, an enzyme found in the stomachs of young mammals. Lactic acid produced by the bacteria creates the correct pH for the rennin to work. The milk **clots**. The solid part (the **curd**) is separated from the liquid (the **whey**). The curds are pressed and moulded and left to mature, or ripen. Sometimes, further bacteria are added to provide flavour, e.g. from copper wires which are drawn through the dried curds.

C. Yeast and alcohol

Yeast is a **fungus** that is added to a sugar solution to make alcohol. For example, to make wine, yeast is added to fruit sugar from grapes; to make **beer**, it is added to maltose from barley. The yeast is allowed to FERMENT the sugar at a **controlled temperature** in a vessel called a **fermenter**. The optimum temperature for the growth of yeast is around 20°C. The yeast converts the sugar to **alcohol** by **anaerobic respiration**, with **carbon dioxide** evolved as a waste product. As the concentration of alcohol rises, it eventually kills the yeast, which must then be filtered from the liquor to produce a yeast-free alcoholic drink. Drinks with a higher alcoholic content, such as spirits, are produced by **distillation** of the original alcoholic drink. For example, brandy is distilled wine.

D. Yeast and bread

A process similar to the one described above occurs in bread-making. Flour and water are used to make a dough, then yeast and a little sugar are added. Although alcohol is produced by the anaerobic respiration of the yeast, it is the **carbon dioxide** which is important. The mixture is left in a **warm** place for around half an hour (depending on temperature) for the dough to 'prove'. The carbon dioxide gas causes the dough to rise, giving it a light texture. The dough is then **baked** at **high temperature** in an **oven**. The high temperature cooks the bread and also evaporates the alcohol produced during fermentation.

Industrial biotechnology

INDUSTRIAL BIOTECHNOLOGY is the use of microorganisms in industrial processes, for example, in the manufacture of **antibiotics** and **single-cell protein** (SCP). Large quantities of end-product (antibiotic or SCP) are required, so the microorganisms involved are grown in very large containers called **fermenters**. A **maximum rate of growth** of the microorganism within the fermenter can be achieved by careful control of:

(i) the **temperature**

(ii) the type and concentration of **substrate** (i.e. the substance on which the microorganism works)

(iii) the **oxygen availability**.

Thus, fermenters are unaffected by climate, soil type or, in temperate regions, time of year. Fermenters must be kept **sterile** to prevent the growth of unwanted species of microorganism which might contaminate the end-product.

Antibiotic production

Pathogenic (disease-causing) bacteria are killed by certain chemicals (**antibiotics**) released by other microorganisms, especially fungi. For example, the **mould fungus** *Penicillium*, which grows naturally on stale bread, may be cultured on a sterile medium in a laboratory. The fungus is then introduced into a **fermenter** for commercial production. The fermenter (up to 100,000 litres in volume) contains a suitable sterile medium on which the fungus can grow.

After an appropriate period of time, when the rate of fungal growth becomes limited by the amount of food available, the contents of the fermenter are crushed and filtered. The liquid part contains the antibiotic (in this case, **penicillin**), which is separated and purified. The rest of the material may be dried and used as cattle feed.

Single-cell protein production

Bacteria and fungi contain cytoplasm, and a major constituent of cytoplasm is **protein**. Therefore, large-scale production of bacteria and fungi involves the large-scale production of protein. The microorganisms can be grown in a fermenter, harvested and used as a protein source, known as SCP. If the microorganisms involved are fungi, then, more accurately, the protein is known as **mycoprotein**.

Many microorganisms will grow successfully on industrial waste materials as a substrate. Examples are: waste from oil refining, waste from sugar refining (molasses), whey from cheese manufacture, and straw.

Insects

Insects are by far the largest group of animals. They are **invertebrates** (i.e. they have no vertebral column) and have the following characteristics:

(i)   They have a body divided into **three** parts (head, thorax and abdomen).

(ii) They have **six legs** attached to the **thorax**.

(iii) They have **wings** (one or two pairs) also attached to the **thorax** (n.b. a very few types of insects are wingless).

(iv) They have **compound eyes**.

(v)   They have **one pair of antennae**.

(vi) They breathe through small pores called **spiracles** which lead to a system of **tracheal tubes** carrying oxygen **directly** to the tissues.

Insects, together with the crustacea (crabs and lobsters), arachnids (spiders and scorpions), and myriapods (centipedes and millipedes), belong to a larger group called the **arthropods**, all of which possess:

1 a flexible **exoskeleton** (containing chitin) with muscles within

2 bodies divided into **segments** (more easily seen in the myriapods)

3 **legs with many** visible **joints**.

Activities of insects which affect the ecosystem

A   Beneficial effects

Pollination. Many flowers rely on insects to bring about pollination. Insects are suited to this process since they:

- **fly** from flower to flower – often of the same species

- are **attracted by the scent and colour** of the flowers

- are able to **follow the nectar guides** on petals

- have **mouthparts** specially **adapted** for collecting the nectar on which they feed (e.g. butterflies)

- have 'hairy' bodies and 'bristly' **legs on which the pollen can stick**. Bees also have 'pollen baskets' on their legs in which pollen is carried since it forms part of the larval bees' diet.

B   Effects which are disadvantageous to Mankind

Some insects carry **pathogenic** organisms (i.e. they act as **vectors** for the organisms). The **mosquito** carries the **malaria** pathogen, the **tse-tse fly** carries the **sleeping sickness** pathogen. Many scavenging insects carry bacteria on their legs from refuse to our food (e.g. the **cockroach and housefly**, which **carry bacteria** responsible for diarrhoea). Houseflies also vomit the remains of their stomach contents onto their food (which could be your sandwich) to digest it before sucking it back up again.

Plants

There are two main types of plants – (i) *Dicotyledonous* and (ii) *Monocotyledonous*. The differences between them are as follows:

	Dicotyledonous	**Monocotyledonous**
Leaves	broad veins form a network	narrow and strap-like veins run parallel
Flowers	petals in fours and fives (or multiples of) sepals distinct from petals	petals in threes (or multiples of) sepals and petals often indistinguishable
Stems	vascular bundles ('veins') form a circle (see Fig. 5b, p. 6)	vascular bundles scattered
Roots	usually a long central 'tap' root with lateral (side) roots	roots fibrous with no tap root
Seeds	have two cotyledons which are often a food store	have one (protective) cotyledon food stored in tissue called endosperm

Plants cultivated for their **fruits** are often dicotyledonous (e.g. mango, apple and citrus). Leguminous plants (peas and beans) are also dicotyledonous and, apart from being important food plants, are important also in the nitrogen cycle since they 'fix' atmospheric nitrogen (see p. 106).

Monocotyledonous plants include all the cereals as well as palm trees. Grass is an important monocot since it is the **producer** in many natural food chains, some of which include animals used as food by Mankind.

TOPIC 17: The Relationship between Organisms and the Environment

Energy flow

The source of energy for all life on the planet is **the sun**. Living organisms use that energy for their activities. So long as the sun continues to shine, life can continue.

The **heat energy** from the sun is used by organisms such as 'cold-blooded' animals to keep their bodies warm. The sun also supplies **light energy**, which is locked away by plants during **photosynthesis** to form **chemical energy** in food molecules. A plant's chemical energy is passed on to an animal when the animal eats the plant. If that animal is eaten by *another* animal, the energy is passed on again.

In this way, the sun's energy **enters** then **flows** through biological (eco)systems, and is gradually **lost** to the environment as it passes from one organism to the next. It is **never recycled**.

Food chains and food webs

Definition

A FOOD CHAIN is a sequence of organisms, starting with a photosynthesising organism (usually a green plant), through which energy is passed as one organism is eaten by the next in the sequence.

An example of a food chain in a large pond:

green algae ⟶ mosquito larvae (e.g. *Anopheles*) ⟶ small fish (e.g. small *Tilapia*) ⟶ heron

Note: Algae are unicellular organisms which contain chlorophyll and photosynthesise.

In any one habitat, such as a pond or mangrove swamp, there will be many organisms living together forming an ECOSYSTEM. The food chains involving all of these organisms will be interconnected.

Definition

A FOOD WEB is made up of interlinked food chains involving organisms within the same ecosystem.

All food chains, and thus all food webs, begin with a photosynthesising organism, the **producer**. When organisms in a food chain/web die, they are decomposed by saprotrophic organisms – usually bacteria and fungi.

Key terms

Term	Definition	Example
PRODUCERS	Organisms which manufacture and supply energy-rich foods, made by photosynthesis, to all organisms in their food chain.	green algae
CONSUMERS	All organisms which rely on the energy supplied by the producer in that chain.	mosquito larvae, small fish, heron
HERBIVORES or PRIMARY CONSUMERS	Consumers which feed directly on the producer.	mosquito larvae
SECONDARY CONSUMERS	Consumers which feed directly on the herbivore.	small fish
TERTIARY CONSUMERS	Consumers which feed on the secondary consumer.	heron
CARNIVORES	All consumers above the level of herbivore, i.e. all meat eaters.	small fish, heron
DECOMPOSERS	Organisms which release enzymes to break down large molecules in dead organic matter into smaller ones which can then be recycled.	bacteria, fungi

Energy loss along a food chain

Some of the energy locked away by producers (plants) is **released** by the producer itself through the process of respiration. Some of the energy is **used** by the producer, for example, in the processes of **cell division**, **growth** and **reproduction**. A lot of energy is still present when a plant dies, and is then available to decomposers. Only about 10% of a plant's available energy is passed on to the herbivores which eat it.

Herbivores then **release the energy** by respiration, and use it for growth, movement and, as heat, to maintain body temperature.

Much of the energy is still present in the faeces of herbivores, and some in the nitrogenous waste. This is available to decomposers. Not all herbivores are eaten, so the amount of energy available to be passed on to carnivores is small, at around 20%. This is only 2% of the amount that originated in the producer.

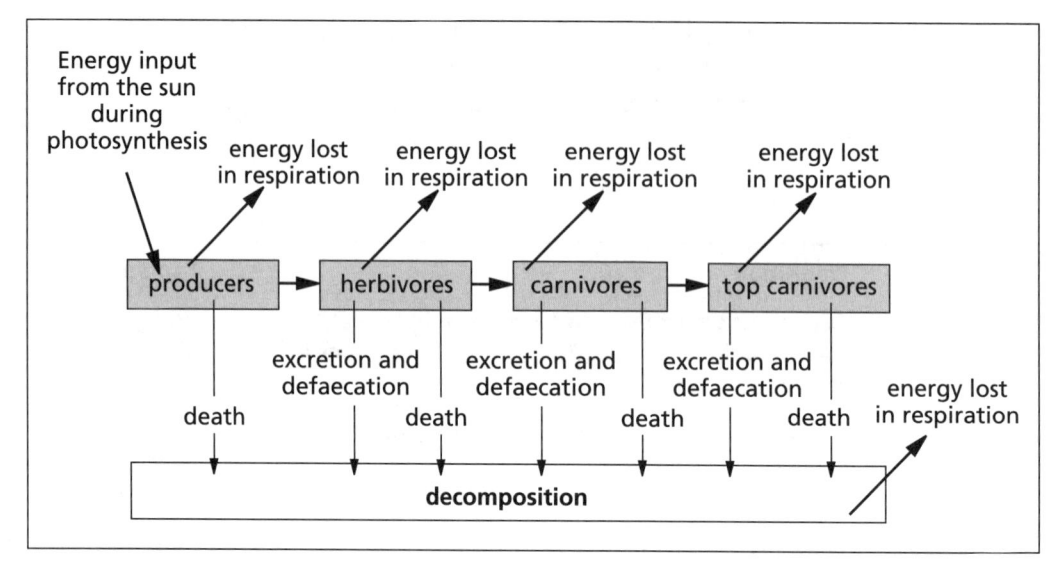

Fig. 60 Energy flow in an ecosystem

The longer the food chain, the less energy available to the carnivore at the end of the chain. **Short** food chains are therefore **much more energy-efficient** than long ones. In order to supply enough energy in food to maintain an ever-increasing world population, it must be realised that far less energy is lost when humans eat green plants than when crop plants are fed to animals which are then eaten by humans.

Pyramids of numbers, biomass and energy

Producers (plants) need to produce enough food – and therefore enough energy – for their own metabolic processes. They must also provide enough food for the herbivores that eat them, and leave enough surviving individuals to reproduce the next generation. Therefore, we would expect there to be **a larger number of producers than primary consumers** (herbivores). For the same reasons, we would expect there to be more primary consumers than secondary consumers, and so on. These decreasing numbers along a food web can be represented in the form of a PYRAMID OF NUMBERS, as shown below.

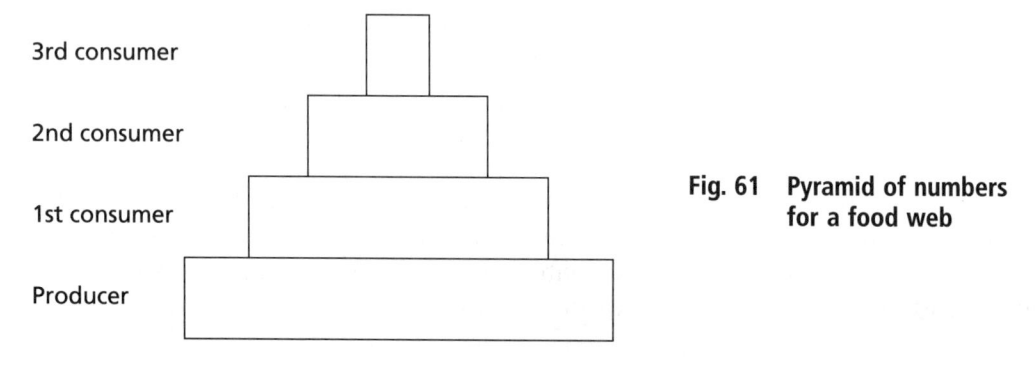

Fig. 61 Pyramid of numbers for a food web

However, this representation of feeding relationships can be misleading: one large plant may sustain a large number of very small herbivores; and one carnivore may sustain a large number of smaller carnivores. If this is the case, we see a 'top heavy' pyramid, as shown below.

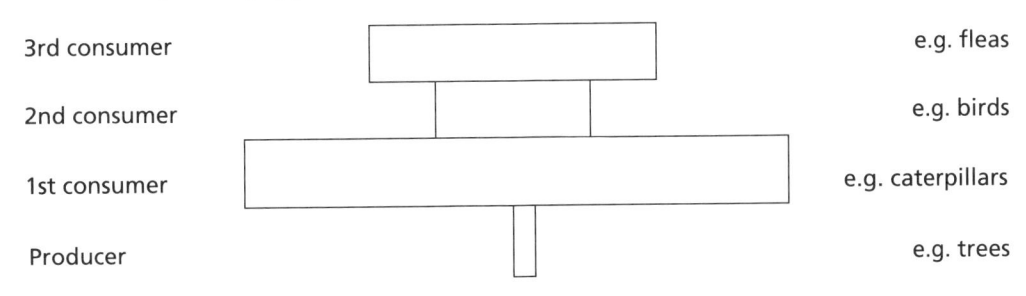

3rd consumer — e.g. fleas
2nd consumer — e.g. birds
1st consumer — e.g. caterpillars
Producer — e.g. trees

Fig. 62 'Top heavy' pyramid of numbers for a particular food chain

A PYRAMID OF BIOMASS is a pyramid constructed using the **dry mass** of organisms at each trophic level in a food chain (or food web). It produces pyramids of a more standard shape (e.g. Fig. 61) and can be constructed by collecting data from population estimates in any particular habitat. Biomass is the total dry mass of a population, i.e. the theoretical mass of chemicals **other than water** in the organisms under consideration (water can vary considerably).

A PYRAMID OF ENERGY is the most reliable of all the representations of the interactions between organisms in a food web. It shows how much **energy** is passed from one trophic level to the next, within organisms in a food web, **over a period of time**. It thus allows for the growth of producers over that period, and thus can show **productivity** (how much organic material is made) and how much energy is passed on, during that period, to the herbivores. Its **shape** is that of a **standard pyramid** (like the pyramid of biomass), but the **information** necessary to construct it **is difficult to obtain**, since it requires knowing how much of all the different foodstuffs are manufactured by the producer, how much energy they contain, and how much of each foodstuff is passed on to each member of the food web.

The carbon cycle

When **decomposition** occurs, carbohydrates in the dead organic matter are used as the substrate for respiration by decomposers (bacteria and fungi). **Carbon dioxide is released** into the atmosphere, as it is in all cases of aerobic **respiration**.

Combustion, the burning of fuels, also **releases carbon dioxide** into the atmosphere. Many of these fuels are **fossil fuels** such as coal, gas and oil.

Photosynthesis absorbs that carbon dioxide and converts it into carbohydrates (which may then be used to make fats or proteins) in a plant.

Animal nutrition involves the transfer of these carbon-containing molecules to animals. Animals and plants **respire**, and eventually die and are decomposed, releasing the carbon dioxide back into the atmosphere, and so the cycle continues.

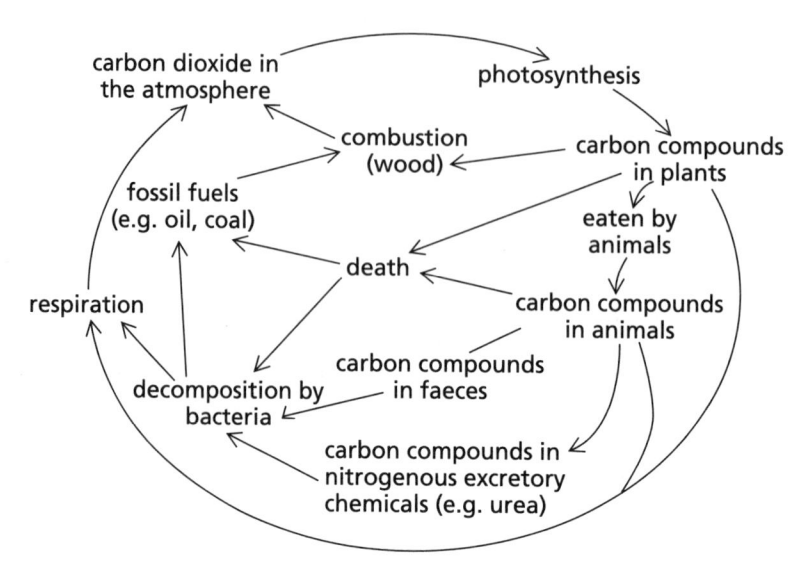

Fig. 63 The carbon cycle

The nitrogen cycle

Decomposition includes the conversion by bacteria of **proteins** to **amino acids**, and the conversion of amino acids and **urea** to **ammonium ions**. This process usually takes place in the **soil**.

Ammonium ions contain **nitrogen** atoms, but before plants can absorb nitrogen from the soil, it must be in the form of **nitrate** ions.

Nitrifying bacteria convert ammonium ions first into **nitrites** then into **nitrates**.

Plants absorb the nitrates and use them together with the carbohydrates made by photosynthesis, to make amino acids and then **proteins**.

Animals eat the protein in plants and excrete, e.g. urea. Both plants and animals die, and decomposition releases ammonium ions again.

Atmospheric nitrogen (79% of the air) cannot be used either by plants or by animals in its gaseous form, but it is used by some bacteria (the **nitrogen fixing bacteria**). These bacteria are found in two forms:

(i) Those which live in swellings called **nodules** on the roots of peas, beans and other **leguminous** plants.

(ii) Those which live freely in the soil.

Nitrogen fixation by these bacteria changes the atmospheric nitrogen, via ammonia, into **proteins**. The nitrogen becomes available to other organisms when these proteins later decompose.

Nitrogen fixation also occurs when **lightning** passes through the nitrogen in the air, converting it to **nitric acid** which forms nitrates in the soil.

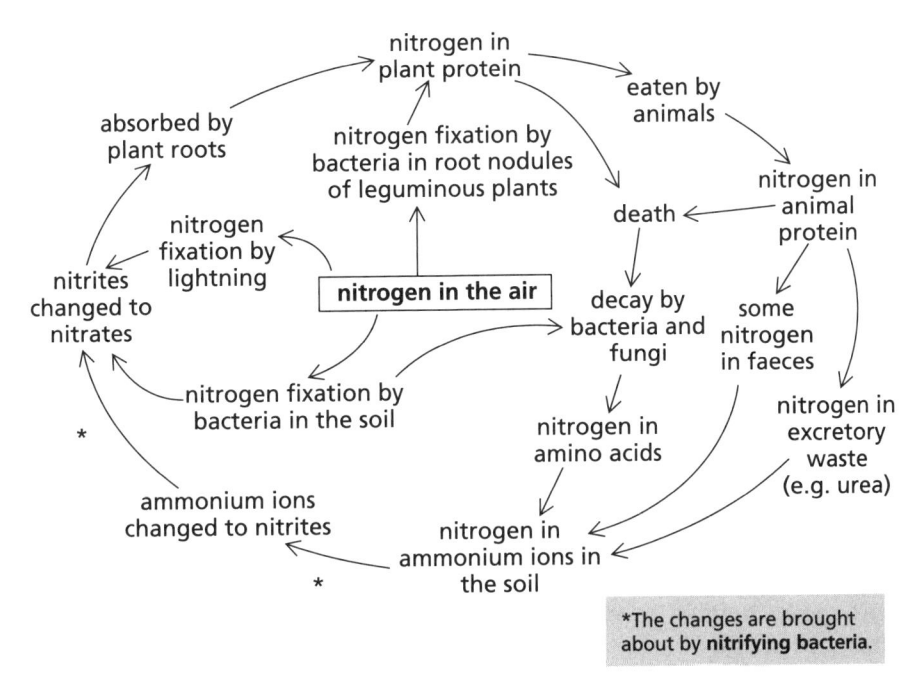

Fig. 64 The nitrogen cycle

The water cycle

Water is a substance essential to life on this planet. It is important for the following reasons:

- It is the medium in which **all metabolic reactions** take place.
- Water is sometimes called 'the universal solvent'.
- It is the means of **transporting** chemicals in plants and animals.
- It is used in **photosynthesis**.
- It is used in **temperature regulation** in many animals.
- It is given off in transpiration and respiration.
- It is a major constituent (**about 85%**) of all cells.

Like carbon and nitrogen, it is a chemical which is recycled.

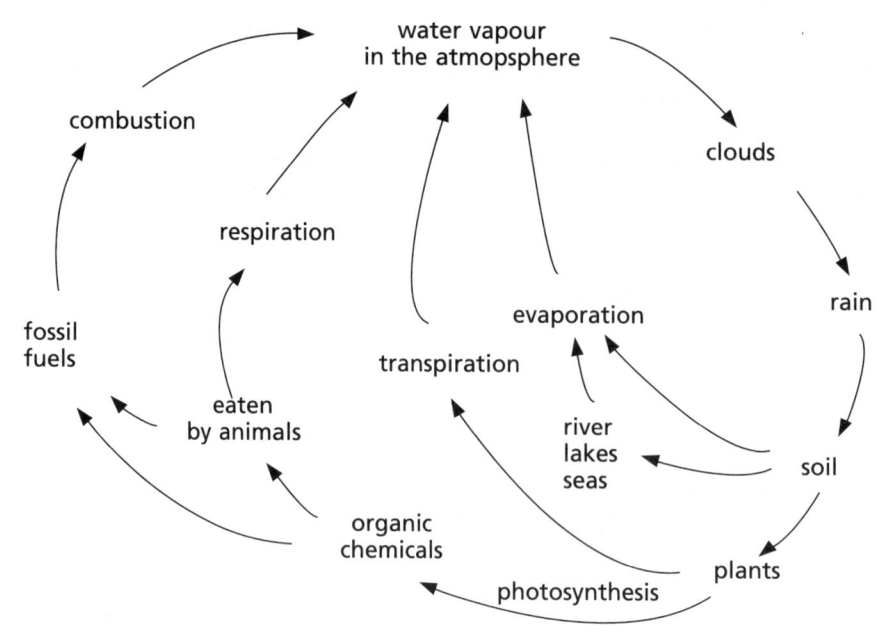

Fig. 65 The water cycle

Parasitism

Definition

A parasite can be defined as an organism which obtains its food from another, usually larger living organism ('host'); the host always suffering in the relationship.

Pathogens are therefore parasites. One such pathogen is the unicellular organism *Plasmodium* which causes **malaria**.

Malaria

Malaria is a disease caused by a **single-celled microorganism** called *Plasmodium* which lives in red blood cells. It is carried from person to person (host to host) by the female *Anopheles* mosquito. The mosquito is described as the **vector**, or carrier, of the microorganism. Usually at night, while the host is asleep, she injects her saliva into a (healthy) person before she starts to suck the blood which she needs for her developing eggs. The saliva contains a chemical to stop the blood from clotting. If the mosquito has previously taken blood from a person **infected** with malaria, it may also contain the parasite *Plasmodium*. The parasite is transferred *from* the **blood** of one host, where it lives and develops, *to* the **blood** of a second host.

Control of malaria

Malaria can be controlled in **three** ways:

A By controlling the mosquito vector.

B By avoiding mosquito bites.

C By treating the parasite in the blood.

A Controlling the mosquito

(i) Cover water tanks with netting to stop mosquitoes laying their eggs in the water.

(ii) Drain swamps where mosquitoes lay their eggs.

(iii) Introduce fish such as *Tilapia* into the swamps to feed on mosquito larvae.

(iv) Cover the surface of the water with light oil. Larvae cannot then use the water film from which they hang as they breathe air from the atmosphere. The larvae therefore suffocate.

(v) Use insecticides or mosquito coils to kill or repel adult mosquitoes inside buildings.

B Avoiding mosquito bites

(i) Place nets over doors and windows.

(ii) Wear clothes which cover wrists and ankles, especially in the evenings, when mosquitoes are most active.

(iii) Use insect repellent sprays.

(iv) Sleep under mosquito nets.

C Protection against the parasite *Plasmodium*

(i) Take drugs **regularly** to kill the parasite if it enters the bloodstream. The correct drug (e.g. Paludrin) must be taken for the particular type of *Plasmodium*.

(ii) Treat patients suffering from malaria with a higher dosage of anti-malarial drug, and isolate them to prevent spreading of the disease.

TOPIC 18: The Effects of Human Activity on the Ecosystem

The human animal is as much part of the ecosystem in which it lives as any other organism in that ecosystem. But humans can be far more destructive than any other organism.

Deforestation

A great deal of natural woodland has been (and is being) destroyed for the following reasons:

(i) to harvest timber for building houses and making furniture
(ii) to make way for roads and industrial development
(iii) to create agricultural land for the growth of crops and the rearing of livestock.

The dangers of deforestation

A The loss of soil stability

(i) The loss of HUMUS in the soil.

Leaves fall to the ground where they decompose, forming humus in the soil. Humus provides a steady supply of **ions**. It acts as a sponge, soaking up and holding water in the soil, and helps to bind the soil together, preventing soil erosion.

(ii) The loss of protection from excessive sun, wind and rain.

Trees form a **canopy** which keeps the powerful sun's rays off more delicate organisms. The canopy also protects the soil from the force of tropical rainfall, and protects the soil, smaller plants and animals from the full force of high winds. Tree **roots** also help to bind the soil. Removal of the trees therefore leads to soil **erosion** caused by wind and water, and soil carried into rivers may lead to **flooding** further downstream as it is deposited on the bed of the river as **silt**.

B The effect on climate

Trees supply enormous quantities of water vapour to the atmosphere through **transpiration**. Transpiration leads to the formation of clouds. Clouds are carried by the prevailing winds and eventually produce rain, usually in an area some distance away from where the vapour was released. Deforestation can therefore lead to distant regions receiving **reduced rainfall**. In the most extreme cases, relatively fertile areas can become **deserts**.

On a global scale, deforestation can reduce the amount of carbon dioxide taken in for photosynthesis. The **levels of carbon dioxide in the atmosphere rise**, acting as a 'thermal blanket' over the planet, preventing the natural escape of heat from our atmosphere. This is known as the **greenhouse effect**. It is believed to lead to **global warming**, which may affect the distribution of plants and animals (and eventually melt the ice caps).

C The effect on local human populations

Deforestation is usually motivated by financial gain. Those who benefit may live outside the country where the deforestation is occurring. Many local residents **lose their homes** and see their **culture destroyed** along with the trees. Many people find it **difficult to adapt** to lifestyles which are geared to commercial success. The people living in the Amazon rainforest of South America are one example. The forest, their home, is one of the largest areas of deforestation in the world.

Pollution

Apart from the effects of deforestation, humans are also responsible for polluting the environment in a number of ways.

A The pollution of water by sewage

Large human settlements create a considerable amount of sewage. Tipping sewage directly into streams and rivers can have these harmful effects:

(i) Sewage contains pathogenic organisms. If the water is used for human consumption, then diseases, such as cholera, spread.

(ii) Very high levels of sewage contain very large numbers of **bacteria** which use up the oxygen in the water for their own respiration. This does not leave enough oxygen for any other water life, so many organisms die.

(iii) Smaller quantities of sewage release ions as it decomposes. The ions encourage rapid growth of water plants (**eutrophication**), which eventually die and decompose. The bacteria of decomposition again use up so much oxygen in the water that no other life can exist.

B The pollution of water by inorganic waste

(i) **Household detergents**, discharged into rivers along with sewage, often contain **phosphates**. These encourage the growth of small water organisms (algae), leading to possible eutrophication.

(ii) **Industrial** wastes such as those which contain **mercury** (e.g. from paper mills) and **copper** ('heavy metals') are highly toxic to all organisms. It is expensive to remove these wastes in a completely safe way, so they, too, are often discharged into rivers.

Polluted rivers discharge into **seas**. Polluted seas lead to contamination of producers in the sea's food chains. One small fish consumes many smaller contaminated food organisms. One large fish eats many smaller fish. In this way, the amount of poison gradually increases in the organisms along the food chain. If a human eats contaminated fish, they may consume harmful levels of poison.

C Air pollution by sulphur dioxide

Sulphur dioxide is a gas which is released whenever fossil fuels are burnt. In industrial areas, the amounts of sulphur dioxide released into the air can be high. It is a gas linked with bronchitis and heart disease in humans.

In the air, sulphur dioxide dissolves in rain and falls to earth as a dilute solution of **sulphuric acid**. This is known as ACID RAIN, and has these effects:

(i) It kills the leaves of some species of plant (e.g. wheat).

(ii) It makes the water of lakes **acidic**. This acidic water dissolves toxic chemicals (such as aluminium salts) present in the mud of the lake, which are insoluble in neutral or alkaline solutions. Fish, for example, are killed by aluminium.

D Pollution due to insecticides

Insects can cause considerable harm to the economy, either as pests on crops or as vectors of disease. They can be killed very effectively by insecticides, but insecticides may pollute the environment, with the following harmful effects:

(i) Useful insects, such as those needed for pollination, may be killed as well.

(ii) If the livers of animals are unable to break down the insecticide, it may be passed from animal to animal along food chains. Animals at trophic level A eat *many* animals from trophic level B, and animals at trophic level B eat *many* animals from trophic level C (which may have been insects affected by insecticide). Therefore, animal A receives a very high, and perhaps very harmful, level of insecticide. For example, some birds are known to have been made sterile.

(iii) Agricultural pesticides can be washed into rivers, entering food chains in the water as well as on land.

TOPIC 19

The Need for Conservation

The threat of extinction

The removal of organisms from an environment at a faster rate than the organism can reproduce itself leads to EXTINCTION of the species. Widespread deforestation can lead to the extinction of plant species; uncontrolled fishing can lead to the extinction of species of fish.

Destruction of habitats, however it may occur, may also lead to the extinction of **animal** species which live among the plants. Animals are protected by plants and are linked to them through food chains.

Plants are the source of many valuable products, such as the insecticide **pyrethrum** extract (from a species of daisy) and **drugs**. Aspirin (for pain relief and treatment of circulatory disorders), quinine (for the treatment of malaria) and many other drugs were first obtained from plants. Deforestation could rob humans of the plant which might bring a cure for diseases such as AIDS.

Maintaining a continuous supply of commodities from trees

Timber, **rubber** and **oils** are commodities, or useful products, supplied by trees.

Most trees that supply commodities grow very slowly: the product they supply may not be ready for harvest until many years after planting. A system of **sustainable management** must therefore be used. This means harvesting only the number of trees that can be replaced by planting.

Maintaining fish supplies

The **oceans** supply many communities with a large part of their food requirements. **Overfishing** can reduce fish populations to a point where they are not able to maintain their numbers. Fishing **quotas** (a legally enforced limit on the amount of fish which can be caught) make sure that stocks remain at sustainable levels, but must be adhered to.

Conservation of other species

To maintain the wide variety (**biodiversity**) of living species on the planet, it is important to identify **threatened species** so that their needs can be addressed before it is too late. This work is carried out by organisations such as the Worldwide Fund for Nature (WWF) and the Convention on International Trade in Endangered Species (CITES). Countries throughout the world must also support these organisations with legislation.

Recycling

Pressure is taken off endangered species if countries encourage a policy of **recycling**.

Many commodities we use every day can be recycled. For example:

(i) Aluminium cans, tin cans and many car parts can be made of recycled **metal**. This reduces the need for mining activity and, consequently, the effect that mining has on the environment. The burning of fossil fuels, used to produce heat to extract metals from their ores, is also reduced.

(ii) Bottles are made from recycled **glass**.

(iii) **Paper** can be recycled so fewer trees need to be cut down for their **fibres** which are used to make paper products.

(iv) **Litter** is also reduced by recycling, making our environment a more pleasant place in which to live. There is less need to bury garbage in landfills, or incinerate it.

(v) When **sewage** is properly treated, it can be recycled to provide an effective fertiliser. The large amounts of water used to carry away the sewage, which would otherwise be wasted, can be purified even to the extent that it can be returned to drinking water supplies!

TOPIC 20

Reproduction

Asexual reproduction

Definition

ASEXUAL REPRODUCTION is the production of genetically identical offspring from one parent.

A population of organisms produced in this way, and all genetically identical, is known as a CLONE.

The **advantages** of asexual reproduction are:

(i) Only one parent organism is required.

(ii) It is a relatively certain method of reproduction.

(iii) Because the parent can survive in that particular habitat, the genetically identical offspring should be suited to the environment as well.

The **disadvantages** of asexual reproduction are:

(i) A lack of variation in offspring prevents evolution.

(ii) Adverse conditions and disease will be likely to affect all members of the population.

(iii) Overcrowding and competition for resources (water, nutrients and, importantly for plants, light).

(iv) Distribution of the species is likely to be limited. However, asexual reproduction in plants is an important **commercial** process, since it:

    (a) produces **large numbers** of offspring

    (b) **quickly**, all of which have

    (c) **known characteristics** (such as flavour, appearance, yield and disease resistance).

Tissue culture

A commercial application of asexual reproduction in plants is the use of a technique called TISSUE CULTURE.

Definition

A technique for keeping alive cells or tissues of living organisms after their removal from an organism.

Plants reproduced in this way include food plants (the **oil palm**, the **date palm** and the **banana**) and horticultural plants such as the **begonia**.

Demonstration 20.1

Method
Some actively dividing ('**meristematic**') cells are taken from the parent plant, and placed on a sterilised **culture medium** in many separate sterilised dishes. The culture medium is a jelly-like substance called **agar** containing **plant growth hormones** and the ions necessary for healthy growth.

The dishes are kept at a suitable temperature, and are covered to prevent the cells drying out.

Results
The cells continue to **divide**, then some of them become modified to produce small ('**adventitious**') **roots** and some become modified to produce small **shoots** bearing lateral **buds**.

These plantlets can then be transferred to compost and will develop into clones of their parent.

The commercial advantages of using tissue culture to produce plants are:
(i)   it is quick
(ii) it is reliable
(iii) it gives plants of guaranteed type
(iv) it is profitable.

Sexual reproduction

Definition

Sexual reproduction is the fusion of male and female nuclei to form a ZYGOTE. Zygotes develop into offspring genetically different from each other, and from their parents.

The nuclei are contained within **gametes**. As a result of a special type of nuclear division ('**reduction division**'), the nuclei of gametes contain only **half** the number of chromosomes found in normal body cells.

Sexual reproduction in plants

The **flowers** of plants are the organs of sexual reproduction.

Flowers have the following parts:

Sepals

Sepals are (usually) green, leaf-like structures which protect the flower when it is in bud.

Petals

Petals may be large, colourful and scented with lines on them (nectar guides) if the flower is pollinated by insects. But if the flower is wind-pollinated, the petals are small and green, or not present at all.

Stamens

These are made up of two parts – a stalk-like **filament** bearing, at its outer end, an **anther**. Anthers contain **pollen sacs** which make and then release pollen grains. Each pollen grain contains the male gamete(s).

Carpels

CARPELS are the **female** part of the flower. Each carpel is made up of a (sticky) **stigma** (for receiving pollen during pollination), connected by a **style** to the **ovary**, in which lie the **ovules** which contain the female gamete.

Pollination

Definition

POLLINATION is the transfer of pollen from an anther to a stigma.

Self-pollination occurs when the anther and stigma are either in the same flower, or in different flowers **on the same plant**.

Cross-pollination occurs when the anther and stigma are in flowers on **different plants of the same species**.

The two most common agents for carrying pollen are the **wind**, and **insects**. Wind- and insect-pollinated flowers have structural differences, adapted according to their method of pollination.

The differences between wind- and insect-pollinated flowers

Structure	Wind-pollinated flowers	Insect-pollinated flowers
Petals	Small or absent No scent Nectar guides absent Nectar absent	Large* Colourful Scented Nectar guides present Nectar present to attract insects (*also act as landing platforms)
Pollen grains	Small Dry and dusty Smooth-coated Light More easily carried by the wind Vast quantities (greater wastage of pollen)	Larger Sticky Rough-coated Relatively heavy More easily carried by insects Smaller quantities (pollination much more certain)
Anthers	Held outside the flower in the wind Relatively large	Protected within the flower where insects will touch them Relatively small
Stigmas	Large surface area Outside flower	Smaller surface area Inside flower

Examples of wind-pollinated flowers are maize and grasses.

Examples of insect-pollinated flowers are beans and black-eyed Susan.

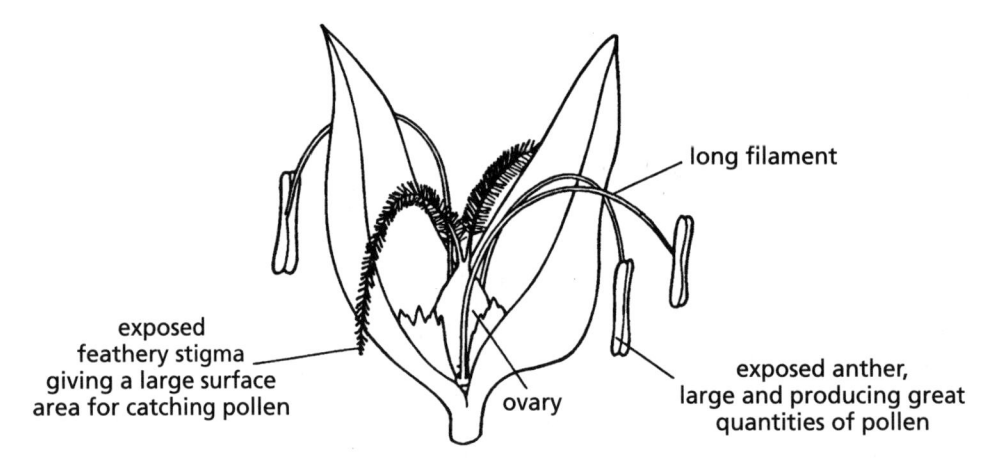

Fig. 66a A wind-pollinated flower (grass flower)

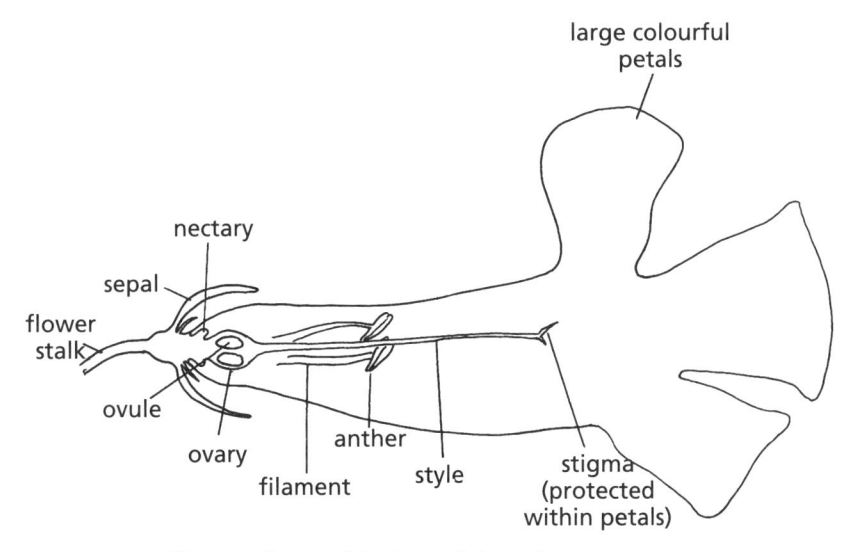

Fig. 66b An insect-pollinated flower (black-eyed Susan)

Fig. 67a Pollen grains of a wind-pollinated plant on a stigma

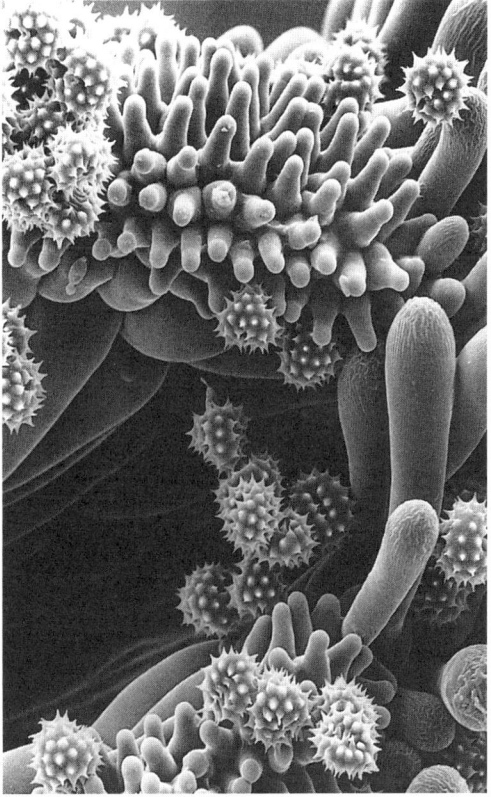

Fig. 67b Pollen grains of an insect-pollinated plant on a stigma

Fertilisation in flowering plants

When the pollen grain arrives on the stigma of the correct species of plant, the sugary solution on the stigma forms a medium in which the pollen grain will **germinate**.

Germination of the pollen grain involves the growth of a POLLEN TUBE, which releases **enzymes** at its tip in order to **digest** the cells of the style beneath. In this way, the cells of the style are removed to allow the pollen tube to **grow** down the **style** towards the **ovary**.

On arrival at the ovary, the end of the pollen tube enters an **ovule** through a small hole called the **micropyle**. Inside the ovule is the **embryo sac** which contains the female **gamete**, within which is the female **nucleus**.

The end of the pollen tube then bursts to release the **male** gamete, which has travelled down the pollen tube from the pollen grain. **Fertilisation** occurs as the **nuclei of the male and female gametes fuse**.

The development of the fruit

Once fertilisation has occurred, the ovule is then called a **seed**. The ovary wall then becomes the PERICARP, and the (**protective**) pericarp with the seed(s) inside is called the **fruit**.

Seed structure

Sugars and amino acids travel through the phloem of the parent plant, and enter the seed. Sugars are converted to starch and, in some cases, fat (e.g. the sunflower). Amino acids are converted to protein. **Starch** and **protein** are then **stored** in the seeds of dicotyledonous plants in two large storage organs called COTYLEDONS. Between the two cotyledons lies the **plumule** (or young shoot) and the **radicle** (young root) of the embryo plant.

The **embryo** within the seed of a dicotyledonous plant is made up of **cotyledons**, **plumule** and **radicle**. The embryo is protected within a seed coat or **testa**.

Fig. 68 A broad bean seed cut in half (with one cotyledon removed)

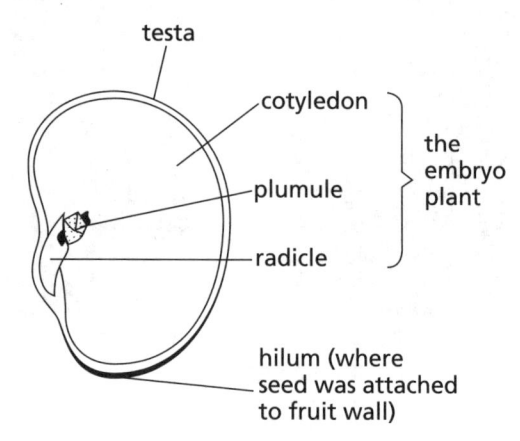

Seed dispersal

Once it has developed within the fruit, the seed containing the embryo plant must break free from the parent and be **dispersed**. In this way, the plant species is able to **colonise new areas**. It also **prevents overcrowding** and **avoids competition** with its fellow offspring for light and for nutrients.

It may be some time before the embryo is in a suitable environment for growth. The food stored in the cotyledons will keep it alive. However, many seeds never find a suitable environment and there is great wastage. There are **two** main agents of dispersal responsible for carrying away the seed (often still part of a fruit and still inside its pericarp): **wind** and **animals**.

Wind-dispersed seeds (or fruits) are usually:

(i) light in weight, and

(ii) have their testa (if it is a seed) or pericarp (if it is a fruit) extended to provide a **large surface area**. This allows the seed or fruit to catch in the wind and be pulled clear of the parent. It also slows the seed's fall to the ground, allowing the wind to carry it some considerable distance away.

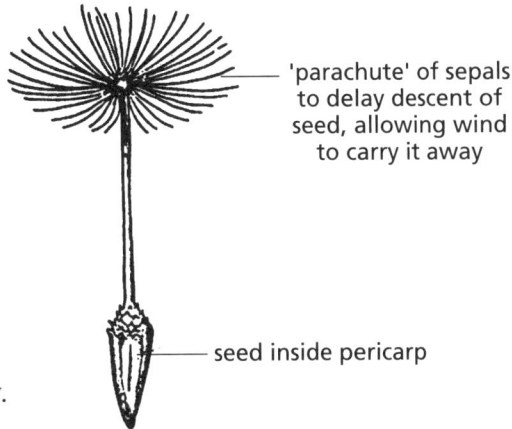

- 'parachute' of sepals to delay descent of seed, allowing wind to carry it away
- seed inside pericarp

Fig. 69 Wind-dispersed fruit
(Reproduced by permission of the University of Cambridge Local Examinations Syndicate)

Animal-dispersed seeds may rely on coloured, sweet and juicy pericarps around them to entice an animal (often a bird) to eat them. In this case, the seeds will also have enzyme-resistant testas, so that they can pass through the animal's intestines intact. They will then be dropped in the animal's faeces at a distance from the parent plant.

Sometimes animal-dispersed seeds or fruits are dry, with hooks on their testas or on the surrounding pericarps. The hooks catch on a small mammal's fur and the seeds or fruits are carried some distance before being removed.

Cross-section through tomato fruit

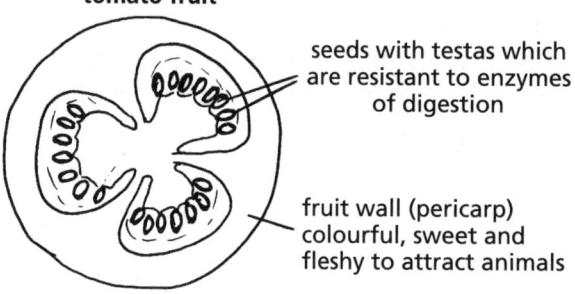

- seeds with testas which are resistant to enzymes of digestion
- fruit wall (pericarp) colourful, sweet and fleshy to attract animals

Fig. 70   Animal-dispersed fruit

Germination of seeds

When suitable environmental conditions are available, the seed will **germinate**. The conditions necessary for seed germination are:

(i) **Water** (to activate the enzymes).

(ii) **Oxygen** (to allow for the release of a great deal of energy from respiration to fuel the greatly increased growth rate).

(iii) A **suitable temperature** (enzymes operate efficiently only if the temperature is suitable for them).

Note: Light is not necessary for seed germination, except in a very few cases.

If conditions are suitable, the enzymes work to digest the food stored in the cotyledons (see the section on enzymes in germination, p. 124). The food is then carried to the **growing regions** of the embryo.

Demonstration 20.2

The need for the conditions described on p. 122 can be demonstrated experimentally, as follows:

Apparatus
- four test-tubes
- cotton wool
- rubber bung
- ignition tube
- alkaline pyrogallol
- cotton
- dry seeds (e.g. green beans)

Method
Set up the experiment as shown in the diagram below, and leave the test-tubes for two to four days.

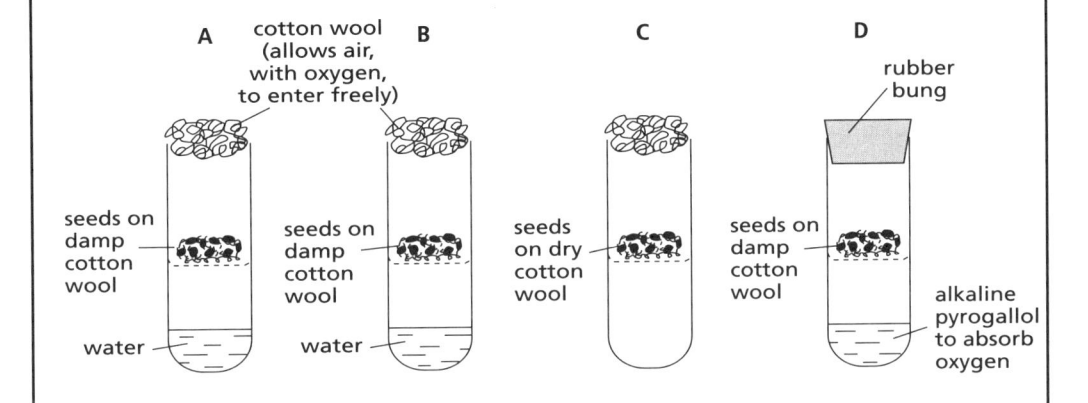

Fig. 71   To demonstrate the conditions necessary for seed germination

A The Control. Seeds left in air at room temperature (a suitable temperature for germination).
B Seeds left in refrigerator (4°C) – not a suitable temperature for germination.
C Seeds left in air at room temperature.
D Seeds left at room temperature.

Results
Only the seeds in tube A, which has access to all the three conditions (room temperature, water and oxygen), will germinate.

Conclusion
A **suitable temperature**, **water** and **oxygen** are all necessary for seed germination.

The use of enzymes in the germination of seeds

Food is stored in seeds in the form of **large, insoluble, organic** molecules, either in **cotyledons**, or (in monocotyledonous seeds) in a special storage tissue called **endosperm**. These large molecules are usually:

(i)   **carbohydrate** (usually in the form of starch)

(ii) **protein**, and sometimes

(iii) **fat**.

When a seed germinates, these food stores must be changed into smaller molecules. These molecules must be able to dissolve in the water which has been absorbed by the seed. They are then transported, **in solution**, to the **growing regions** of the seedling to make new cells.

Enzymes, present in the seeds and activated by the absorbed water, bring about these chemical conversions.

Substrate	Enzyme	Product
Starch	Amylase	Glucose
Protein	Protease	Amino acids
Fats	Lipase	Fatty acids and glycerol

The **glucose** is used in **respiration** to provide the **energy** for the process of growth.

The **amino acids** are used to build up **proteins** in the **cytoplasm of the new cells**.

The **fatty acids and glycerol** recombine to form fats which are used to make important components of cell membranes. Fats also provide a considerable amount of **energy**.

The enzymes shown in the table above, like many other enzymes, work by digesting larger molecules. In this process, molecules of water are used to split (or **hydrolyse**) large **substrate** molecules into smaller **product** molecules. The enzymes are said to bring about **hydrolysis** of the larger molecules.

TOPIC 21: Sexual Reproduction in Human Beings

Although a baby is born with a full set of reproductive organs, these organs are not functional during the first 12 (or so) years of life. Under the influence of **hormones** from the **pituitary** gland, the organs become active at the time known as PUBERTY.

The male reproductive system

The male nuclei involved in the process of human sexual reproduction are located within male GAMETES (sex cells) called SPERMS (an abbreviation for 'spermatozoa'). The male reproductive system is designed to manufacture sperms and to deliver them to the place where one of them will be able to fuse with a female nucleus.

Testes (singular: 'testis')

The testes are the GONADS of the male. Gonads are the organs which produce the gametes, in this case the sperms. The testes are made of millions of tiny coiled tubes. The cells forming the walls of these tubes are constantly dividing to produce up to 100,000,000 sperms per day. The testes work more efficiently at just below body temperature, so they are held outside the body in the **scrotum** (or scrotal sac).

Sperm ducts

Sperm ducts are tubes which carry the sperms away from the testes. They join with one another and with the tube bringing urine, at a position just under the bladder. Each sperm duct bears a SEMINAL VESICLE for sperm storage.

Prostate gland

The prostate gland is about the size of a golf ball. It surrounds the junction between the sperm ducts and the tube from the bladder. It manufactures, and adds to the sperms, a nutrient fluid (SEMINAL FLUID) in which the sperms are able to swim (sperms + seminal fluid = SEMEN).

Urethra

The urethra is a tube that carries both urine and semen along the **penis** to be released from the body.

Penis

The penis is the organ for introducing sperms into the female. It contains spongy tissue which fills with blood to make the penis firm (an 'erection') so that it can more easily be guided into the female.

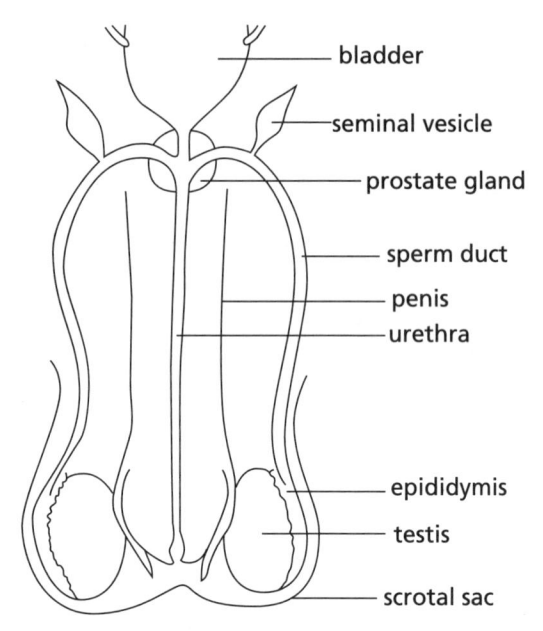

Fig. 72 The human male reproductive organs

The female reproductive system

The female nuclei which are involved in the process of sexual reproduction are located in the female **gametes** called OVA (singular: 'ovum'). The functions of the female reproductive system are:

(i) to produce ova and ensure that they are fertilised by the male gametes
(ii) to protect and nourish the embryo until it is born.

Ovaries

The ovaries are the female **gonads**, making and releasing the female gametes (ova). There are two ovaries, each a little smaller than a ping-pong ball, lying in the lower abdomen. The female releases one ovum every four weeks from alternate ovaries, that is, each ovary releases one ovum every eight weeks.

Oviducts

The oviducts are the tubes which carry the ova away from the ovaries. They are lined with cilia (see trachea, p. 70 and section (iii) p. 94) which, together with a little muscular assistance, help to move the ova gently along. If fertilisation occurs, it usually does so about **one-third** of the way along the oviduct.

Uterus

The uterus is a pear-shaped organ lying behind and slightly above the bladder. Its walls contain **involuntary muscle** (i.e. muscle that cannot be consciously controlled). The embryo develops in the uterus during **pregnancy**.

Cervix

The cervix is the 'neck' of the uterus, where the uterus joins the vagina. It supplies mucus to the vagina.

Vagina

The vagina is the part of the female system which receives the penis during **copulation**. It is muscular and stretchable (it forms part of the birth canal) and it connects the cervix with the slit-like **vulva** opening to the outside.

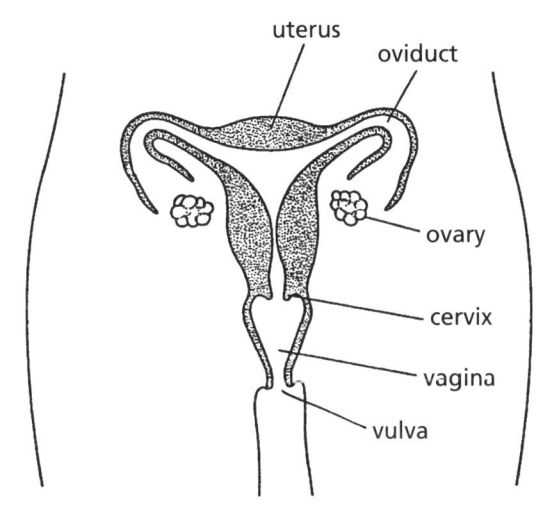

Fig. 73 The human female reproductive organs
(Reproduced by permission of the University of Cambridge Local Examinations Syndicate)

A comparison of male and female gametes

Male gametes	Female gametes
Released in millions	Released one at a time
Able to move	Unable to move on their own
Very small (0.05 mm – of which around 80% is tail)	Comparatively large (0.1 mm in diameter)
Very little cytoplasm	A lot of cytoplasm which contains nourishment for the **zygote** if the ovum is fertilised
Nucleus contains either an X or a Y chromosome (see p. 146)	Nucleus always contains an X chromosome

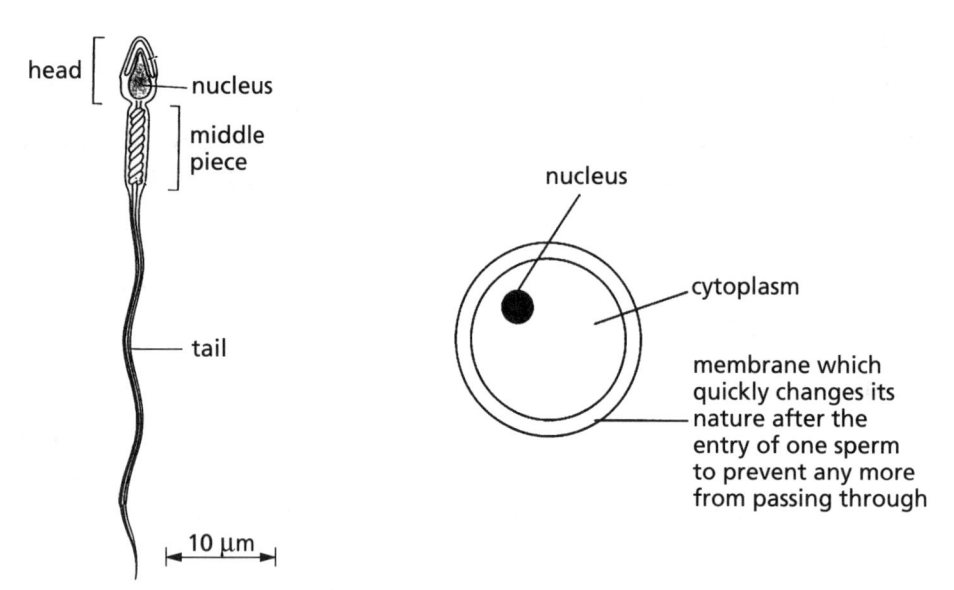

Fig. 74a A human sperm
(Reproduced by permission of the University
of Cambridge Local Examinations Syndicate)

Fig. 74b A human ovum

The menstrual cycle

Once a female reaches puberty, she will start to release ova from her ovaries (i.e. she will start to **ovulate**). Ovulation is one stage in her **menstrual** or monthly cycle, described below:

1. Over a period of about 14 days, the walls of the female's uterus develop a **spongy lining**, containing many blood capillaries.

2. When the spongy lining is ready, ovulation occurs. The ovum passes down the oviduct. If the ovum is not fertilised by a sperm, it passes through the uterus and vagina and out of the vulva.

3. The spongy lining then peels away from the uterus wall, damaging the blood capillaries. The lining is passed out of the vagina and vulva, together with blood. This is MENSTRUATION or the monthly period. Menstruation lasts for about four days, and occurs about two weeks after ovulation.

4. Once the uterus wall has recovered, it begins to rebuild its spongy lining, under the influence of a hormone from the ovary. Meanwhile, a new ovum is maturing in the ovary, under the influence of a hormone from the pituitary gland. When mature, the ovum is released (ovulation), at around two weeks after menstruation. The cycle continues in this way as long as the female remains healthy.

If an ovum is fertilised, and the woman becomes pregnant, her menstrual cycle stops until after the baby is born. When a female reaches the MENOPAUSE, usually at around 50 years of age, she stops ovulating and can no longer become pregnant.

Factors affecting the menstrual cycle

- **Stress** – At times of emotional stress the menstrual cycle may become irregular.

- **Diet** – An inadequate diet can lead to an irregular cycle, and starvation can suppress the cycle completely.

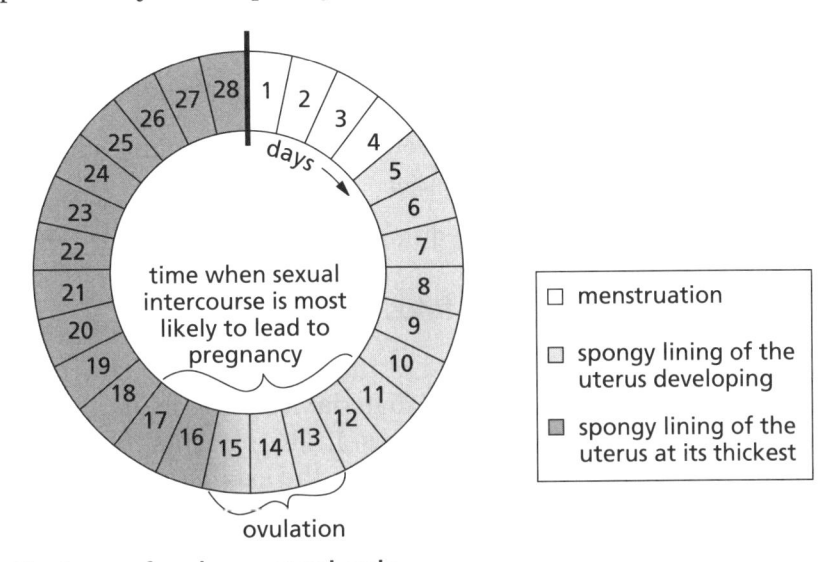

Fig. 75 The human female menstrual cycle
(Reproduced by permission of the University of Cambridge Local Examinations Syndicate)

Fertile and infertile phases of the menstrual cycle

When there is no ovum in the oviducts, fertilisation cannot occur. It is unlikely to occur if the ovum is not in the correct position in the oviduct, however, sperms can live in the oviduct for a few days, allowing the ovum a chance to arrive. A woman's **most fertile** period is therefore **from a few days before ovulation** (allowing for the possible survival of sperms in the oviduct) **to a few days after ovulation**. Outside this time, she is less likely to become pregnant.

Human fertilisation

During copulation, sensitive cells near the end (glans) of the penis are the receptors for a **reflex** action leading to the release (**ejaculation**) of semen. The sperms are deposited near the cervix of the female, then swim through the uterus and up the oviducts. If they meet an ovum, around one-third of its way from the ovary, **one** of the sperms may fuse with the ovum to form a **zygote**. This is the moment of **fertilisation**.

Development of the embryo

The zygote, a single cell formed from equal nuclear contributions from both parents, now begins to divide, eventually to form a **hollow ball of cells**. This stage in embryonic development is called the BLASTOCYST.

The embryo initially absorbs nourishment secreted by the cells of the uterus, but it soon embeds itself (**implantation**) in the spongy lining of the uterus. Further division of the cells turns the blastocyst into a FETUS. The fetus is surrounded by a membrane (the AMNION) which forms the **amniotic sac** enclosing the fetus in a water bath (the AMNIOTIC FLUID).

Functions of the amniotic fluid

(i) To protect the embryo from physical damage, e.g. if mother falls over.

(ii) To support the embryo, keeping even pressure all round it, allowing organs to develop without restriction.

(iii) To allow the fetus some restricted movement.

The nutrition and excretion of the fetus

Both nutrition and excretion are carried out through a special structure called the PLACENTA. This is made up partly of material from the fetus, and partly of material from the spongy lining of the uterus. In the placenta, **blood** in the mother's capillaries runs **very close** to blood in the capillaries of the fetus. However, their blood **does not mix** – mother and child may be different blood groups.

Diffusion of substances takes place between the two blood systems.

Diffusing from mother to fetus	Diffusing from fetus to mother

Dissolved nutrients:
  Glucose
  Amino acids
  Ions
  Vitamins
  Water
	Nitrogenous waste:
	  Urea

Dissolved gas:
  Oxygen
	Dissolved gas:
	  Carbon dioxide

The placenta is connected to the fetus by the UMBILICAL CORD, inside which run **fetal** blood vessels. The umbilical **vein** brings substances *to* the fetus; the umbilical **artery** carries substances **from** the fetus.

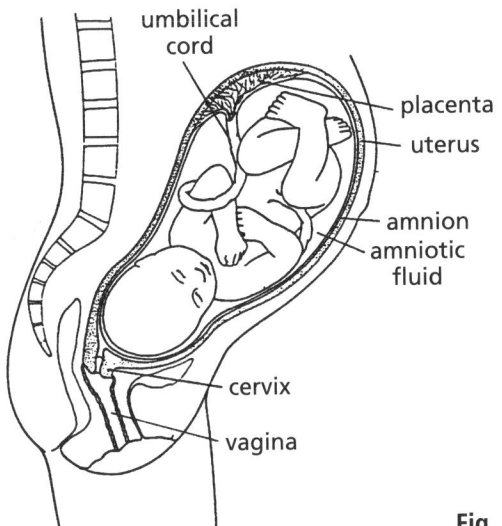

Fig. 76 A fetus inside a pregnant woman
(Reproduced by permission of the University of Cambridge Local Examinations Syndicate)

The dietary needs of a pregnant woman

An embryo's development depends on the food eaten by its mother, so a pregnant woman must adjust her diet accordingly. She should ensure that the levels of the following constituents are higher than in her normal intake:

(i)   **Protein*** for the manufacture of embryonic tissues.

(ii) **Carbohydrate*** for additional respiration in embryonic tissues.

(iii) Vitamin C for making proteins in the embryo.

(iv) Vitamin D and **calcium** for making bones and teeth of embryo.

(v)   Iron for making embryo's blood.

*These should be raised to the approximate levels required by a very active woman who is not pregnant.

The value of breast feeding

After the birth of the baby, **milk** from the mother's **mammary glands** supplies the ideal food for the first months of development. The milk:

(i)   is **cheap**
(ii) **readily available**
(iii) contains *all* the necessary **constituents**, in the **correct proportions**
(iv) is at the **correct temperature**
(v)   contains some **antibodies** which protect the baby against disease.

Breast feeding also helps to develop the bond between mother and baby.

Some babies may suffer harmful reactions to the substitute formula milk powders which are used in bottle feeding.

Birth control

The world population has risen alarmingly over the last few decades. It is already difficult to supply enough food to all areas of the world. A solution lies in BIRTH CONTROL. The main methods are:

A 'Natural' method (or rhythm method)

Sexual intercourse (copulation) is limited only to those times in the menstrual cycle when fertilisation is less likely.

However, a woman's menstrual pattern may not be a reliable indicator of her fertility. Severe **anxiety** and **malnutrition** can **suppress** the menstrual cycle **completely**. Varying degrees of anxiety and dietary deficiency can lead to an erratic menstrual pattern.

Not all healthy and perfectly happy women have predictable and regular periods – particularly when **teenagers** or when approaching the **menopause**. Often the most accurate prediction can only be that ovulation usually occurs somewhere between 12 and 16 days before the start of menstruation.

The 'natural' method of birth control is therefore not a reliable method of avoiding pregnancy.

B Chemical method

Chemicals which kill sperms ('**spermicides**') are put into the vagina of the female before intercourse. This is not a very effective method of birth control when used on its own.

C Mechanical methods

(i) Where some form of **barrier** is put between the sperms and the ova. The barrier may take the form of:
-   (a) a **condom**, a sheath placed over the penis before intercourse to catch the sperms when ejaculated
-   (b) a **femidom** which lines the vagina of the female with the same result
-   (c) a **diaphragm** which fits over the cervix of the uterus, preventing the entry of sperms. A diaphragm is usually used with a spermicide.

Barrier methods are popular and quite effective.

(ii) Where there is **no** barrier between the sperms and the ovum:
   (a) an **intra-uterine device** (IUD) which is fitted inside the uterus. It does not stop fertilisation, but it prevents implantation of the blastocyst. This is an effective method of birth control.

D Hormonal method

This method is otherwise known as **the pill**. The **woman** takes a tablet which contains a hormone. When taken **regularly**, the pill prevents ovulation, so that no ova are present to be fertilised. This is an effective method of birth control if the routine is followed carefully.

E Surgical methods

(i) In the **male**: cutting the sperm ducts (the operation is called **vasectomy**) – an effective method but rarely reversible.

(ii) In the **female**: tying the oviducts to prevent the passage of ova – an effective method and usually reversible.

Sexually transmitted diseases

During the act of sexual intercourse, the bodies of the partners are brought into close contact. PATHOGENS can easily pass from one infected person to another. Diseases spread through sexual contact are called sexually transmitted diseases (STDs). Three examples are **syphilis**, **AIDS** and **gonorrhoea**.

Syphilis

Syphilis is caused by a **bacterium**. Symptoms of the disease include: sores on the penis, or around the vulva, a slightly raised temperature, rash and headache. This disease can eventually destroy the tissues of the brain, skeleton and other major organs. However, it may be treated with antibiotics.

Syphilis can be controlled by limiting sexual contact to one partner, and using a condom during intercourse.

Gonorrhoea

Gonorrhoea is caused by a bacterium. Symptoms include severe pain on urination (particularly in the male) since the bacterium invades the tissues of the urethra. There is a discharge of pus from the urethra (from the end of the penis in the male). The infection may spread to produce inflammation of the uterus in the female and of the epididymis in the male. The disease is not life-threatening, but it may lead to sterility. Methods of treatment, prevention and control are similar to those described for syphilis.

AIDS

Acquired immune deficiency syndrome (AIDS) is caused by the human immuno-deficiency virus (HIV). The virus affects the body's ability to fight infection. It lives in **body fluids** such as **blood** and **semen**.

Transmission

HIV may be transmitted in the following ways:

(i) From host to host when intravenous drug users **share unsterilised needles**. A small amount of blood may enter the needle and syringe when a person injects a drug. If another person uses the same, unsterilised needle, they will receive the blood of the first user, who may be infected.

(ii) In **semen**, from one partner to the blood of another, if there is any tearing of tissues during intercourse.

(iii) From an infected mother's blood to her baby's blood during the **birth** process.

(iv) In untreated blood during **blood transfusion**.

Disease control

Although the drug AZT can slow the progress of the disease, there is, as yet, no cure for AIDS. It can, however, be controlled by:

(i) **Educating** the public about how it is spread, and what precautions can be taken.

(ii) **Never** sharing needles.

(iii) **Avoiding sex with prostitutes** because they are often carriers of the disease. Staying with **one** STD-free partner.

(iv) **Always using a condom** or other barrier method of contraception which prevents direct contact between the body fluids of the two partners.

(v) **Treating** all blood and blood products used in transfusions to destroy the AIDS virus.

TOPIC 22: Inheritance

Variation

Sexual reproduction leads to **variation** in the offspring, that is, each individual has different characteristics. No two offspring from the same parents, produced by sexual reproduction, are genetically identical. An exception occurs when the offspring develop from the **same ovum and sperm**, in which case they are 'identical twins'.

Two types of variation are seen:

A   CONTINUOUS, and
B   DISCONTINUOUS.

A   Continuous variation

Continuous variation is the result of the interaction of **two** factors:

(i)   the genes that are inherited by an individual
(ii) the effect of the environment on the individual.

The **environmental** factors involved might include:

(i)   the availability and type of food (in animals)
(ii)   disease
(iii) the climate – amount of sunlight
                   – temperature
                   – amount of available water
(iv)   the ions present in the soil (in plants)
(v)   competition from other organisms in the environment.

In continuous variation, individuals show a **range** between the two extremes. Every possible form between the two extremes will exist.

Examples of continuous variation are:

(i)   body mass
(ii)   height
(iii) foot size.

B   Discontinuous variation

This is the result of **inheritance only**. There are *few* types, with *no* intermediates.

Examples of discontinuous variation are:
(i) blood groups
(ii) the ability to roll the tongue into a 'U' shape (either you can or you cannot!).

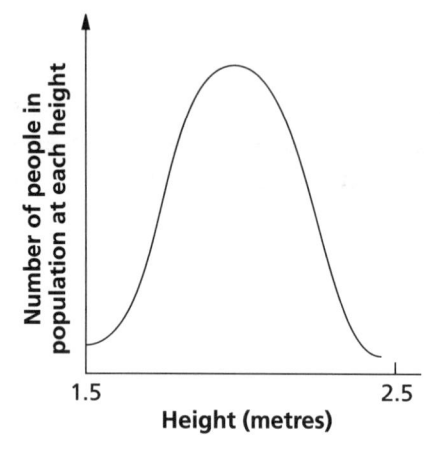

Fig. 77a Continuous variation (with every possible intermediate between two extremes)

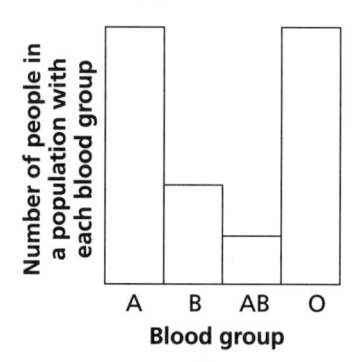

Fig. 77b Discontinuous variation (no intermediates)

The chemical structure of chromosomes

Chromosomes, situated in the **nuclei** of all living cells (except bacteria, which have no true nucleus) are made of the chemical substance **DNA**. The DNA molecule, looking rather like a very long, twisted rope ladder, is made up of two strands (of alternating sugar and phosphate units) held together by pairs of chemical units called **bases** (the rungs of the ladder – see the upper section of the diagram below). The molecule is described as *a double helix* (Greek 'helix' = a spiral).

There are *four bases* only:

A   (Adenine)

C   (Cytosine)

G   (Guanine)

T   (Thymine)

These bases link with one another in the following ways ('The Rule Of Base Pairing')

A always with T

C always with G

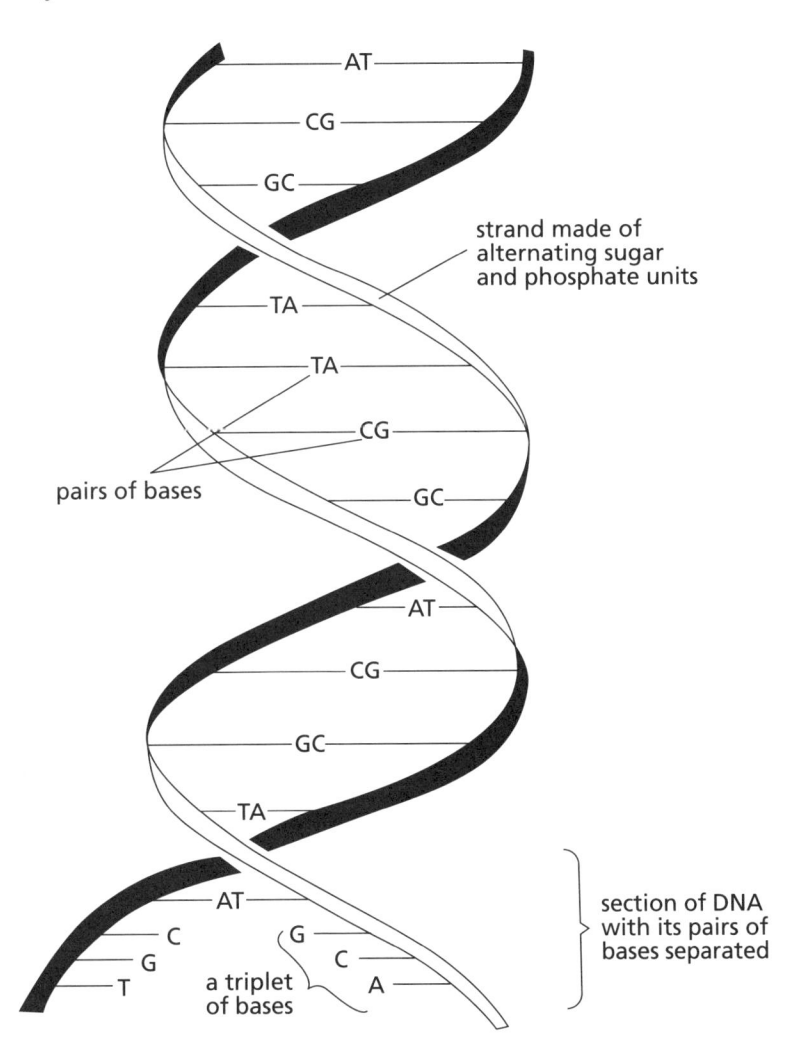

Fig. 78a Part of a molecule of DNA

The unit of inheritance

All living organisms manufacture proteins in their cells. These are used either for structural purposes within the cell or as **enzymes** to control chemical processes in the cell. All proteins are made up of linked **amino acids**.

The sequence of bases (e.g. CATGCTAGCCTA) on *one* of the two strands is a **code**. When protein molecules are made in the cytoplasm of a cell, a copy of the bases on a section of a DNA strand is made and passed out into the cytoplasm of the cell. The sequence of bases is first split into **triplets** (CAT, GCT, AGC, CTA). Each triplet is then responsible for lining up one particular amino acid in the sequence of amino acids that will link to form a protein. Each of the 22 amino acids has its own triplet.

Since the sequence of bases on DNA molecules is different for each (sexually produced) individual, it follows that no two individuals will make protein molecules with exactly the same sequence of amino acids.

The length of chromosome which contains the bases necessary to make **one** protein molecule is otherwise known as a **gene**.

Definition

A GENE is defined as a unit of inheritance.

For the purpose of understanding the mechanism of simple inheritance, it is convenient to imagine a chromosome as a string of beads, like that shown below, each bead represents one gene.

Fig. 78b   Representation of a chromosome

Genes are passed on from parent to offspring via chromosomes in the nuclei of the parents' **gametes**.

Genetic inheritance

Every member of the same species has the same number of chromosomes in each (healthy) cell of their body. These chromosomes exist in matching pairs. For example, human beings have 23 matching or **homologous** pairs of chromosomes, a total number of 46. Of each pair of matching chromosomes, one is inherited from a person's mother and one is inherited from their father.

The genes of homologous chromosomes *also* match. In other words, if we look at two strings of beads, like those shown in Fig. 79, the order of the different shapes of beads is the same on both strings.

Matching genes on homologous chromosomes are called ALLELES.

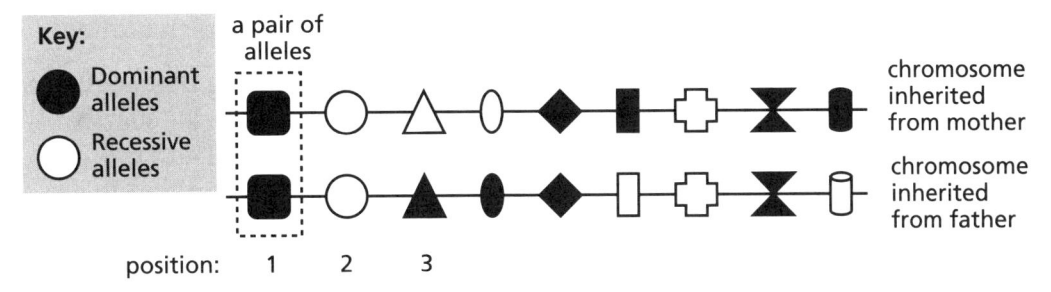

Fig. 79 Representation of alleles on homologous chromosomes

You can see in Fig. 79 that a pair of beads (like the two ■ shown at position 1) always match in shape, but do not always match in colour. This is a way of showing that one pair of alleles controls one character, but each allele may exist in two forms: they may be dominant or recessive.

In Fig. 79, the alleles in position 1 are both dominant, in position 2 they are both recessive and in position 3, there is one of each.

For a particular character, an offspring may therefore inherit either:

- **Two dominant** alleles, one from each parent. The offspring is described as HOMOZYGOUS **dominant**.

- **Two recessive** alleles, one from each parent. The offspring is described as HOMOZYGOUS **recessive**.

- **One dominant** and **one recessive** allele. The offspring is described as HETEROZYGOUS.

These are the three possible GENOTYPES of the individual.

If at least **one** dominant allele is present in the genotype, the individual will show the dominant feature in their appearance (or PHENOTYPE). Thus the homozygous dominant and heterozygous genotypes will give the same phenotype. The homozygous recessive individual will have the alternative (or '**contrasting**') phenotype.

Variation as a result of mutation

Genes and chromosomes are always subject to change (or MUTATION) as a result of environmental forces acting upon them. These forces are known as **mutagens**, and include **X-rays**, **atomic radiation**, **ultraviolet light** and some **chemicals**. Exposure to higher doses of any of these mutagens will lead to a greater rate of mutation.

> **Definition**
>
> A mutation is a spontaneous change in the structure of a gene or chromosome.

Gene mutation

Sickle-cell anaemia is an example of a condition caused by a gene mutation.

Both parents pass on a **mutated** (and recessive) allele for making **haemoglobin** in red blood cells. The homozygous recessive offspring cannot make effective haemoglobin, and cannot carry sufficient oxygen in their blood. Their red blood cells also take on a distorted shape. A person with this condition is likely to die at an early age.

Chromosome mutation

Down's syndrome is an example of a condition caused by a chromosome mutation.

As described on p. 138, there are 46 (23 pairs of) chromosomes in every normal cell of the human body; there are 23 **unpaired** chromosomes in each gamete. Forty-six is known as the **diploid** number, and 23 as the **haploid** number.

If, in the production of gametes by one of the parents, one **extra** chromosome enters one of the gametes, then there will be 24 (instead of 23) chromosomes in that gamete. If this gamete is involved in the process of fertilisation, there will be 47 (instead of 46) chromosomes in the zygote. In older parents, there is a greater tendency for chromosome number 21 not to separate properly as gametes are being made.

A child who inherits the extra chromosome will suffer from Down's syndrome. Their physical and mental development will be slow, and they will have a distinctive facial appearance.

Monohybrid inheritance

Organisms inherit alleles for thousands of different contrasting characters, for example, human hair is either curly or straight, and we either can or cannot smell the scent of certain flowers. MONOHYBRID INHERITANCE refers to only **one pair** of contrasting characters, such as curly or straight hair, controlled in the individual by **one pair** of alleles.

There are **two types** of monohybrid inheritance:

A   with COMPLETE DOMINANCE, and
B   with CODOMINANCE.

A With complete dominance

This is where the presence of only **one** dominant allele will decide the appearance (or **phenotype**) of the individual.

Example: coat colour in mice

In mice, brown coat colour is dominant over grey coat colour. In an experiment, a **homozygous dominant** (or 'pure-breeding') **brown** male mouse mated with a **homozygous recessive** (also pure-breeding) **grey** female mouse. All their offspring (that is, the F_1 or **first filial generation**) were found to be **brown**.

The offspring of the F_1 generation were then allowed to freely interbreed. It was found that their offspring (the F_2 generation) were **brown** to **grey** in a 3 : 1 ratio. This can be explained in a **genetic diagram**, set out below.

Genetic diagrams

Genetic diagrams are a way of looking at the combinations of alleles produced by two parents. In constructing genetic diagrams, the letters of the alphabet (rather than beads) are used to represent alleles. A dominant allele is represented by a **capital** letter (like A, B, C) and its recessive allele is represented by a small (or **lower case**) version of the same letter (like a, b, c).

For example:

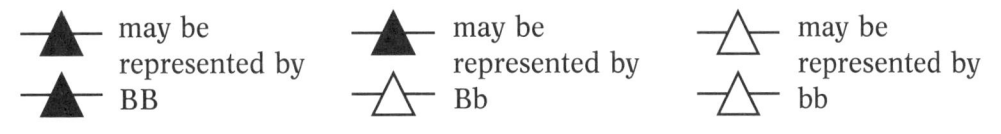

▲▬ may be represented by ▲▬ BB

▲▬ may be represented by △▬ Bb

△▬ may be represented by △▬ bb

Genetic diagram: cross between homozygous brown-coated mouse and homozygous grey-coated mouse

Key to alleles

- 'B' represents the dominant allele for **brown** coat colour in mice.
- 'b' represents the recessive allele for **grey** coat colour in mice.

■ **Parents**   male   x   female

       genotype: BB   bb
       phenotype: brown   grey

Alleles found
in gametes: B   B   b   b

(*Note:* Statistically, there is an exactly equal chance of either of the alleles from the male combining with either of the alleles from female at the time of fertilisation.)

■ F_1 **generation**

Gametes		of the male	
		B	B
of the female	b	Bb	Bb
	b	Bb	Bb

       genotype: all Bb
       phenotype: brown

F_1 'selfed'   Bb   x   Bb
(allowed to interbreed)

Gametes: B   b   B   b

■ F_2 **generation**

Gametes		of the male	
		B	b
of the female	B	BB	Bb
	b	Bb	bb

       possible genotypes: BB   Bb   Bb   bb
       phenotypes: brown   brown   brown   grey

Ratio in a **large** sample: 3 brown   :   1 grey

Note: The results are given as a statistical ratio in a **large** sample. The **smaller the sample**, the **less likely** that the ratios will be the same as shown.

In humans, where only **one** offspring is likely to be produced at a time, the **probability** of that offspring inheriting a particular feature is often given. Probability is usually expressed as a **percentage**.

Example: cystic fibrosis in humans

Cystic fibrosis is an inherited condition that affects the type of mucus found in people's lungs. Most people produce normal protein in the mucus of their lungs. They possess at least one dominant allele, which may be called 'F'. The homozygous recessive person, suffering from cystic fibrosis, has the genotype 'ff'. Their lungs contain a particularly thick and sticky mucus, which makes gaseous exchange difficult.

Genetic diagram: both parents heterozygous for cystic fibrosis

In the diagram below, there are two parents who are both **heterozygous** for cystic fibrosis (their genotype is 'Ff'). If they have a child, the probability of this child having the genotype ff, and therefore suffering from cystic fibrosis, is 25%.

Gametes	F	f
F	FF	Ff
f	Ff	**ff**

The test (or back) cross

Of the brown mice in the F_2 generation in the example given on p. 142, approximately one-third of them will be homozygous dominant (BB), and two-thirds will be heterozygous (Bb). There is no way of telling from their phenotype which type they are. Therefore, a TEST (or 'back') CROSS is performed.

In a test cross, the individual is mated with a homozygous recessive (bb) partner.

If the individual is **heterozygous** (Bb):

- *Parents*

	genotypes:	Bb	x	bb
	phenotypes:	brown		grey

Gametes: B   b   b   (b)

	B	b
b	Bb	bb

- *Offspring*

	genotypes:	Bb	bb
	phenotypes:	brown	grey

Ratio in a large sample: 1 brown   :   1 grey

If the individual is **homozygous dominant** (BB):

- *Parents*

	genotypes:	BB	x	bb
	phenotypes:	brown		grey

Gametes: B (only)   b (only)

	B
b	Bb

- *Offspring*

	genotypes:	All Bb
	phenotype:	brown

B   With codominance

Sometimes both alleles have an equal effect on the phenotype of an individual. When this happens, the alleles are said to be **codominant**. The individual which is heterozygous will therefore show a **third** phenotype – different from the two homozygous possibilities.

Example: the inheritance of human blood groups

This is also an example of monohybrid inheritance, but this time, there exist **three** possible alleles, only **two** of which are possessed by any one person.

The alleles are described as: I^A, I^B and I^o.

Both I^A and I^B are **dominant** over I^o, but are **codominant** to one another. The following combinations of alleles are possible, resulting in the blood groups (phenotypes) shown:

Genotype	Phenotype
$I^A I^A$	blood group A
$I^A I^o$	blood group A
$I^B I^B$	blood group B
$I^B I^o$	blood group B
$I^o I^o$	blood group O
$I^A I^B$	blood group AB

An example of the inheritance of blood groups in humans can be shown in the following genetic diagram:

- **Parents**

genotypes:	$I^A I^o$	x	$I^B I^o$
phenotypes:	group A		group B

Gametes: I^A I^o I^B I^o

	I^A	I^o
I^B	$I^A I^B$	$I^B I^o$
I^o	$I^A I^o$	$I^o I^o$

- **Offspring**

possible genotypes:	$I^A I^B$	$I^A I^o$	$I^B I^o$	$I^o I^o$
phenotypes:				
– blood groups	AB	A	B	O
– probability	25%	25%	25%	25%

Key terms

Variation	The different characteristics produced in an individual by sexual reproduction.
Continuous variation	Where both inherited and environmental factors determine the characteristics of an individual (e.g. body mass, height).
Discontinuous variation	Where inheritance *alone* determines the characteristics of an individual (e.g. blood group).

Gene	A unit of inheritance, forming part of a chromosome. Passed on from parent to offspring via chromosomes in the nuclei of the parents' gametes.
Gametes	Male or female sex cells.
Alleles	A pair of matching genes.
Dominant alleles	The presence of a *single* dominant allele will have the same effect on the phenotype of an individual as the presence of an identical pair of them.
Recessive alleles	Characters determined by these genes will not appear in an individual unless two recessive (no dominant) alleles are present.
Genotype	The genetic combination of an individual.
Homozygous dominant	Offspring with two dominant alleles, one from each parent, for a particular character.
Homozygous recessive	Offspring with two recessive alleles, one from each parent, for a particular character.
Heterozygous	Offspring with one dominant and one recessive allele for a particular character.
Phenotype	An inherited feature in an individual's appearance. The homozygous dominant and heterozygous genotypes give the same phenotype. The homozygous recessive individual will have a contrasting phenotype.
Mutation	Change in genes or chromosomes through environmental forces, or mutagens (e.g. X-rays, atomic radiation).
Monohybrid inheritance	Inheritance involving only one pair of contrasting alleles.
Complete dominance	When the presence of a *single* allele will have the same effect on the phenotype of an individual as the presence of an identical pair of alleles.
Codominance	When both alleles have an equal effect on the phenotype of the offspring.

The inheritance of sex

Whether a child is born male or female is determined at the moment of fertilisation.

Of the 23 pairs of chromosomes in a human nucleus, **one** pair is known as the SEX CHROMOSOMES. In the female, the sex chromosomes are **identical** and are called 'X' chromosomes.

In the male, they are **not identical**. One of them is an 'X' chromosome, exactly like those in the female, but the other is a (shorter) 'Y' chromosome.

The sex chromosomes are:

> XX for a female
>
> XY for a male

The **gametes** contain 23 **single** chromosomes, and therefore only **one** of the two sex chromosomes that exist in normal body cells.

In **females**, **all gametes** contain an 'X' chromosome (she has no other type to give).

In **males**, 50% of the gametes contain an 'X' chromosome and 50% contain a 'Y' chromosome.

There is an exactly equal chance of the 'X' chromosomes in the ovum:

(i) fusing with an 'X'-carrying sperm to produce a daughter, or

(ii) fusing with a 'Y'-carrying sperm to produce a son.

■ *Parents*   father   x   mother

sex chromosomes
   in body cells: XY   XX

   in gametes: X   Y   X (only)

At fertilisation:

	X	Y
X	XX	XY

■ *Offspring*

   chromosomes: XX   XY
                       female   male
   probability: 50%   50%

Selection

Examples of the variation shown by members of a population in a given habitat include:

(i)   the shade of colour of a leaf-eating insect

(ii) the sharpness of vision in a bird of prey

(iii) the speed at which a gazelle can run.

In all of these examples, the variation can have some effect on the success or even on the chances of survival of that organism in its environment:

(i) The leaf insect with better camouflage may escape the notice of a hungry predator.

(ii) The bird of prey with sharper vision is more likely to find a meal – particularly important when food is scarce.

(iii) The faster the gazelle can run, the more chance it has of escaping from a hungry lion.

All organisms are therefore in **competition** with other members of their species in that particular environment. The winners in that competition **survive** to **reproduce**. The losers provide food for predators, or fail to obtain enough food to remain alive.

It is the environment which 'decides' which organisms survive. The process is called NATURAL SELECTION.

Variation is controlled by the genes possessed by the organisms. Surviving individuals are able to hand on their advantages, via their genes, to the next generation.

Evolution

The offspring of the survivors also show variation, so the process is repeated over **many generations**. For example, through natural selection, lions may improve their stealth and camouflage over several generations. As they do so, more species become threatened by the lion. Thus, ecosystems are constantly changing – and organisms may have to adapt to climatic change as well.

This gradual change by natural selection is known as EVOLUTION. During the process, a population of organisms may become separated and form two isolated branches. Each of the populations will adapt to different environmental changes, and **new species** may evolve.

Artificial selection

In the process of ARTIFICIAL SELECTION, humans – not the environment – perform the selecting. That is, people deliberately choose to breed organisms with particular characteristics.

Many crop plants and farm animals are the result of **selective breeding** programmes. Some examples are:
- increased milk production in cows
- increased meat production in farm animals
- increased yield from cereals
- increased disease resistance in many crops.

As a result, greater profits are made from greater quantities of better quality produce.

Selective breeding follows this procedure:

1 The individuals showing the quality required are selected.

2 Those individuals are used as breeding stock.

3 Only those offspring showing the desired quality *to the greatest extent* are selected.

4 These selected individuals are used for breeding.

5 This process is continued over *many* generations.

There is a danger, however, that this form of 'inbreeding' will increase the chances of two recessive alleles coming together. This may give rise to a genetically-controlled deformity (e.g. a heart defect).

Genetic engineering

Since we are now able to identify specific genes (i.e. lengths of DNA which encode for the production of a particular protein), that gene can then be isolated and inserted into another organism.

In this way, genes for disease resistance existing in a crop plant with low yield can be introduced into a crop plant with a high yield but low disease resistance. Where a person inherits a genetically-controlled condition (e.g. cystic fibrosis), it may be possible to improve their condition by the introduction of genes from a healthy person. In both these examples, gene transfer is between organisms of the *same* species.

Gene transfer between organisms of **different** species is commonly used in the production of the hormone **insulin**. In this example, a bacterium is used as the 'host' organism. The gene for insulin production is taken from a healthy person and (using enzymes) attached to the bacterium's chromosome. Every time the bacterium divides, it makes a further copy of the inserted gene. A culture of the bacteria will then not only be manufacturing all the proteins it needs for its own survival, it will also produce an ample supply of insulin molecules. Insulin is now commercially produced using such a process.

Public concern over genetic engineering

Genetic engineering can increase food production and help to control disease, but there is much concern over the possibility that bacteria with 'introduced' genes may be accidentally released. Those which make a plant resistant to disease or to pesticides may find their way into pests. There is worry over the safety of foods which have been genetically engineered to improve their flavour and texture. 'Watchdog' committees have been set up to monitor gene transfer experiments.

Review Questions

Multiple choice

1. Which of the following graphs shows how temperature change affects enzyme activity?

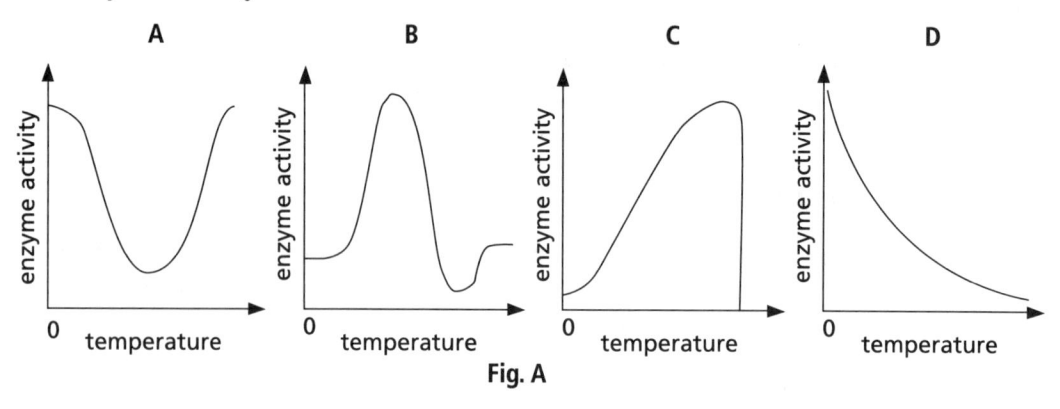

Fig. A

2. Figure **B** shows a plant cell. Which part controls the movement of chemicals into and out of the cell?

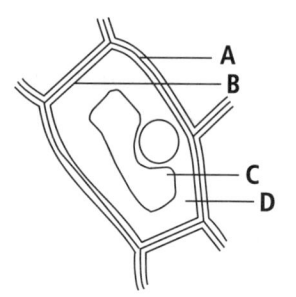

Fig. B

3. Which structures in a plant cell contain DNA and cellulose?

	DNA	cellulose
A	cell wall	cytoplasm
B	chloroplast	nucleus
C	cytoplasm	chloroplast
D	nucleus	cell wall

4. Figure **C** shows a bag made of a partially permeable material and filled with concentrated sugar solution. The solution has been coloured with a dye and the bag has been submerged in a beaker of water. The same experiment is then shown six hours later.

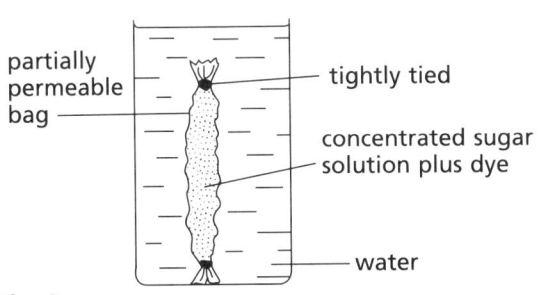

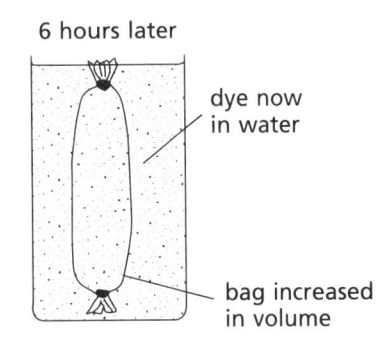

Fig. C

Which explains how the molecules of water and dye have moved during the six-hour period?

	water	dye
A	active transport	diffusion
B	diffusion	active transport
C	osmosis	diffusion
D	osmosis	osmosis

5. A flexible cell membrane is necessary for which one of the following to carry out its function?

   A   palisade cell
   B   red blood cell
   C   root hair cell
   D   xylem vessel

6. Circular muscle in the walls of the intestine is an example of which of the following?

   A   an organ in an organ system
   B   an organ system in an organism
   C   cells in a tissue
   D   tissues in an organ

7. A student carries out tests on a food substance using biuret solution and iodine solution. If the food contains protein only, what colours will be seen in the test-tubes at the end of each test?

	biuret solution	iodine solution
A	blue	blue/black
B	blue/black	milky white
C	purple	yellow
D	red	blue

8. When carrying out the starch test on a leaf, why is it important to boil the leaf in alcohol?

   A to dissolve the waxy cuticle
   B to make the cells more permeable to iodine solution
   C to remove the chlorophyll
   D to stop chemical reactions in the cells

9. Which food contains the highest amounts of fat and fibre?

   A bread
   B groundnuts
   C meat
   D potatoes

10. A chemical molecule contains sulphur and phosphorus. Which of the following could it be?

    A a carbohydrate
    B a fatty acid
    C a protein
    D glycerol

11. Figure **D** shows bubbles being released by a water plant exposed to light.

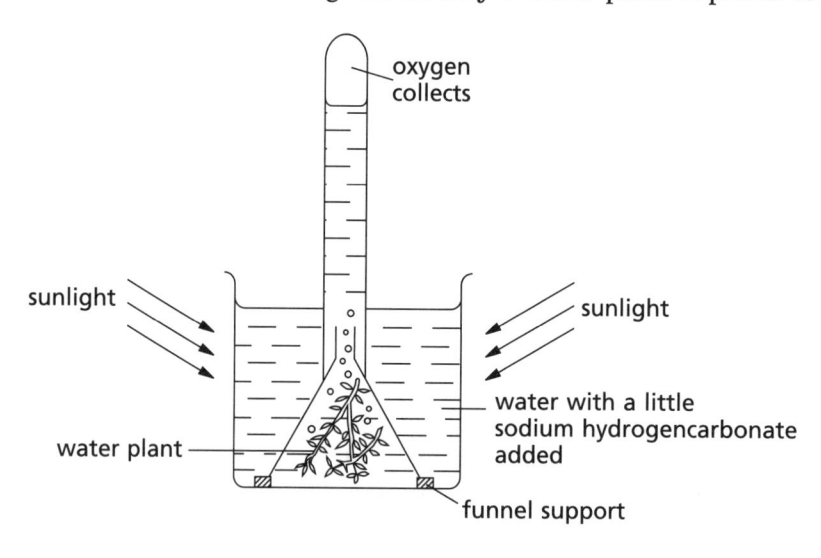

Fig. D
(Reproduced by permission of the University of Cambridge Local Examinations Syndicate)

Under which conditions would the plant produce fewest bubbles?

	light	temperature
A	bright	15°C
B	bright	25°C
C	dim	10°C
D	dim	20°C

12. Figure **E** shows a section through a leaf. Which of the cells contains some, but not a large number, of chloroplasts?

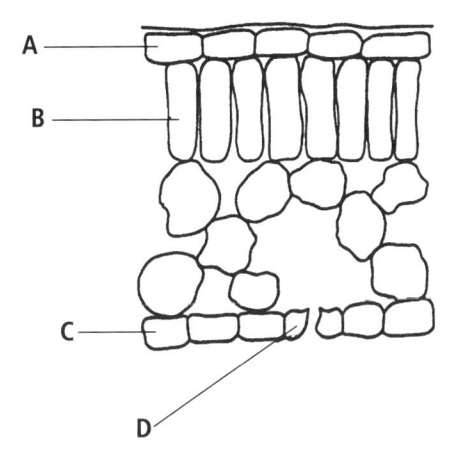

Fig. E
(Reproduced by permission of the University of Cambridge Local Examinations Syndicate)

13. Figure **F** shows a section through a plant stem. Before the section was taken, the plant had stood for six hours in sunlight in an atmosphere containing radio-active carbon dioxide. Which region of the stem would be first to show signs of radio-activity?

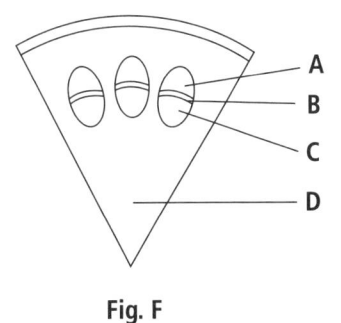

Fig. F

14. Pancreatic juice contains enzymes which digest:

   A proteins and carbohydrates only
   B proteins and fats only
   C fats and carbohydrates only
   D proteins, fats and carbohydrates

15. Which states where bile is secreted and stored?

	secreted	stored
A	bile duct	liver
B	gall bladder	liver
C	liver	bile duct
D	liver	gall bladder

16. Where are proteins first digested in the alimentary canal?

    A colon
    B duodenum
    C mouth cavity
    D stomach

17. Figure **G** shows the structure of a villus.
    Where will the most amino acids be present?

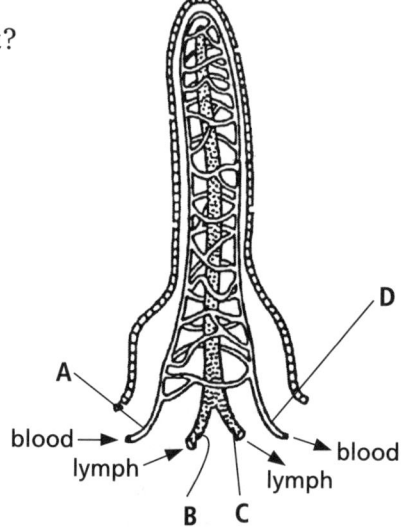

    Fig. G
    (Reproduced by permission of the University of Cambridge Local Examinations Syndicate)

18. Which region of the alimentary canal does food pass through immediately before entering the rectum?

    A anus
    B colon
    C duodenum
    D ileum

19. Which arteries carry blood to the heart?

    A coronary
    B hepatic
    C pulmonary
    D renal

20. Which blood vessel carries the least carbon dioxide?

    A hepatic vein
    B pulmonary artery
    C pulmonary vein
    D vena cava

21. Which of the following is correct for the process of anaerobic respiration?

	carbon dioxide always produced	a lot of energy released
A	no	yes
B	no	no
C	yes	no
D	yes	yes

22. Figure **H** shows the heart in section (front view).

    What is the function of **P**?

    A It allows pressure to build up in the ventricle.
    B It pushes blood from the atrium to the ventricle.
    C It stops blood passing from the atrium to the aorta.
    D It stops blood returning to the ventricle from the aorta.

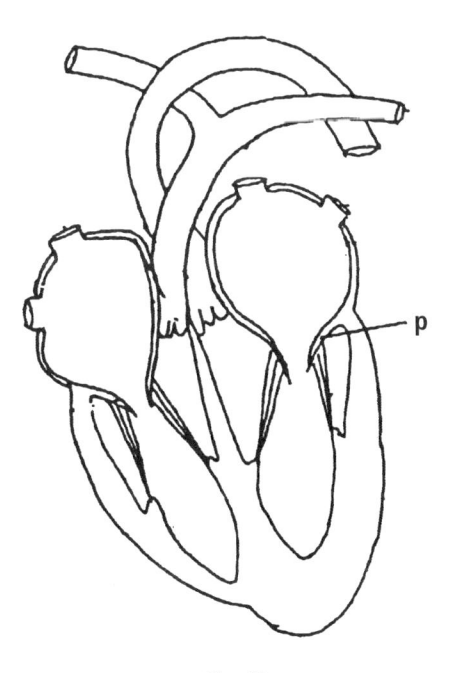

    Fig. H

23. Figure I shows structures associated with breathing. Which structure contains cartilage?

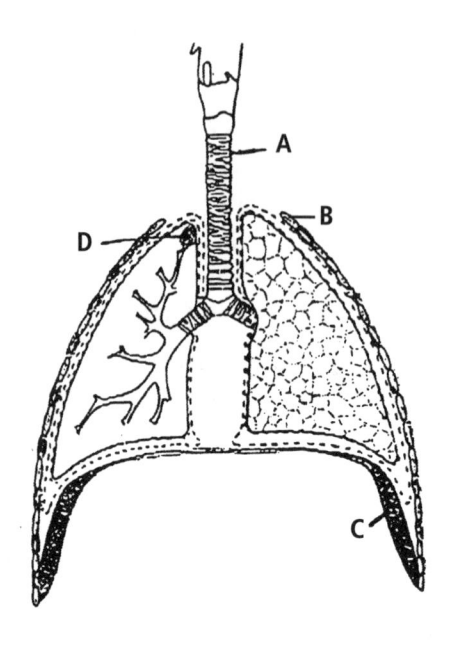

Fig. I
(Reproduced by permission of the University of Cambridge Local Examinations Syndicate)

24. Which of the following increases in muscle cells when they are lacking in oxygen?

    A   carbon dioxide
    B   hydrogencarbonate (bicarbonate) ions
    C   lactic acid
    D   urea

25. Figure J shows a kidney and associated structures. Which part contains the highest concentration of urea?

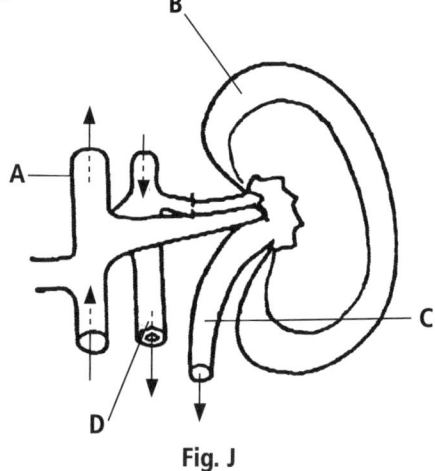

Fig. J

26. Defaecation, sweating, urination and expiration are all ways in which the body loses:

    A   heat and water
    B   salts and water
    C   urea and heat
    D   urea and salts

27. Figure **K** shows a section through human skin. Which structure is not directly affected as a result of a change in atmospheric temperature?

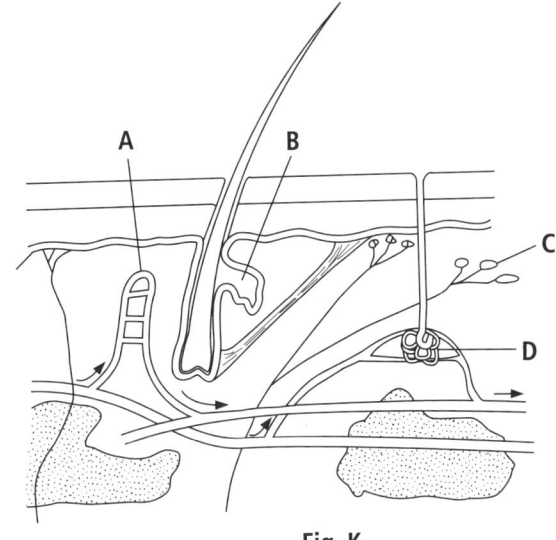

    Fig. K

28. After a sharp blow below the knee cap, impulses travel to the thigh muscles. Which shows the route taken by the impulses?

    A   sensory neurone ⟶ receptor ⟶ synapse ⟶ motor neurone
    B   sensory neurone ⟶ synapse ⟶ motor neurone ⟶ receptor
    C   receptor ⟶ motor neurone ⟶ synapse ⟶ sensory neurone
    D   receptor ⟶ synapse ⟶ sensory neurone ⟶ motor neurone

29. Which is a target organ of both adrenaline and insulin?

    A   heart
    B   ileum
    C   liver
    D   pancreas

30. On a very hot day, which of the following would occur?

    A   Less blood would travel to the brain.
    B   Less blood would travel to the skin.
    C   More blood would travel to the intestines.
    D   More blood would travel to the kidneys.

31. Which of the following are decomposers of dead organisms?

	bacteria	fungi	viruses
A	no	yes	yes
B	yes	no	yes
C	yes	yes	no
D	yes	yes	yes

32. Of the energy eaten in its food by a herbivore, 55% is lost in its faeces, 40% is lost as heat and 5% is used for growth. How many kJ of energy would be absorbed into its blood for every 10 kJ of energy consumed by the herbivore?

   A 0.5 kJ
   B 4 kJ
   C 4.5 kJ
   D 5.5 kJ

33. Figure L represents part of the carbon cycle.

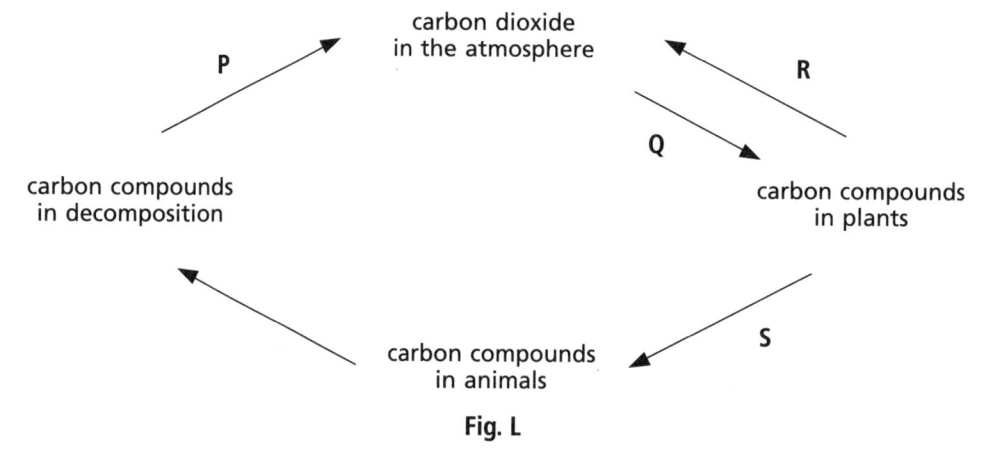

Fig. L

Which letters represent the process of respiration?

   A P and R
   B P and S
   C R and Q
   D R and S

34. What provides the energy which then flows through a food chain?

   A glucose
   B oxygen
   C respiration
   D sunlight

35. Which disease is not normally associated with smoking?

   A emphysema
   B heart disease
   C liver damage
   D lung cancer

36. Which pollutant, released into the air during combustion, is the greatest contributor to acid rain?
   A carbon dioxide
   B soot
   C sulphur dioxide
   D water

37. Figure **M** shows a grass flower. Which part receives the pollen during pollination?

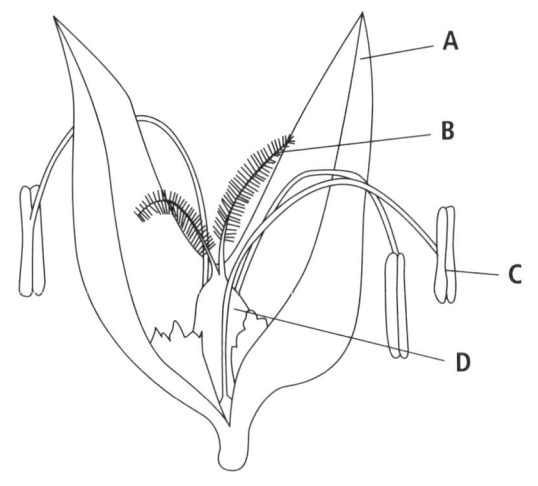

Fig. M

38. What happens to the fresh mass of a seed (the total mass, including water) during the first few days of germination?

   A decreases steadily
   B decreases then increases
   C increases steadily
   D increases then decreases

39. What changes take place in the composition of a mother's blood as it passes through the placenta?

	glucose	carbon dioxide	urea
A	less	more	more
B	less	more	less
C	more	less	less
D	more	less	more

40. Asexual reproduction is:

A a fusion of specialised cells
B a method by which all types of organism reproduce
C a method of producing genetically identical offspring
D a way of avoiding competition

41. Figure **N** shows a fruit of a plant.

This plant is likely to have:

A animal dispersal
B insect pollination
C wind dispersal
D wind pollination

Fig. N

(Reproduced by permission of the University of Cambridge Local Examinations Syndicate)

42. Figure **O** shows the human male reproductive organs.

Which structures make sperms and seminal fluid?

	sperms	seminal fluid
A	V	X
B	W	Y
C	X	W
D	Y	V

Fig. O

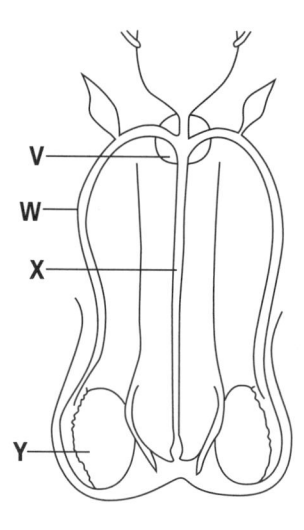

43. The sex of a child is determined by which of the following?

   A the length of the mother's pregnancy
   B the length of time between ovulation and copulation
   C the presence of an X chromosome in an ovum
   D the presence of a Y chromosome in a sperm

44. In fruit flies, the allele for long wings is dominant to the allele for short wings. Long-winged individuals may be homozygous or heterozygous. When long-winged males of the two genotypes are crossed with short-winged females, which percentages of short-winged offspring are expected?

Expected percentages of short-winged offspring

	short-winged female crossed with homozygous long-winged male	short-winged female crossed with heterozygous long-winged male
A	0%	50%
B	25%	25%
C	50%	0%
D	75%	75%

45. A pregnant woman has an equal chance of her baby being blood group A or blood group AB. Which one shows the possible genotypes of the woman and the father of her child?

   A $I^A I^A$ and $I^B I^o$
   B $I^A I^B$ and $I^B I^o$
   C $I^A I^o$ and $I^B I^o$
   D $I^A I^B$ and $I^A I^o$

46. A man has a recessive gene on all his X chromosomes. What is the probability of this gene being present in his first daughter?

   A 25%
   B 50%
   C 75%
   D 100%

47. The palisade cells of a species of plant contain 28 chromosomes. How many chromosomes will there be in each gamete produced by the plant?

   A 56
   B 28
   C 14
   D 4

48. Which of the following may be used to obtain an F_2 generation?

    A allowing flowers on a parent plant to be self-pollinated
    B allowing flowers on an F_1 plant to be self-pollinated
    C cross-pollinating an F_1 plant with a parent plant
    D cross-pollinating two parent plants

Answers

1 – C.	13 – A.	25 – C.	37 – B.
2 – B.	14 – D.	26 – A.	38 – C.
3 – D.	15 – D.	27 – B.	39 – A.
4 – C.	16 – D.	28 – B.	40 – C.
5 – B.	17 – D.	29 – C.	41 – C.
6 – D.	18 – B.	30 – A.	42 – D.
7 – C.	19 – A.	31 – C.	43 – D.
8 – C.	20 – C.	32 – C.	44 – A.
9 – B.	21 – B.	33 – A.	45 – A.
10 – C.	22 – A.	34 – D.	46 – D.
11 – C.	23 – A.	35 – C.	47 – C.
12 – D.	24 – C.	36 – C.	48 – B.

Questions from past examination papers

1. Figure **A1** shows a cyclinder of potato tuber immersed in water. Figure **B1** shows an identical cyclinder in concentrated salt solution. Both cyclinders are fixed to a support at one end and have identical weights firmly attached to the opposite ends. (All figures are drawn to the same scale.)

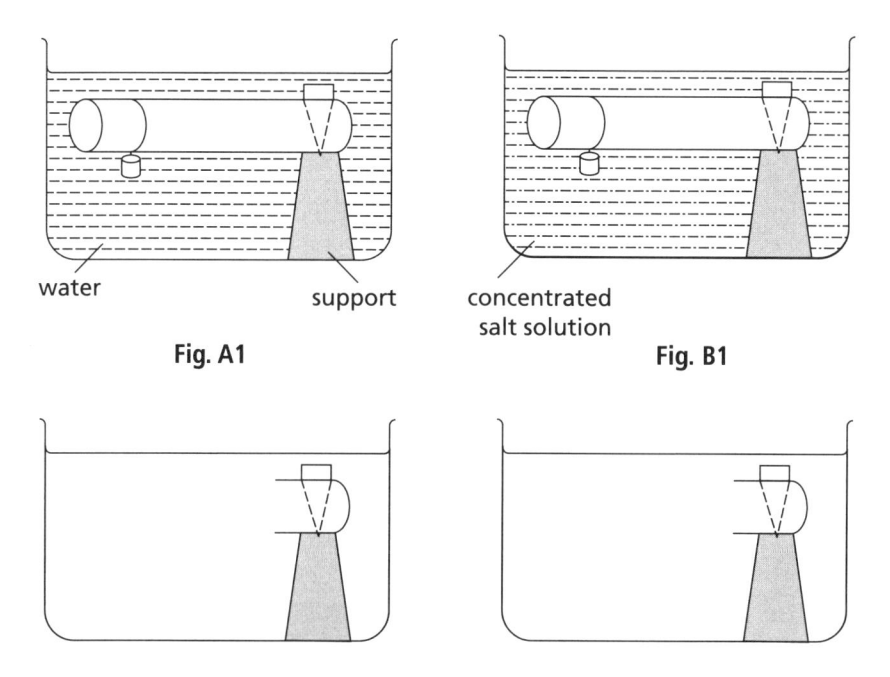

Fig. A1

Fig. B1

Fig. A2

Fig. B2

(Reproduced by permission of the University of Cambridge Local Examinations Syndicate)

    (i)   (a) Complete Figs. **A2** and **B2** above to show how the cyclinders would appear several hours later.
           (b) Explain what has happened in Figs. **A2** and **B2**.
           (c) Name the process responsible for any changes in appearance of the cyclinders.
    (ii)   (a) Suggest how pressure within a plant cell may reach higher levels than those usually found within animal cells.
           (b) What is the value of this pressure to the shoot of a seedling?

2. (i) For each of the following, describe how structure is related to function:
       (a) root hair cells
       (b) red blood cells.

(ii) A student examined root hair cells and red blood cells in distilled water on a microscope slide. She looked at them at regular intervals throughout the lesson. Describe, with reasons, what she would have seen.

3. Figure **C** shows the proportions of the main chemical substances found in the human body.

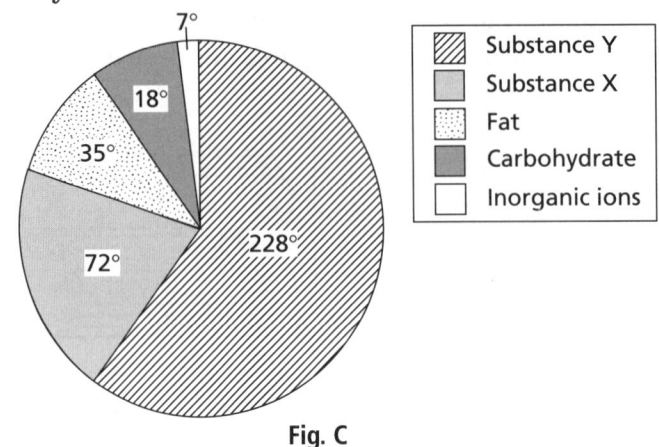

Fig. C

(i) What is the percentage of carbohydrate? Show your working.
(ii) What are substances **X** and **Y** most likely to be?
(iii) Name **two** inorganic ions and, for each one, state its functions in the body.

Figures **D** and **E** show the effects of two diseases caused by dietary deficiency.

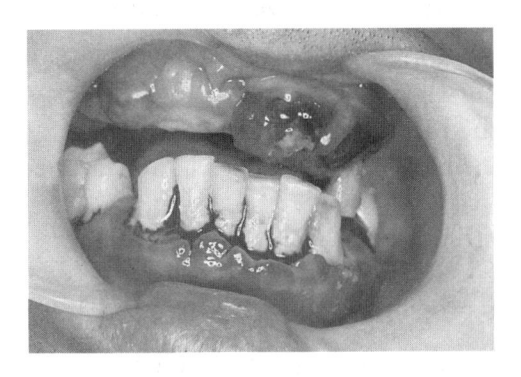

Fig. D

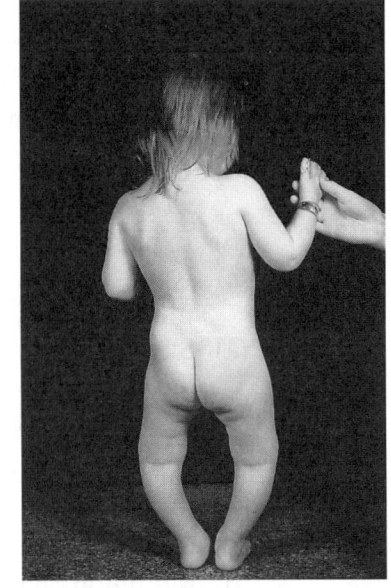

Fig. E

Complete the table below by:
(a) identifying each disease
(b) stating which constituent was lacking in the diet.
(c) naming a food which could have prevented the disease.

	Disease	Constituent	Food
Fig. D			
Fig E			

4. Figure **F** shows a section through a green leaf.

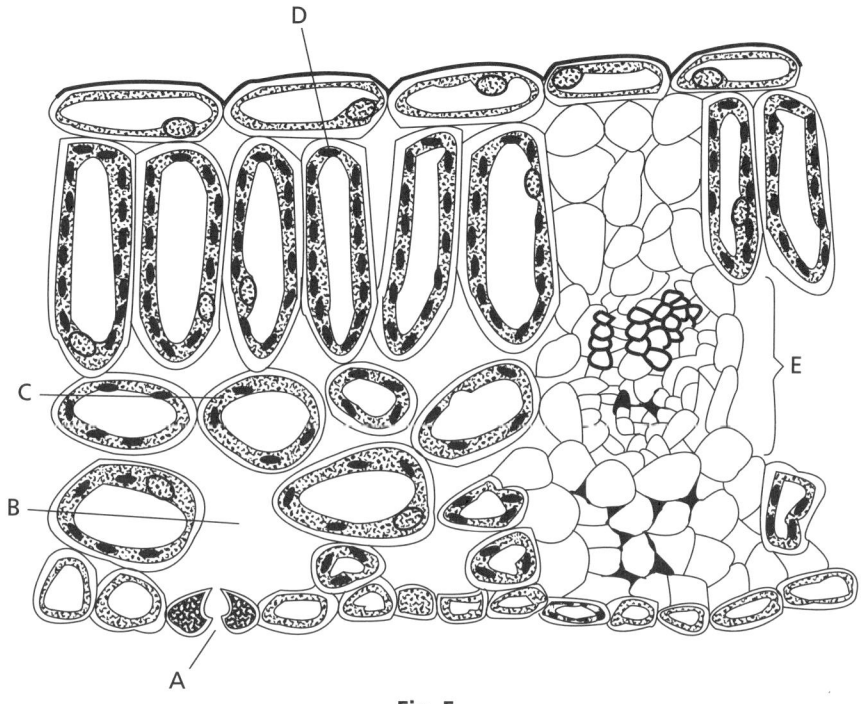

Fig. F
(Reproduced by permission of the University of Cambridge Local Examinations Syndicate)

(i) With reference to the parts **A** to **E**, explain how a leaf is involved in the manufacture of carbohydrates.
(ii) Explain how these carbohydrates are distributed to the rest of the plant.

5. (i) (a) Name the biological process by which a plant loses water to the air.
(b) State **two** other processes which are involved in the movement of water from the roots to the leaves.

Figure **G** shows the rate of water uptake by a plant over a period of three days.

(ii) Using the information in Fig. **G**:
(a) Account for the rate of water uptake at midnight.
(b) Suggest reasons for the differences between the rates of water uptake on days 2 and 3 compared with day 1.

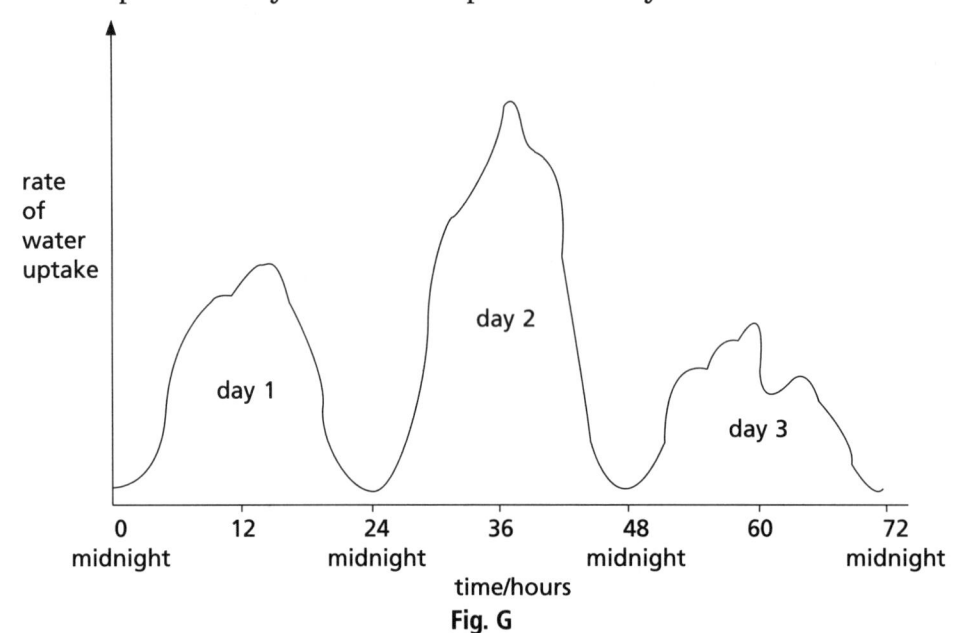

Fig. G

(Reproduced by permission of the University of Cambridge Local Examinations Syndicate)

6. (i) What is the advantage to a herbivore, such as a cow, of chewing its food?

(ii) Describe:
(a) how a molecule of digested food from the gut enters the bloodstream
(b) the pathway by which it eventually reaches cells in the hand.
(*Names of the heart chambers are not required.*)

(iii) How can diet which is rich in fat lead to heart disease?

7. Figure H shows a photograph of a blood clot taken using an electron microscope.

(i) Identify structure **X**.
(ii) (a) What is the function of structure **X**?
(b) Complete the table on the next page by stating how the listed features help structure **X** to carry out this function.

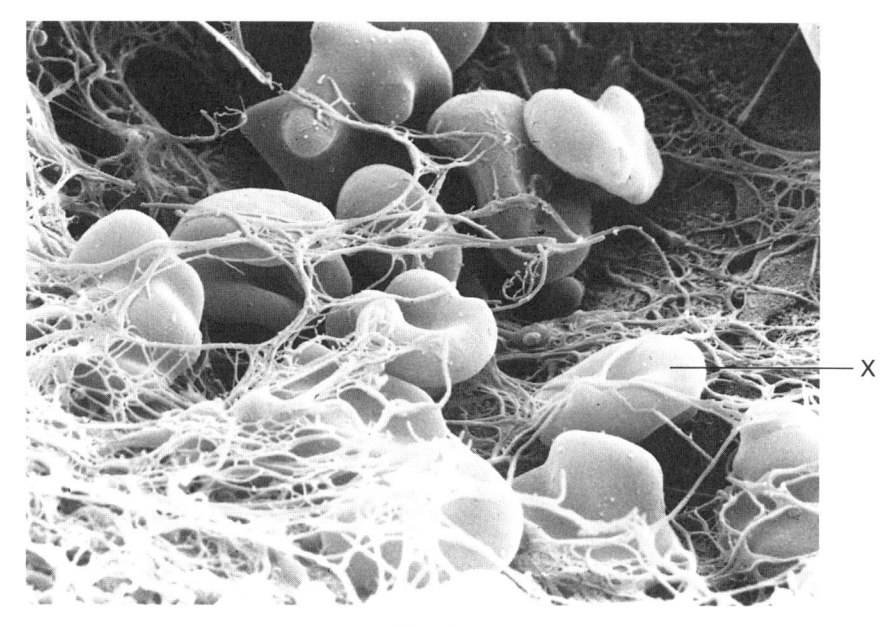

Fig. H

	Feature of X	How it helps the function of X
1.	Thin cell membrane	
2.	Flexible cell membrane	
3.	Shape	

Long, insoluble threads are shown in Figure **H**, and are formed as the blood clots over a cut in the skin. Figure **I** shows how the insoluble threads are formed.

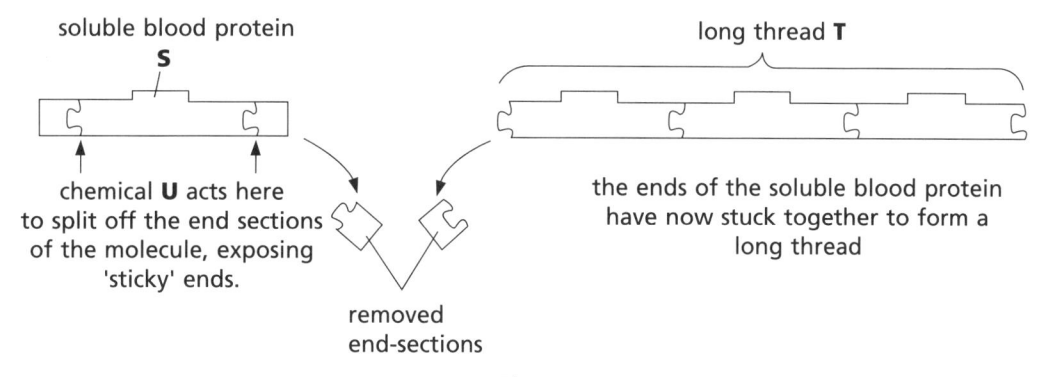

Fig. I

(iii) (a) Name the soluble protein **S**.
(b) Name the long insoluble thread **T**.
(c) Suggest what type of chemical **U** is likely to be.

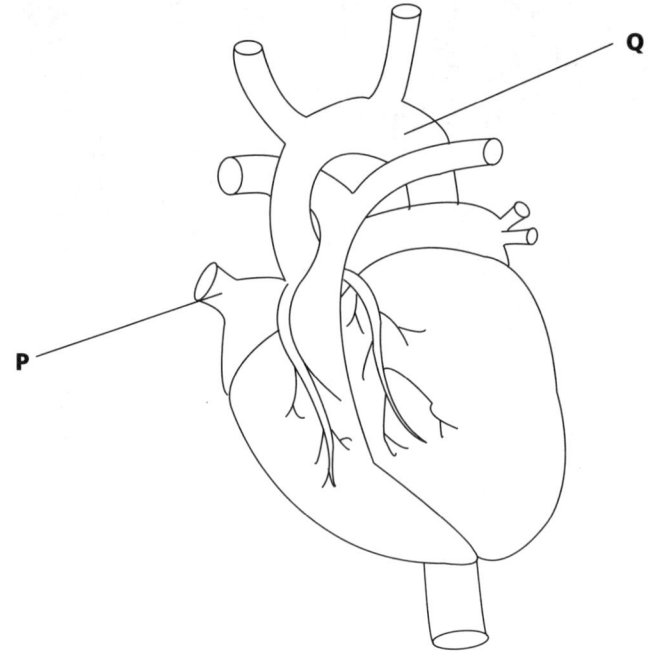

8. Figure **J** shows a ventral ('front') view of the human heart.

Fig. J
(Reproduced by permission of the University of Cambridge Local Examinations Syndicate)

   (i)   Describe and explain the flow of blood through the heart from the time that it arrives at **P** to the time that it leaves at **Q**.
   (ii)   Explain the relationship between blood and tissue fluid.

9. Figure **K** shows a diagram of a kidney and associated structures. The tables list the percentages of certain components found within structures **B** and **C**.

In structure B

Component	Concentration %
urea	0.03
glucose	0.10
amino acids	0.05
salts	0.72
proteins	8.00

REVIEW QUESTIONS 169

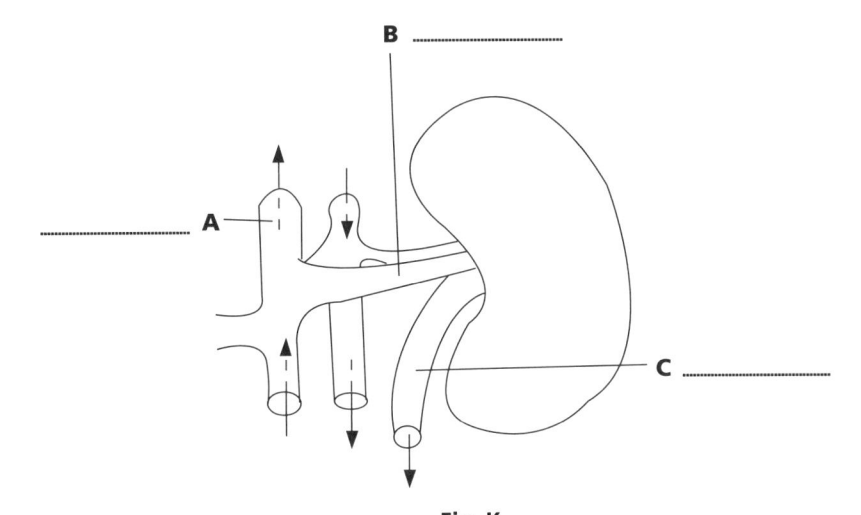

Fig. K
(Reproduced by permission of the University of Cambridge Local Examinations Syndicate)

In structure C

Component	Concentration %
urea	2.00
glucose	0.00
amino acids	0.00
salts	1.50
proteins	0.00

(i) On the diagram, label structures **A**, **B** and **C**.

(ii) Which chamber of the heart first receives the contents of structure **A**?

(iii) Using **only** the information in the tables in Fig. **K**, deduce the functions of the kidney.

(iv) Explain how the proportions of the components present in **C** would change:
   (a) after eating meat
   (b) if a person suffering from diabetes had not taken enough insulin.

10. (i) What is meant by the term 'pupil reflex'?

   (ii) (a) Explain how the image of a distant object is focused on the retina of the eye.

(b) Describe the changes which take place if the eye then focuses on a near object.

11. Figure **L** shows the apparatus used for collecting some of the substances in cigarette smoke.

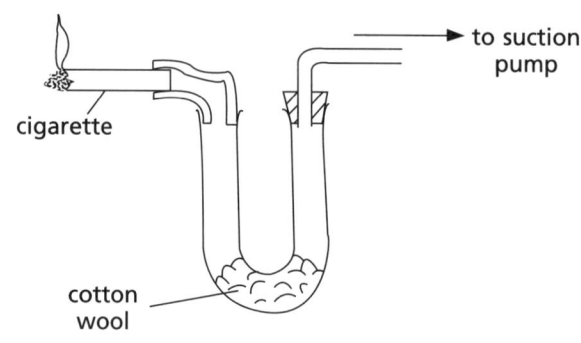

Fig. L
(Reproduced by permission of the University of Cambridge Local Examinations Syndicate)

As the cigarette burns, the cotton wool turns brown.

(i) (a) Name the substance which causes the cotton wool to change colour.
(b) The cotton wool provides a large surface area on which this substance collects. What structures in the lungs does the cotton wool represent?
(c) Explain how smoking affects the amount of oxygen taken up by the blood.
(d) State two ways in which smoking can damage the smoker's health.

(ii) What are the effects on an embryo if the mother smokes during pregnancy?

12. (i) (a) Define the term 'drug'.
(b) State the medicinal uses of **two named** drugs.

(ii) Explain the link between the misuse of drugs and AIDS.

(iii) Why is heroin regarded as a drug of abuse?

13. Figure **M** shows one method of birth control which can be used by a woman.

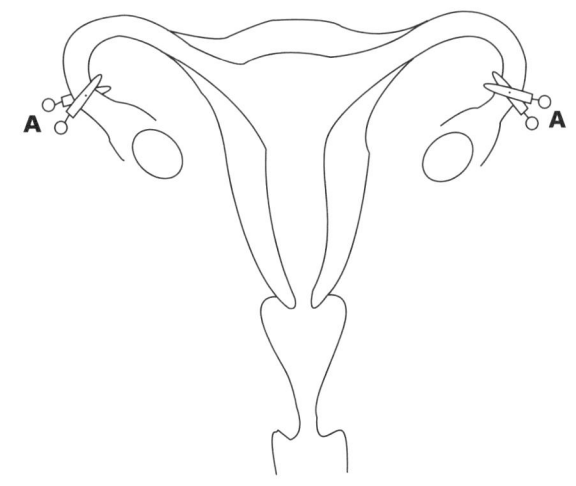

Fig. M
(Reproduced by permission of the University of Cambridge Local Examinations Syndicate)

(i) (a) Explain how the treatment at point **A** prevents conception.
(b) Draw in and label, on the diagram, the position in which a contraceptive cap (diaphragm/barrier) could be fitted.

(ii) On Figure **M**, indicate with an **X** the place where sperms would normally be deposited, and with a **Y** the place where fertilisation would normally occur when no method of birth control is being used.

14. (i) Figure **N** shows the structure of a flower, in section, which has been partly labelled.

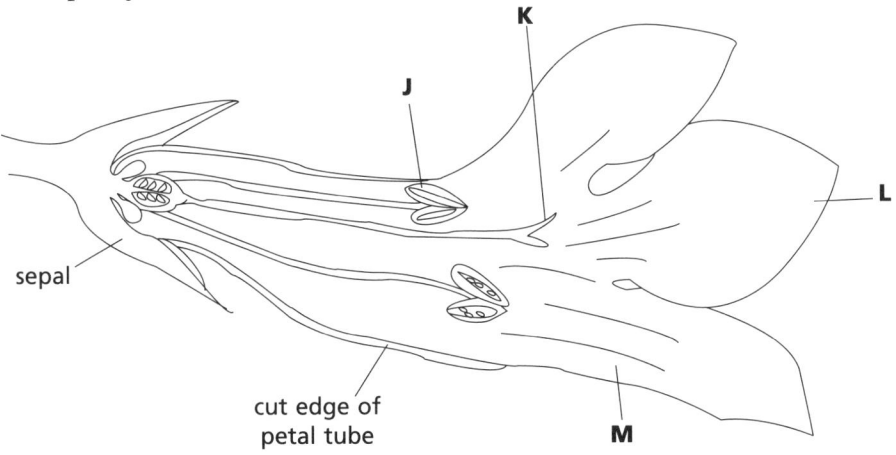

Fig. N
(Reproduced by permission of the University of Cambridge Local Examinations Syndicate)

Describe how the process of pollination is most likely to be carried out in this flower. In your answer, you should identify **J**, **K**, **L** and **M**.

  (ii) In what ways is fertilisation in a plant:
  (a) similar to fertilisation in a mammal?
  (b) different from fertilisation in a mammal?

15. Figure **O** shows the results of some breeding experiments on mice.

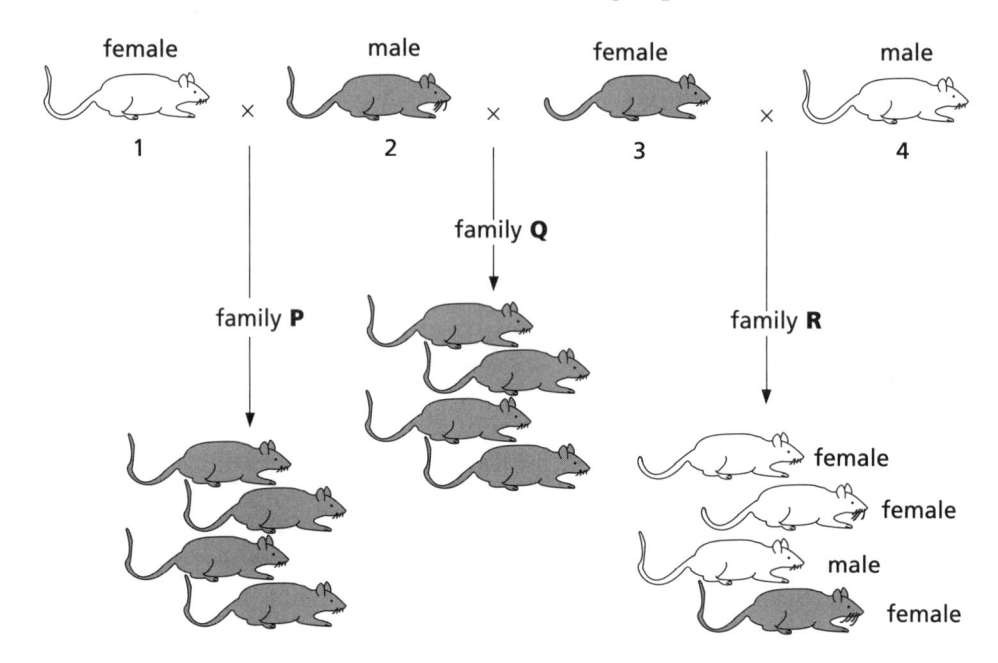

Fig. O
(Reproduced by permission of the University of Cambridge Local Examinations Syndicate)

  (i) (a) Complete the table below to show the sex chromosomes present in the gametes of parent mice 2 and 3.

Mouse 2	Mouse 3

  (b) If mice 3 and 4 had a second family, what is the percentage chance that the first mouse born would be female?

Coat colour in these mice is controlled by a single pair of alleles showing complete dominance.

  (ii) Which of the parent mice 1 to 4 is likely to be:
  (a) homozygous dominant for coat colour?
  (b) heteroxygous for coat colour?

(iii) Mouse 5 later bred with a mouse of similar genotype to its mother (mouse 3). Draw a full genetic diagram to show how coat colour would be inherited in this new family.

(iv) (a) The mice in Fig. **O** show some examples of pairs of inherited characters, in addition to coat colour. Identify **one** of these pairs of inherited characters.
  (b) Assume that the inheritance of the pair of characters you have identified is due to one pair of alleles showing complete dominance. Draw a full genetic diagram to explain the inheritance **in family R**.

16. (i) Distinguish clearly between 'complete dominance' and 'codominance'.

(ii) Explain how a man with blood group A and a woman with blood group B can have a child with blood group O.

(iii) The presence of hair on the stems of a certain species of plant is controlled by a single pair of alleles. When a pure-breeding plant with a hairy stem is crossed with a pure-breeding plant with a smooth stem, all the offspring have hairy stems. Use a genetic diagram to show a cross which would produce offspring with hairy stems and smooth stems in a ratio of 1:1 and explain the symbols you use.

Answers

1. (i) (a) **A2** cylinder should appear straight and no shorter or thinner than **A1**. **B2** should curve downwards and be no longer or fatter than **B1**.
  (b) Water enters cylinder **A2** whilst water leaves cylinder **B2**. The cell membranes are partially permeable. There should be some reference to water potential either being higher in the water or lower in the concentrated solution than in the cell sap, and to a high (turgor) pressure inside the potato cells in **A2** and a low pressure in **B2**.
  (c) Osmosis.
 (ii) (a) Plant cells are surrounded by an elastic cell wall.
  (b) It helps to support seedlings since they have not yet had chance to manufacture much xylem.
2. (i) (a) A large surface area is provided by their long, thin extensions which are surrounded by soil water containing dissolved salts. Water is absorbed by osmosis whilst mineral salts (e.g. nitrates) are absorbed by active uptake (or active transport).
  (b) Red blood cells are very small and numerous and biconcave in

shape. They therefore offer a very large surface area for the uptake of oxygen. Haemoglobin in their cytoplasm forms oxyhaemoglobin so that oxygen can be efficiently carried.

(ii) In both, water enters by osmosis because of the lower water potential within the cells and the fact that both possess a partially permeable (cell) membrane. Root hair cells swell and because of the cell wall, the cell contents increase in pressure. In the blood cells, with no cell wall, the pressure causes the cell membrane to burst.

3. (i) $\dfrac{18}{360} \times 100 = 5\%$

(ii) X is protein, Y is water.

(iii) Iron for making haemoglobin, calcium for strong bones and teeth.

(iv) (a) **D** is scurvy; **E** is rickets.
(b) **D**: the diet was lacking in vitamin C; **E**: the diet was lacking in vitamin D.
(c) **D**: (fresh) fruit e.g. oranges; **E**: eggs, dairy produce or fish oils

4. (i) You must link each point you make with the appropriate letter wherever possible. **A** is a stoma through which carbon dioxide diffuses. Its size is controlled by guard cells. **B** is an intercellular space which allows the carbon dioxide to reach the mesophyll cells. Carbon dioxide then dissolves in the water on the cell walls of cells **C**, then diffuses through the cell walls to the chloroplasts (**D**). **C** is a spongy cell, **D** is a palisade cell. Chlorophyll in the chloroplasts absorbs light energy for the process of photosynthesis. **E** is a vein containing xylem which brings the water for this chemical reaction which makes carbohydrate.

(ii) Sugar (sucrose) is carried away from the leaf in solution through the phloem to the stem and root.

5. (i) (a) Transpiration.
(b) Osmosis causing root pressure and capillarity are the two main processes, but the fact that molecules stick together (molecular cohesion) is also important.

(ii) (a) At night time it is dark, and therefore the stomata are almost completely closed, greatly reducing water loss.
(b) Day 2 may be brighter, windier, warmer or less humid than day 1. Day 3 may be less bright, calmer, cooler or more humid than day 1. The more uneven shape of the graph might suggest more variable conditions during day 3. (All these conditions will affect the rate of water loss by the plant, therefore also the rate of water uptake.)

6. (i) Chewing breaks open the plant cells by grinding the cellulose walls, thus releasing the nutrients (mostly carbohydrates and some proteins) in the cytoplasm.

(ii) (a) Digested foods are in solution so they can diffuse through the very thin walls of the villi which line the ileum. Amino acids and glucose enter the blood in the capillaries, while fatty acids and glycerol enter the lacteals, joining the blood stream via the lymph system.

(b) The capillaries join to form the hepatic portal vein which takes the food to the liver. From the liver, it travels via the hepatic vein and the (inferior) vena cava to the heart. It then travels along the pulmonary artery to the lungs before returning to the heart via the pulmonary vein. The aorta then takes it to an artery in the arm which supplies the capillaries in the hand. The food then diffuses in solution from the capillaries via the tissue fluid to the cells.

(iii) Fat may deposit on the walls of the coronary artery (atheroma), blocking the artery and starving the heart muscle of oxygen and glucose.

7. (i) **X** is a red blood cell.
   (ii) (a) To carry oxygen.
   (b) The thin membrane allows oxygen to diffuse through it easily, the flexible membrane allows it to pass more easily through capillaries, and its shape gives it a large surface area for greater oxygen uptake.
   (iii) (a) Fibrinogen.
   (b) Fibrin.
   (c) An enzyme (protease).

8. (i) **P** is the entrance to the right atrium. Blood flows from here to the right ventricle through the tricuspid valve which then closes to prevent blood returning to the atrium. The right ventricle contracts to force the blood through the pulmonary artery to the lungs. Semi-lunar valves prevent blood returning to the ventricle. The pulmonary vein then leads blood to the left atrium which empties, via the mitral (bicuspid) valve into the left ventricle. When the left ventricle contracts, blood is forced out of the heart along the aorta **Q**, and its return to the heart is prevented by another set of semi-lunar valves.

(ii) Tissue fluid bathes the cells. It is the fluid part of the blood plasma which passes out of the leaky capillary walls carrying with it dissolved molecules such as glucose and oxygen. Larger molecules such as blood proteins do not pass out.

9. (i) **A** – (inferior) vena cava; **B** – renal vein; **C** – ureter.
   (ii) Right atrium.
   (iii) The kidney extracts urea and salts from the blood and sends them in the urine along the ureter. Glucose, amino acids and proteins are not passed from the blood into the urine.

(iv) (a) The urea content would be higher since more amino acids from the protein in the meat will have been deaminated. The salt content may also be a little higher.
 (b) There would be glucose in **C** since without insulin, blood glucose would not have been turned to glycogen for storage. The kidney then attempts to reduce the blood glucose level.

10. (i) The pupil reflex is an automatic response of the muscles of the iris to a change of light intensity.
 (ii) (a) The ciliary muscles of the eye relax, causing the suspensory ligaments to be stretched and pulled tight. They pull on the sides of the lens making it thinner and giving it a longer focal length. The transparent cornea refracts (bends) the light rays as they pass through, and the transparent lens makes a final adjustment to the rays to focus an image on the retina.
 (b) Accommodation must now occur. The ciliary muscles contract reducing the tension on the suspensory ligaments, allowing the lens to bulge. This gives it a short focal length allowing the near object to be focused on the retina.

11. (i) (a) Tar.
 (b) Alveoli.
 (c) Tar covers the moisture coating to the alveoli preventing the diffusion of oxygen through the alveolus wall into the blood. Carbon monoxide combines with the haemoglobin preventing the uptake of oxygen into red blood cells.
 (d) Lung cancer, bronchitis, smoker's cough, emphysema, increased risk of thrombosis and heart attack are all possible diseases resulting from smoking.
 (ii) Less oxygen is carried to the baby which may be born prematurely, underweight or miscarried. Babies born to mothers who smoke during pregnancy may also be less intelligent.

12. (i) (a) A drug is a chemical which is taken into the body and which then affects the body's metabolism.
 (b) Any two drugs could be given, but two examples are: 1. Aspirin (or paracetamol) which is taken to relieve pain, and 2. Paludrin (or other malarial drug) taken either to reduce the risk of contracting malaria or to treat the disease after the symptoms have appeared.
 (ii) AIDS is caused by HIV (a virus) which exists in the blood of those with the infection and is transmitted from person to person through shared needles and through sex with an infected person.
 (iii) Heroin is used medicinally for pain relief, but the sense of well-being which it produces causes it to be abused. Unrestricted used leads to a craving for the drug and distressing withdrawal symptoms if the

craving is not satisfied. Increased dosages become necessary in order to obtain the same effect. The user may resort to a life of crime to fund their habit. Apart from the risk of AIDS, death will often follow for the untreated user.

13. (i) (a) The oviducts have been cut. The ovum, after release from the ovary, cannot meet a sperm which would be unable to pass through the cut portion.
    (b) The cap should be drawn fitting over the cervix so that it blocks the entrance to the uterus.
  (ii) An 'X' should be drawn towards the top of the vagina, and a 'Y' in an oviduct somewhere between the scissors and the muscular wall of the uterus.

14. (i) The flower is insect-pollinated. Insects land on the large petals (**L**), attracted by their colour and, probably also, scent. As an insect reaches down to the nectary, directed by the nectar guides (**M**), any pollen which may be on the insect's body is transferred to the stigma (**K**). At the same time, pollen from the anthers (**J**) will be dusted onto the insect to be carried away to the next flower it visits, bringing about cross-pollination.
  (ii) (a) Similarities: the fusion of nuclei in gametes, both occur in the female part of the organism, the male gamete moves (or is moved) to the female gamete and a zygote is produced which develops into an embryo.
    (b) Differences: there is pollination in a plant, copulation in a mammal. There is no equivalent in a plant to the oviduct in a mammal. In the mammal, the male gametes (sperms) swim, while in the plant, self-fertilisation is possible.

15. (i) (a) X Y | X (X)
    (b) 50%
  (ii) (a) Mouse 2.
    (b) Mouse 3.
  (iii) Using the letter B to respresent the gene for the dominant coat colour – black – and the letter b for its recessive allele, then

Parents				
genotypes:	Bb	×	Bb	
phenotypes:	(black)		(black)	
Gametes:	B b		B b	
Offspring	BB	Bb	Bb	bb
	(black)	(black)	(black)	(white)
Ratio:		3 black : 1 white		

(iv) (a) Either long and short whiskers or long and short tail.
  (b) Using the letter L to represent the gene for the dominant short whiskers / long tail, and the letter l for its recessive allele, then

  Parents   Ll   ×   ll

  Gametes: L   l   l   l

  Offspring: Ll   ×   ll

  (short whiskers) or (long whiskers)
  (long tail)   (short tail)

  Ratio: 1 : 1

(*Note*: Since the numbers of offspring involved does not represent a large sample, it would be possible, but unlikely, for long whiskers and short tail to be the dominant phenotypes. You might be expected to explain this point if you chose to answer the question in this way.)

16. (i) When only one allele in a heterozygous individual controls the phenotype (appearance), then that allele is said to be dominant (e.g. the allele for blood group A – I^A is dominant over the allele I^o). When both alleles in a heterozygous individual have an effect on the phenotype, then the alleles are said to be codominant (e.g. in the genotype $I^A I^B$ which produces the phenotype blood group AB).

(ii) If the father has blood group A and the genotype $I^A I^o$ and the mother has blood group B, with the genotype $I^B I^o$, then both are able to produce gametes containing the allele I^o. They may therefore have an offspring with the genotype $I^o I^o$ whose phenotype will be blood group O.

(iii) If H represents the dominant gene for hairy stems, and h represents its recessive allele, then:

Parents
Genotypes: Hh   ×   hh
Phenotypes: hairy   smooth

Gametes: H   h   h   h

Offspring   Hh   Hh   hh   hh
               hairy   smooth

Ratio: 1 : 1

Glossary

ACCOMMODATION: the changing of the shape and therefore the focal length of the lens in the eye in order to focus on objects at different distances.

ACID RAIN: a dilute solution of acids that falls to earth when mainly oxides of nitrogen and sulphur in the atmosphere dissolve in rain.

ACTIVE SITE: section on the surface of an enzyme where a substrate molecule fits exactly and is split into product molecules. The 'lock' in the 'lock and key hypothesis'.

ACTIVE TRANSPORT: an energy-consuming process where substances are transported through living membranes against a concentration gradient.

ADRENAL GLAND: gland situated above the kidneys. Produces the hormone adrenaline.

ADRENALINE: hormone produced by the adrenal glands that produces the body's response in times of fear or anger.

AEROBIC RESPIRATION: the release of relatively large amounts of energy by using oxygen to break down foodstuffs. Usually takes the form of the oxidation of glucose in the cytoplasm of living cells.

AIDS: acquired immune deficiency syndrome. Caused by HIV, a virus that affects the body's ability to fight infection.

ALLELES: a pair of matching genes.

ALVEOLI (singular: 'alveolus'): air sacs of the lungs.

AMINO ACIDS: simple, soluble units. A few linked together form a polypeptide; many linked together form a protein. Used in cells for building up proteins as the cells grow, and for making special proteins such as enzymes.

AMNION: membrane that surrounds a developing fetus. It forms the amniotic sac, enclosing the fetus in amniotic fluid.

AMNIOTIC FLUID: a water bath that encloses a developing fetus.

AMYLASE: an enzyme that digests starch to sugars.

ANAEMIA: a lack of haemoglobin, often caused by low levels of iron in a person's diet.

ANAEROBIC RESPIRATION: the release of relatively small amounts of energy by the breakdown of food substances. Occurs in the absence of oxygen.

ANTAGONISTIC MUSCLES: two muscles that provide opposing forces for movement. One of the pair contracts while, at the same time, the other relaxes.

ANTIBIOTICS: drugs (e.g. penicillin) used to treat diseases caused by bacteria.

ANTIBODIES: chemicals, produced by lymphocytes, that 'stick' to bacteria and clump them together, ready for ingestion by phagocytes.

ANTITOXINS: types of antibodies produced by lymphocytes. They neutralise toxins in the blood.

ARTERY: vessels with thick, muscular walls that carry blood, under high pressure, away from the heart. A large artery is called an aorta; a small one is called an arteriole.

ARTIFICIAL SELECTION: the deliberate breeding of organisms with particular characteristics.

ASEXUAL REPRODUCTION: the production of genetically identical offspring from one parent.

ATHEROMA: fatty deposits that form on the walls of arteries, produced by a combination of saturated (animal) fats and cholesterol.

ATRIA (singular: 'atrium'): two upper chambers of the heart that receive blood from the body and the lungs.

AUTOTROPHIC: describes organisms (e.g. plants) able to produce their own food by using small molecules in the environment to build large organic molecules.

AUXINS: a group of plant hormones. They control the enlargement of plant cells (after division), and the modification of the new cell to carry out a particular function. Can be produced synthetically.

BACTERIA (singular: 'bacterium'): unicellular organisms.

BALANCED DIET: food and drink consumed by a person which has the correct amount of each constituent (e.g. proteins, carbohydrates) to enable them to be healthy.

BALL AND SOCKET JOINT: type of joint which allows free movement in many planes (e.g. at the shoulder).

BENEDICT'S SOLUTION: used to test for the presence of certain sugars including maltose and glucose (i.e. 'reducing' sugars).

BIRTH CONTROL: methods of preventing pregnancy, e.g. through the use of contraceptives.

BIURET SOLUTIONS: used to test for the presence of proteins.

BLASTOCYST: a stage in embryonic development after the zygote has divided to form a hollow ball of cells.

BLIND SPOT: the point in the eye where the retina is joined to the optic nerve. There are no rods or cones, so images formed here are *not* converted into impulses and relayed to the brain.

CAPILLARIES: microscopic blood vessels that carry blood from arterioles to venules.

CAPILLARITY: the movement of liquids upward through very narrow tubes.

CARBOHYDRATE: organic chemicals containing only the elements carbon, hydrogen and oxygen. Ratio of hydrogen atoms to oxygen atoms is always 2 : 1.

CARNIVORES: all consumers above the level of herbivore, i.e. all meat eaters.

CARPELS: the female parts of a flower – a stigma, connected by a style to the ovary, in which lie the ovules which contain the female gamete.

CATALYSTS: particular chemicals that can affect how quickly chemical reactions occur (usually speed up reactions).

CELL MEMBRANE: outer covering of the cell that controls the passage of substances into and out of the cell.

CELL WALL: a 'box' made of cellulose that encloses the cell – not present around animal cells.

CENTRAL NERVOUS SYSTEM (CNS): the body's coordinating centre, made up of the brain and the spinal cord. Receives information about the environment from receptors and directs a response to effectors (muscles or glands).

CHLOROPHYLL: a green pigment found within the chloroplasts of plant cells. Traps sunlight for use in the process of photosynthesis. Contains magnesium.

CHLOROPLAST: small bodies lying in the cytoplasm of those plant cells involved in photosynthesis. Green in colour because they contain chlorophyll.

CHROMOSOME: possesses genes which are responsible for programming the cytoplasm to manufacture particular proteins.

CLONES: a population of organisms produced by asexual reproduction, and all genetically identical.

CLOT: a clump of blood cells trapped in a mesh of fibrin. It prevents the entry of bacteria at a wound. It dries and hardens to form a scab.

CNS: central nervous system.

CODOMINANCE: a type of monohybrid inheritance, when both alleles have an equal effect on the phenotype of the offspring.

COMPLETE DOMINANCE: when the presence of a *single* allele will have the same effect on the phenotype of an individual as the presence of an identical pair of alleles.

CONCENTRATION GRADIENT: when a region of (relatively) high concentration of molecules or particles is next to a region of (relatively) low concentration. Must be present for diffusion to occur.

CONES: light-sensitive cells in the retina of the eye that provide a picture with greater detail and in colour. They convert light energy into electrical energy.

CONSUMER: any organism which relies on the energy supplied by the producer in its food chain.

CONTINUOUS VARIATION: where both inherited and environmental factors determine the characteristics of an individual (e.g. body mass, height).

CONTROL: apparatus and materials identical to those in an experiment but lacking in the one feature being investigated. Used to make a comparison with the experiment in order to make the results of the experiment valid.

CORNEA: transparent part of the eye that allows light rays to enter and refracts them toward each other.

CORONARY ARTERY: vessel that supplies oxygenated blood to the heart muscle.

COTYLEDONS: organs in seeds, often used for storing starch and protein.

CYTOPLASM: a jelly-like substance in which the chemical reactions of the cell take place.

DEAMINATION: process by which excess amino acids are broken down in the liver to produce the excretory chemical urea.

DECOMPOSERS: organisms which release enzymes to break down large molecules in dead organic matter into smaller ones which can then be recycled.

DEFICIENCY DISEASE: conditions caused by a lack of a constituent (e.g. vitamin C, vitamin D, calcium or iron) in a person's diet.

DERMIS: lower layer of skin containing most of the skin structures (e.g. sweat glands, venules, arterioles).

DETOXIFICATION: the removal and breakdown of toxins (e.g. alcohol) from the blood. A major function of the liver.

DIFFUSION: the movement of molecules from a region of higher concentration to a region of lower concentration, down a concentration gradient.

DISCONTINUOUS VARIATION: where inheritance *alone* determines the characteristics of an individual (e.g. blood group).

DISSOLVE: mix a substance into a liquid so that it is absorbed into the liquid.

DRUGS: externally-administered substances which modify or affect chemical reactions in the body.

ECOSYSTEM: a community of organisms living together in a habitat and connected through food webs.

ENZYMES: biological catalysts that control chemical reactions in living organisms. Each has a specific shape and works most effectively at a particular temperature and pH.

ETHANOL: alcohol used to test for the presence of fats; a waste product of anaerobic respiration in yeast.

EUTROPHICATION: the abundant growth of water plants. Accelerated when nitrate levels increase in waterways.

EVOLUTION: gradual change in the characters of a species through natural selection. Takes place over many generations.

EXCRETION: the removal of waste products of metabolism from organisms.

EXPIRATION: the breathing out of air into the atmosphere.

EXTENSOR: one muscle in an antagonistic pair that contracts to straighten a limb at a joint. As it does so, the antagonistic flexor muscle relaxes.

EXTERNAL DIGESTION: method of nutrition, characteristic of saprotrophs, by the release of enzymes onto an organic substrate ('food').

EXTINCTION: the elimination of all members of a particular species of organism.

FATS: soluble organic molecules containing the elements carbon, hydrogen and oxygen only. Ratio of hydrogen to oxygen is much higher than 2 : 1. Formed by the joining of a glycerol molecule with fatty acid molecules.

FATTY ACIDS: insoluble molecules that, when joined with glycerol, form fat.

FERMENTATION: the anaerobic decomposition of some organic substances (e.g. of sugar to alcohol). Carbon dioxide is a waste product.

FETUS: a developing embryo in its mother's uterus.

FIBRIN: an insoluble, stringy protein formed by fibrinogen and enzymes released by damaged cells. It forms a mesh which traps blood cells and becomes a clot.

FIBRINOGEN: a soluble protein found in blood that plays a part in blood clotting.

FLACCID: used to describe cells, tissues or organs when they lose their shape and firmness (turgor).

FLEXOR: one muscle in an antagonistic pair that contracts to bend a limb at the joint. At the same time, the extensor muscle relaxes.

FOOD CHAIN: a sequence of organisms, starting with a photosynthesising organism (usually a green plant), through which energy is passed as one organism is eaten by the next in the sequence.

FOOD WEB: interlinked food chains involving organisms within the same ecosystem.

FOVEA: a very sensitive part of the retina that has far more cones than rods. Also called the yellow spot.

FUNGI (singular: 'fungus'): parasitic or saprotrophic multicellular organisms that feed on organic matter by digesting and absorbing it. They do not photosynthesise.

GAMETES: male or female sex cells.

GASEOUS EXCHANGE: the simultaneous absorption and release of gases by an organism. For example, mesophyll cells in plants absorb carbon dioxide and release oxygen during photosynthesis; cells of the alveoli pass oxygen from the lungs into the blood and carbon dioxide in the opposite direction.

GENE: a unit of inheritance, part of a chromosome.

GENETIC ENGINEERING: artificially changing the genetic make-up of cells.

GENOTYPE: genetic combination of an individual. Three possibilities are: homozygous dominant, homozygous recessive, heterozygous.

GLYCEROL: molecule that, when joined with fatty acids, forms fat.

GLYCOGEN: a carbohydrate with large, insoluble molecules. It is stored in the cells of the liver and muscles and in fungal cells. The conversion of glucose to glycogen takes place in the liver of mammals. This process is controlled by the hormone insulin, secreted by the pancreas.

GONADS: the organs which produce gametes (reproductive cells) – the testes in males; ovaries in females.

HAEMOGLOBIN: iron-containing pigment found in the cytoplasm of red blood cells. It carries oxygen around the body by combining with it in the lungs to become oxyhaemoglobin.

HERBIVORES: consumers which feed directly on the producer in their food chain.

HETEROTROPHIC: obtaining food requirements 'second-hand' either by eating plants, or by eating other animals which have eaten plants.

HETEROZYGOUS: having a pair of dissimilar alleles for a particular character.

HIGH WATER POTENTIAL: dilute solutions with a relatively large number of water molecules.

HINGE JOINT: joint which allows movement in one plane only (e.g. at the elbow).

HIV: human immuno-deficiency virus.

HOMEOSTASIS: the maintenance of a constant internal environment in the body. Performed by organs of homeostasis (e.g. the skin).

HOMOZYGOUS: having a pair of similar alleles for a particular character (e.g. both dominant, or both recessive).

HORMONE: a chemical substance, produced by a gland and carried by the blood, which alters the activity of one or more specific target organs. It is then destroyed in the liver.

HUMUS: formed when dead organic matter decomposes in the soil. Humus provides a steady supply of ions. It acts as a sponge, soaking up and holding water in the soil, and helps to bind the soil together, preventing soil erosion.

HYDROLYSIS: enzyme-controlled chemical reaction that involves the introduction of a water molecule in order to split a substrate molecule. The newly exposed ends of product molecules are 'sealed' so they will not re-join after being split. Common in digestion.

HYPOTHALAMUS: the part of the brain responsible for monitoring changes in the blood.

INDUSTRIAL BIOTECHNOLOGY: the use of microorganisms in industrial processes.

INSOLUBLE: unable to be mixed into and absorbed by a liquid (dissolved).

INSPIRATION: the taking in, or breathing in, of air from the atmosphere.

INSULIN: hormone produced by the Islets of Langerhans in the pancreas, involved in the uptake of glucose by cells and its conversion into glycogen.

IODINE SOLUTION: used to show the presence of starch (by turning blue/black), also as a temporary stain for plant cells.

IRIS: part of the eye that controls the intensity of light falling on the retina. It has an antagonistic arrangement of circular and radial muscles.

IRON DEFICIENCY: low levels of iron in a person's diet. Leads to a lack of haemoglobin, which is necessary for carrying oxygen around the body.

ISLETS OF LANGERHANS: cells in the pancreas that produces insulin.

KIDNEY DIALYSIS: the use of a machine to perform the functions of a kidney. It removes chemicals with small molecules (urea, toxins and ions) from blood but does not allow larger molecules (e.g. plasma proteins) to leave.

LENS: transparent, elastic part of the eye responsible for focusing an image on the retina.

LIGNIN: chemical that helps to strengthen the walls of xylem vessels in plants.

LIMITING FACTORS: particular factors that limit the rate of photosynthesis in plants, even when all other factors may be optimum. Examples are: light, carbon dioxide, water and temperature.

LIPASE: an enzyme that digests fats to fatty acids and glycerol.

LIPIDS: organic chemicals including fats and oils. Stored in special storage cells in the skin and around the kidneys.

LOW WATER POTENTIAL: concentrated solutions with fewer water molecules.

LYMPHATIC SYSTEM: a system of vessels for returning lymph (tissue fluid plus fats absorbed by the lacteals of the villi) to the blood system.

LYMPHOCYTES: a type of white blood cell, made in the lymph glands. They produce antitoxins and other antibodies which 'stick' to bacteria and clump them together for ingestion by phagocytes.

MAGNESIUM IONS: a form of magnesium absorbed by plants from the soil through the root hairs.

MENOPAUSE: when a female stops ovulating and can no longer become pregnant. Usually occurs at around 50 years of age.

MENSTRUATION: stage in the menstrual cycle when blood and the lining of the uterus are passed out of the vagina and vulva.

MESOPHYLL CELLS: palisade and spongy cells in a leaf, involved in photosynthesis.

METABOLISM: all the chemical reactions occurring in cells.

MICROORGANISMS: organisms so small that they can be studied only by using a microscope (e.g. viruses, bacteria and some fungi).

MILK TEETH: a person's first set of teeth that last for around 10–12 years, then are pushed out by the permanent teeth.

MITOSIS: a process of cell division when each chromosome forms an exact replica of itself. The two cells formed are identical to each other, and to the original cell.

MONOHYBRID INHERITANCE: inheritance involving only one pair of contrasting alleles.

MULTICELLULAR: living organisms that have many cells.

MUTATION: a spontaneous change in the structure of a gene or chromosome.

NATURAL SELECTION: the survival of those organisms most effectively adapted to their environment.

NEGATIVE FEEDBACK: a system which automatically brings about a correction in the body's internal environment (e.g. temperature), regardless which side of the optimum the change has occurred

NEURONES: individual nerve cells with their own cytoplasm, cell membrane and nucleus.

NITRATE ION: a form of nitrogen that plants absorb from the soil through root hairs.

NITROGEN FIXATION: conversion of atmospheric (gaseous) nitrogen into nitrogen compounds which can be used by living organisms.

NUCLEUS: The part of the cell that controls its growth and development. It contains a number of chromosomes made of the chemical DNA.

OPTIMUM: the best; particularly refers to a state (e.g. temperature, pH level) when processes can take place most efficiently.

ORGAN: several tissues working together to produce a particular function.

ORGAN SYSTEM: a collection of different organs working together to perform a particular function.

ORGANISM: a collection of organ systems working together.

OSMOREGULATION: the maintenance of a constant concentration (e.g. of blood plasma, performed by the kidneys).

OSMOSIS: the passage of water molecules from a region of high water potential, to a region of lower water potential, through a partially permeable membrane.

OVA (singular: 'ovum'): female gametes produced in the ovaries.

OXYHAEMOGLOBIN: constituent of red blood cells, formed by the combination of oxygen and haemoglobin.

PARASITE: an organism which obtains its food from another, usually larger living organism ('host'), the host always suffering in the relationship.

PATHOGEN: a disease-causing organism (e.g. virus, bacterium).

PENIS: male organ for introducing sperms into the female.

PERICARP: ovary wall that protects a fertilised plant seed. A pericarp with a seed(s) inside is a fruit.

PERISTALSIS: waves of muscle contractions. Occurs in the oesophagus (pushing boli towards the stomach), and through the duodenum, ileum and colon (pushing food toward the rectum).

PHAGOCYTE: a type of white blood cell, made in the bone marrow. It has a lobed nucleus and is capable of movement. Its function is to ingest bacteria.

PHAGOCYTOSIS: the ingestion of potentially harmful bacteria by phagocytes. Prevents or helps to overcome infection.

PHENOTYPE: inherited feature in an individual's appearance.

PHLOEM: tissue for transporting sugars and amino acids within a plant.

PHOTOSYNTHESIS: a process performed by green plants, in which light energy is converted into chemical energy.

PLACENTA: a special structure which carries out the exchange between the mother and fetus of the chemicals involved in the fetus' nutrition, respiration and excretion.

PLASMA: watery component of blood that carries dissolved chemicals, blood cells and heat.

PLASMODIUM: a single-celled organism, parasitic in human blood, which causes malaria.

PLASMOLYSIS: when a cell's cytoplasm is pulled away from the cell wall as a result of osmosis. Occurs when the cell is placed in a solution of lower water potential, and water is drawn from the vacuole.

PLATELETS: fragments of cells made in the bone marrow. They play a part in blood clotting and help to block holes in damaged capillary walls.

POLLEN TUBE: structure produced by a germinating pollen grain. The pollen tube grows down the style toward the ovary by releasing enzymes at its tip to digest the cells of the style beneath.

POLLINATION: the transfer of pollen from an anther to a stigma.

POLYPEPTIDES: formed by a few amino acids linked together. Enzymes in the body break down proteins to polypeptides, and polypeptides to amino acids.

PRIMARY CONSUMER: (also 'herbivore') a consumer which feeds directly on the producer in its food chain.

PRODUCERS: organisms which manufacture and supply energy-rich foods, made by photosynthesis, to all organisms in their food chain.

PRODUCT: the molecules produced as a result of enzyme action on substrate molecules.

PROTEASE: an enzyme that digests proteins to amino acids.

PROTEINS: contain the elements carbon, hydrogen, oxygen and nitrogen. Often contain other elements such as sulphur and phosphorus. Built up from amino acids.

PROTOPLASM: the cytoplasm and the nucleus of a cell.

PUBERTY: a stage in life when the release of hormones activates the reproductive organs. In humans, this occurs around the age of 12 years.

PYRAMID OF BIOMASS: a diagram constructed using the dry mass of organisms at each trophic level in a food web, with the producer at the base of the pyramid and the top consumer at the apex (top).

PYRAMID OF NUMBERS: a pyramid-shaped diagram showing the structure of a food web where there is a larger number of producers than primary consumers, more primary consumers than secondary consumers, and so on.

RBC: red blood cell.

RECESSIVE GENES: characters determined by these genes will not appear in an individual unless two recessive (i.e. no dominant) alleles are present.

RED BLOOD CELLS: small, biconcave and flexible cells that carry oxygen around the body.

REDUCING SUGARS: a group of sugars, including maltose and glucose, that, when reacting with Benedict's solution, act as chemicals known as 'reducing agents'.

REFLEX: a fast, coordinated, automatic response to a specific stimulus.

RENNIN: an enzyme in the stomach of young mammals for coagulating (clotting) the protein in milk.

RESPIRATION: the release of energy from food substances, that takes place in all living cells to perform all their functions.

RETINA: the innermost, light-sensitive layer of the eye.

RICKETS: a deficiency disease of bones caused by a lack of vitamin D in a person's diet.

RODS: light-sensitive cells found in the retina of the eye. Important when light intensity is low. They convert light energy into electrical energy.

ROOT HAIR CELL: plant cell specially adapted to absorb water and mineral ions (salts) from the soil.

ROOT PRESSURE: created by the process of osmosis carrying water across the root to the vascular bundle of the stem. The pressure forces water into the xylem, and pushes it along the root towards the stem.

SAPROTROPH: organism that feeds on dead organic matter through external digestion.

SCAB: a dried and hardened clot which covers a wound until the skin beneath has repaired.

SCURVY: a deficiency disease of the gums and skin caused by a lack of vitamin C in a person's diet.

SECONDARY CONSUMER: a consumer which feeds directly on the herbivore in its food chain.

SEMEN: sperms and seminal fluid.

SEMINAL FLUID: a nutrient fluid in which sperms are able to swim.

SEX CHROMOSOMES: one pair of chromosomes that determine the sex of an offspring.

SEXUAL REPRODUCTION: the fusion of male and female nuclei to form a zygote. Zygotes develop into offspring genetically different from each other, and from their parents.

SPERM: an abbreviation for 'spermatozoon' – the male gamete (or sex cell).

STAMEN: the anther and filament of a flower, involved in the production of pollen grains.

STARCH: insoluble carbohydrate produced by plant cells from glucose. Stored in the chloroplasts of photosynthesising cells and many storage organs of plants.

STOMATA (singular: 'stoma'): pores through which gases diffuse into and out of a leaf.

SUBSTRATE: molecule on which a catalyst works, changing it into product molecules. The 'key' in the 'lock and key hypothesis'. Also, the food on which organisms such as bacteria and fungi grow.

SYNAPSE: the gap between the dendrites (nerve endings) of neighbouring neurones.

TEMPERATURE REGULATION: function performed by the skin to maintain body temperature, in humans, at 37°C. Includes sweating, dilation or constriction of arterioles, and the control of blood flow to the skin.

TENDON: a cord of connective tissue that attaches muscle to bone.

TERTIARY CONSUMER: a consumer which feeds directly on the secondary consumer in its food chain.

TEST CROSS: a genetic cross involving one homozygous recessive parent.

TISSUE: many similar cells working together and performing the same function.

TISSUE CULTURE: commercial application of asexual reproduction in plants, in which pieces of tissue are removed from an organism and grown in an artificial medium in sterile conditions.

TISSUE FLUID: blood without red blood cells, plasma proteins and some white blood cells. It bathes the body's cells.

TISSUE REJECTION: when the body's immune system fails to accept a transplanted organ (e.g. heart or kidney) and attempts to destroy it as a harmful protein.

TOLERANCE: the ability of an organism to take progressively increased dosages of a drug.

TOXINS: poisons.

TRANSLOCATION: the movement of chemicals around a plant.

TRANSPIRATION: the evaporation of water from the mesophyll cells of a leaf, and the removal of that vapour through the stomata of the leaf.

TRANSPIRATION PULL: a force created by transpiration, where water is drawn up to the leaf to replace the water that has been lost.

TRANSPIRATION STREAM: a continuous stream of water and ions that travels up a plant.

TURGOR: the pressure created as water enters a plant cell, causing the cytoplasmic lining of the cell to press against the cell wall. Helps to make plant cells firm (turgid).

UMBILICAL CORD: connection between placenta and fetus. The fetal blood vessels run within it.

UNICELLULAR: made up of one cell only, as in the simplest living organisms.

UREA: a nitrogenous waste product which passes in the blood from the liver to the kidneys for excretion in urine.

URINE: waste solution containing urea, ions, toxins and water.

VACUOLE: a large, central space in plant cells that contains cell sap, a solution made up mostly of sugars. Also called the 'sap vacuole'.

VASCULAR BUNDLES: contain the tissues for transport within a plant – xylem (for carrying water and ions) and phloem (for carrying sugar and amino acids).

VEIN: vessel which carries blood under low pressure towards the heart – thinner walls than arteries. A large vein is a vena cava; a small one is a venule.

VENTRICLES: two lower chambers of the heart that pump blood out of the heart.

VILLI: microscopic finger-like projections found on the walls of the ileum. Designed to maximize surface area to allow food absorption.

VIRUSES: very small, parasitic organisms that cause disease. They cannot be treated with antibiotics. They do not possess all the characteristics of living organisms.

WILT: When a plant loses its rigidity as a result of a loss of turgidity in its cells. Occurs when the transpiration rate exceeds the rate that water can be absorbed from the soil, and water starts to be lost from the plant's cells.

WITHDRAWAL SYMPTOMS: unpleasant effects that result when someone stops taking a drug to which they are addicted (e.g. heroin).

XYLEM VESSELS: tube-like structures in plants specially adapted to conduct water and ions from the roots to the stem, leaves, flowers and fruits. Also provide support for the parts of the plant above the ground.

ZYGOTE: formed by the fusion of male and female nuclei during sexual reproduction. Zygotes develop into offspring genetically different from each other, and from their parents.